T0330073

Information Systems and the Economics of Innovation

Information Systems and the Economics of Innovation

Edited by

Chrisanthi Avgerou

London School of Economics, UK

Renata Lèbre La Rovere

Federal University of Rio de Janeiro, Brazil

Edward Elgar

Cheltenham, UK • Northampton, MA, USA

© Chrisanthi Avgerou and Renata Lèbre La Rovere 2003

All rights reserved. No part of this publication may be reproduced, stored in a retrieval system or transmitted in any form or by any means, electronic, mechanical or photocopying, recording, or otherwise without the prior permission of the publisher.

Published by
Edward Elgar Publishing Limited
Glensanda House
Montpellier Parade
Cheltenham
Glos GL50 1UA
UK

Edward Elgar Publishing, Inc.
136 West Street
Suite 202
Northampton
Massachusetts 01060
USA

A catalogue record for this book
is available from the British Library

Library of Congress Cataloguing in Publication Data
Information systems and the economics of innovation / edited by Chrisanthi Avgerou, Renata Lèbre La Rovere.
p. cm.
Includes bibliographical references and index.
1. Information technology—Economic aspects. 2. Information technology—Technological innovations. I. Avgerou, Chrisanthi. II. Rovere, Renata Lèbre La, 1961–

HC79.I55 I5368 2003
303.48'33—dc21

2002037949

ISBN 1 84376 018 5

Printed and bound in Great Britain by MPG Books Ltd, Bodmin, Cornwall

Contents

Figures

Tables

Contributors

Chrisanthi Avgerou is Senior Lecturer in Information Systems at the London School of Economics. Her research interests include the relationship between information technology and organizational change, and the role of ICT in socio-economic development. She is the author of *Information Systems and Global Diversity* (Oxford University Press, 2002).

Abiodun O. Bada is Assistant Professor of Information Systems in the School of Business at Virginia State University. His research interests include the application of resource-based and institutional theories to information systems phenomena, IT-enabled distance learning and the implementation of IT in developing countries. He is a member of the International Federation for Information Processing (IFIP) Working Group 9.4 on the Social Implications of Computers in Developing Countries.

Subhash Bhatnagar is leading an initiative to mainstream e-government applications into the activities of the World Bank, while on a sabbatical from the Indian Institute of Management, Ahmedabad, where he has held the CMC Chair Professorship in Information Technology. His research focus is on IT for development, e-government and e-commerce. He has published 80 research papers and seven books, including *ICT and Development: Cases from India* (Sage Publications, 2000). He founded and chaired the IFIP Working Group 9.4 on the Social Implications of Computers in Developing Countries and is Editor of the *International Journal of IT and Development* and a newsletter on IT in Developing Countries. He is also a recipient of the IFIP Silver Core and the Fellowship of the Computer Society of India.

James Cornford is Senior Lecturer in the Business School at the University of Newcastle. He is based in the university's Centre for Urban and Regional Development Studies (CURDS), where he was previously a principal research associate. His research interests are focused on the implications of information and communication technologies for organizations, cities and regions. He has undertaken research for the European Commission, the European Investment Bank, the OECD and the UK Economic and Social

Research Council. He is currently researching the implementation of electronic government among local authorities in the UK.

Tony Cornford is Senior Lecturer in Information Systems at the London School of Economics. His research and teaching are associated with understanding the implementation and use of information systems in varied and contrasting contexts. Recent research has included studies of information systems innovations in the health sector, knowledge management issues associated with the impetus towards sustainability in the construction industry, and how home computers are negotiated and understood within family life.

Renata Lèbre La Rovere is Associate Professor at the Institute of Economics at the Federal University of Rio de Janeiro. Her main lines of research involve the importance of small and medium-sized enterprises (SMEs) for economic development, the use of ICT in SMEs and support policies for SMEs. She obtained her Ph.D. in Economics at the Université Paris 7, her M.Sc. in Economics at Université Paris 7 and her degree in Economics at the Catholic University of Rio de Janeiro. She has worked as a visiting scholar in the Management and Information Systems Department and the Latin American Area Studies of the University of Arizona. She has also undertaken post-doctoral research on ICT diffusion policies for SMEs at the University of Rostock, Germany.

Shirin Madon is Lecturer in Information Systems at the London School of Economics. Her main research interest is studying the impact of information systems on planning and administration in developing countries. She has carried out extensive fieldwork in India as part of her doctoral studies, and subsequently worked on a research project that studied the impact of different structures of local government on the implementation of information systems. From 1998 to 2000, she worked on a British Academy-funded project studying 'information flows' for local governance in the city of Bangalore, focusing on reform of the property-tax system. She is currently working on a project entitled 'E-governance for Development', which aims to carry out a sociological, comparative study of a selection of ongoing e-governance initiatives in India concerned with development planning, city management, electronic payment centres and telecentre projects.

Rodrigo Magalhães' main professional activity since 2000 has been in management consulting but he is also active in research and writing about organizational knowledge and culture, and the role of information systems and technology within these areas. He is a partner in T2C Ltd in Portugal and

EUROSIS in Mozambique, two small strategic consulting firms specializing in organizational and implementation issues, with a special focus on information systems and technology. He is also a guest professor at the Portuguese Catholic University in Lisbon, where he lectures regularly in the MBA programme.

Victor Prochnik is Associate Professor at the Institute of Economics at the Federal University of Rio de Janeiro (UFRJ). His main fields of research involve economics of networks, economics of information and the economic performance of ICT industries. He obtained his Ph.D. in Production Engineering at the UFRJ's Center for Post-graduate Programs and Research in Engineering. He also has an M.Sc. in Economics from the UFRJ and a degree in Statistics from the National School of Statistical Sciences of the Brazilian Institute of Geography and Statistics.

Paulo Bastos Tigre is a full Professor at the Institute of Economics at the Federal University of Rio de Janeiro (UFRJ). His main research interests involve the importance of ICT for competitiveness, the economic performance of ICT industries and science and technology policies. He completed his Ph.D. in Economics at the Science Policy Research Unit at Sussex University, his M.Sc. in Production Engineering at UFRJ's Center for Post-graduate Programs and Research in Engineering and his degree in Economics also at the UFRJ. He has also carried out post-doctoral research on ICT diffusion and electronic commerce at the Center for Latin American Studies of the University of California at Berkeley.

Maurício Yoshinori Une is an economist at the Federal University of Rio de Janeiro and is a student in the Master Degree Course on Economics at the Federal University of Rio Grande do Sul in Brazil.

Preface

This book resulted from a collaboration between scholars in the Institute of Economics of the Federal University of Rio de Janeiro, Brazil (Instituto de Economia, Universidade Federal do Rio de Janeiro) and in the Department of Information Systems, London School of Economics (LSE), UK. As with many fruitful exchanges of ideas in the academic world, the origin of this collaboration was our meeting at international conferences; in our case, it was a series of conferences on 'IT and development' organized by the International Federation of Information Processing (IFIP), Working Group 9.4 on the Social Consequences of Computers in Developing Countries. Sharing the curiosity of understanding the processes of innovation in the context of development, we noticed our different disciplinary allegiances had equipped us with different perspectives, concepts and logics, which we thought would be interesting to explore.

The opportunity for such an exploration came through a grant offered by The British Council and the Brazilian National Council for Research (CNPq). This gave us the means for a series of visits and seminars of scholars from the Instituto de Economia to the Information Systems department of the LSE and vice versa, between 1998 and 2000. We thus established that our disciplinary realms offered complementary knowledge on the phenomenon of information and communication technology innovation, which we thought would be useful to elaborate with a collection of representative articles in a book; so, we invited authors to contribute accordingly.

We would like to take the opportunity to thank the funding bodies of this collaborative project: CNPq, the British Council and the LSE Department of Information Systems. We owe sincere thanks to Malcolm Peltu for his excellent editorial work, and to Luke Adams and Edward Elgar for their support and encouragement to create this publication.

Chrisanthi Avgerou
Renata Lèbre La Rovere
July 2002

Introduction

Chrisanthi Avgerou and Renata Lèbre La Rovere

The significance of technical innovation has attracted a great deal of attention in the field of economics since the early 1980s. In the long-established theoretical preoccupations of mainstream economics, technical change has been treated as one of the 'exogenous' forces, peripheral to economic growth processes. However, a vibrant new research stream has diverged from the orthodox conceptualizations and modelling efforts of the field of economics and placed its focus on technical and institutional innovation (Dosi et al., 1988; Lundvall, 1992; Foray and Freeman, 1993; Nelson, 1993; Hobday, 1995; Archibugi and Michie, 1997; Archibugi et al., 1999).

This new research direction, led by what are known as 'evolutionary' or 'neo-Schumpeterian'[1] economists, has produced a wealth of knowledge on the process of technical innovation, competitiveness and productivity growth, both at the firm and country levels. A number of valuable lessons have been derived from this approach, often by challenging the principles of economics, a discipline that aspired to be the 'theoretical physics of social sciences'. These lessons include:

- identifying the conceptual distinctions between invention, innovation and diffusion;
- overcoming the conceptual and methodological barriers between micro-economic (firm-level) and macro-economic (country-level) model-driven theory;
- highlighting the significance of learning and knowledge, and of the identification of tacit and codified knowledge as necessary distinct elements in the innovation process;
- linking technical and organizational change; and
- revealing the significance of interactions among actors involved in the innovation process and their capacity to generate positive externalities that will spur economic growth.

Within this rich stream of evolutionary economics research, particular attention has been dedicated to information and communication technology

(ICT). The advent and diffusion of this cluster of technologies is considered a major force of productivity and economic growth (Antonelli, 1993). Theoretical views that implicate ICT innovation in fundamental socio-economic changes have been proposed, and are captured in concepts such as the 'information economy' or the 'knowledge society' (Foray and Lundvall, 1996; Mansell and Wehn, 1998).

In particular, ICT has been identified as an important part of the present 'techno-economic paradigm'. The concept of techno-economic paradigm was developed in the eighties by economists (Dosi, 1982; Freeman, 1982; Perez, 1983) who wanted to explain how the creation, use and diffusion of new technologies affect companies' competitive strategies and the dynamics of economic development. The techno-economic paradigm is a combination of technical, organizational and institutional innovations that provoke transformations in the whole economy and have a considerable influence in its behaviour.

A new techno-economic paradigm involves the creation of new sectors and activities, new ways to create and diffuse information and knowledge, new modes of commercialization, new strategies and policies and new modes of operation of public and private institutions. In the currently prevailing techno-economic paradigm, firms are dealing with technology-intensive and knowledge-intensive products that have diminished life-cycle times and often require flexible production processes. In this context, it is considered essential for any enterprise to define an adequate competitive strategy and to monitor its performance so that the strategy can be frequently adjusted. ICT is an important part of the new techno-economic paradigm because it supports managerial processes in firms as well as in public institutions. In addition, ICT-related industries are developing very fast and inducing economic growth in several countries (Lastres and Ferraz, 1999).

At the same time that evolutionary economists were proposing new ways of viewing the firm by enhancing the role of innovation, other economists looked at the way firms were organized by studying the institutional and hierarchical relationships that condition the behaviour of economic agents (Williamson, 1985; Alchian and Woodward, 1988; Williamson, 1990). From this stream of research came the 'transaction costs' theory, which defines the firm as a system of contracts between individual economic agents that is formed because of market imperfections and the asymmetry of information (Coriat and Weinstein, 1995). In this line of research, ICT has been recognized by economists as including tools to organize information and eventually reduce transaction costs (Brousseau, 1993). Thus, several different perspectives have been developed within economics since the 1980s to study the relationship between information and economic growth (Petit, 1998).

The period in which these new approaches to innovation in economics were being developed also saw the emergence of information systems (IS) as the academic field concerned with the processes of developing and deriving value from ICT applications within organizations. In many respects, the IS field has followed a very different intellectual journey in the study of technical innovation than that pursued by scholars in economics. Rather than breaking the rigid theoretical frameworks of a well-founded discipline, as researchers in economics had to do, information systems grew almost without a theoretical tradition, responding mainly to concerns of practitioners (systems developers and business managers) by picking and mixing conceptual perspectives from diverse areas of knowledge, such as engineering, organizational sociology, economics, psychology or anthropology. Such an eclectic approach often met with suspicion within the institutional context of academia. However, this was how information systems allowed for the development of the 'requisite variety' of intellectual constructs to comprehend the complex phenomenon of ICT innovation without, a priori, limiting its elucidation to the norms of particular scientific fields. As a result, IS produced a mass of detailed perspectives on the processes of taking up ICT and exploiting its potential within, mainly, business organizations in industrialized societies.

Research in information systems has dealt with a broad spectrum of thematic areas, including: ICT applications to support the functioning of an organization, such as decision-support systems; the process of information systems development; information systems management; the organizational value of ICT innovation; and the societal impact of ICT (Avgerou, 1999). One of the major conceptual characteristics of information systems studies in all these areas – or at least one of the most important schools of thought within this field – is to consider its object of study as social systems involving technologies, rather than technologies per se. In this way, the study of ICT innovation in information systems avoided the pitfalls of technology determinism, although it often subordinated the process of innovation to a rather impoverished business rationality and only gradually started developing a credible socio-theoretical perspective.

A great deal of research in information systems during the 1970s and 1980s was concerned with understanding and formalizing the process of the development of ICT applications to meet an organization's information requirements. The main outcome of that stream of research effort was the development of professional knowledge for the diffusion of the then-new ICT applications. As a by-product, but perhaps more importantly, research on the systems development process addressed questions about the nature of technical innovation interventions in an organization's context, and laid the foundations of a field oriented towards studying ICT innovation more generally (Avgerou and Cornford, 1998).

In the 1990s, the codified knowledge about the development of customized ICT applications lost its main utility as a prescription of professional activities and its central position in the information systems research field. Most organizations no longer develop customized ICT applications in-house. Instead, they purchase and implement packaged software with generic functionalities. Moreover, new flexible technologies – such as computer-supported collaborative work (CSCW) and Internet-based information communication and transaction systems – tend to be developed idiosyncratically, deviating in many respects from the 'good practice' norms laid down for the development of rather inflexible transaction-processing ICT applications. In this context of ICT innovation, the major contribution of the IS field stems from elaborating on a broader understanding of the way organizations accommodate ICT implementation processes, the way such processes do or do not contribute economic value to an organization and the way they impinge on processes of social change. To that end, information systems research in the 1990s was enriched by drawing from contemporary social theory, with particular influence (as several of the chapters in this volume demonstrate) from the sociology of technology and structuration theory.

Among the many lessons derived by research in the information systems field, we consider the following as especially worth mentioning here:

- The process of ICT innovation in organizations is only partly technical/rational. Political, cultural and cognitive features of the organizational context are significant determinants for the implementation of ICT (e.g., Walsham, 1993).
- ICT innovation is intertwined with organizational change. Rare are the cases where ICT 'automates' existing production or administration activities while leaving their broader organizational processes unaltered. Indeed, the main value of ICT is understood to lie in enabling changes in the socio-organizational arrangements, whether they are perceived as 'work processes' or 'business processes'.
- The intertwined ICT innovation and organizational change process can only partly be formally planned and controlled in a top-down manner. To a large extent, this is a situated process involving a great deal of improvisation, contestation and appropriation by various stakeholders (Orlikowski, 1996; Ciborra and Associates, 2000).
- The economic value of ICT innovation is not limited to productivity gains. Alternative criteria, such as profitability and competitiveness, are more frequently the benefits targeted by ICT investment.

- The significance of ICT innovation cannot be adequately captured in concepts of economic value; ICT is implicated in social changes that are not driven by norms of economic rationality.

I.1 A COMMON FRAMEWORK OF ANALYSIS

The economics and information systems fields of inquiry outlined above have not, of course, been developed in total isolation from each other. The two research communities often found themselves preoccupied with the same research challenges, for instance in their efforts to explain the 'productivity paradox'[2] pointed out by mainstream economists or in their use of common concepts, such as the resource-based theory (see Chapter 10) that was first proposed in management studies and then adopted by evolutionary economists and IS researchers. There are frequent cross-citations in the literature of both fields, even if only to strengthen the legitimacy of their distinct research questions and findings, rather than to sustain a substantial interdisciplinary debate.

On the whole, the study of ICT innovation in economics follows a predominantly 'outside-in' orientation, concerned more with questions relevant to 'institutional policy' for fostering ICT innovation and diffusion, rather than 'business actions' for ICT innovation. Economists focus on innovation as the *result* of interactions and, consequently, as a factor for the competitive performance of firms, while information systems scholars are concerned with the *process* of the interactions that constitute innovation.

The 'outside-in' approach taken by economists does not mean that they do not consider the impacts of ICT innovation on individual firms and on relations between firms. More recently, economists have been tackling the issue of business strategy by applying mainstream micro-economic analysis to the production of information (Shapiro and Varian, 1999). Other authors have been using transaction-cost economics to analyse ICT-based systems of communication between firms (Brousseau, 1993). In general, most economics studies of ICT acknowledge that the results of ICT innovation and diffusion in a country's economy depend on the conditions of individual firms, and therefore analysis of organizational factors – or processes – is essential for defining appropriate policy. It is understood that diffusion policies focusing on the supply of ICT, such as those oriented towards training and enhancement of technological capabilities, need to be accompanied by policies oriented towards demand, i.e., the competitive behaviour of firms.

The study of ICT innovation in information systems has an opposite, 'inside-out' orientation and is concerned primarily with informing management action on ICT innovation. Nevertheless, it considers contextual conditions, such as government policy, structural economic factors and broader societal characteristics, which are essential for understanding effective initiatives by organizational actors. Also, as organizational boundaries often become blurred and the development of communication networks and information technology (IT) applications play an instrumental role in new forms of organizational interactions, information systems studies have expanded in scope, becoming increasingly concerned with the wider socio-economic context within which an organization is embedded.

This book's main objective is to engage in a dialogue between the two streams of research outlined above. It brings together practising researchers of the two communities, each contributing particular perspectives of the ICT innovation processes and consequences. As mentioned in the Preface, the book is a result of discussions that took place in seminars with scholars from these fields. The seminars were organized around a simple linear ICT diffusion framework suggested by Gillespie et al. (1995). In this framework, ICT innovation and diffusion can be seen as a series of 'translations': from infrastructure investment to service and applications provision; from such provision to firms' awareness; from awareness to adoption; from adoption to effective usage; and from effective usage to competitive advantage.

This framework provides a basis to discuss ramifications of diffusion policy and associate them with organizational action. For example, supply-oriented diffusion policies can be seen as aiming to ensure the first translation, while demand-oriented diffusion policies are concerned with influencing the other translations. The framework can also be used to map empirical data on the diffusion process. In this way, it has been observed that policies tend to support the diffusion process up to the third translation. The last two translations of demand are more difficult to stimulate because they depend on a firm's ability for technology innovation; and it is these two translations that can be seen as the domain of information systems, i.e. the intertwined innovation of technology and organizational action in its social setting.

Closer analysis of the processes of ICT innovation reveals complexities that are difficult to fit into tidy concepts of diffusion, such as Gillespie et al's model. Indeed, the chapters of this book contribute to a much more sophisticated understanding of the efforts involved in exploiting the potential of ICT. Thus, the value of this framework for opening the dialogue between the two research fields lies exactly in this provision of an overall structure of ideas and accumulated knowledge across the macro/micro spectrum of analytical focus. In the book's conclusions, we revisit and critique the linear view of ICT innovation and diffusion, highlighting the main lessons suggested by the authors of chapters in the main three parts.

A note on the presentation style of this volume is necessary at this point. The reader will notice that the authors use varying terminology, e.g. some authors refer to IT, others to ICT, others to IS. Such differences reflect not only the conceptual and theoretical differences between the two disciplines from which the authors primarily draw, but also the semantic ambiguity inherent in the study of very fast changing technologies, related industries and socio-organizational practices. Indeed, some authors carefully explain their choice of terminology and the meaning of the particular concepts deployed in their analysis. Others use various terms interchangeably. We felt that the variety and inconsistency of terminology is indicative of the current state of the debate within and between the two academic communities, and therefore editorial interventions for a uniform language across the chapters would be inappropriate.

I.2 STRUCTURE OF THIS BOOK

I.2.1 Part I: Infrastructures, Awareness Building and Development of Capabilities

In the first part of the book, the authors show that the translation from infrastructure to service and application provision depends not only on institutional factors which define government policies, but also on the socio-economic context within which users are embedded. Various such aspects of user context are explored in the analyses of these chapters.

James Cornford's examination of ICT and regional development (Chapter 1) points out the fallacy of focusing policies on ICT infrastructure provision, because there are significant differences between regions' capabilities to adopt and use ICT. In his analysis, the kind of capabilities necessary to foster ICT innovation and economic growth is captured in the concept of the 'learning region', which implies the significance of a historically-developed capacity of learning-by-interacting and learning-by-doing – in short, on the 'social capital' of a region.

Subhash Bhatnagar (Chapter 2) examines three experiments for the provision of telecommunications and Internet access to rural communities in India and Bangladesh. Lessons are drawn from these case studies to understand how telecommunications access to rural areas can be harnessed for development. At the start of the 21st Century, such access is poor and would require huge investment to cover large parts of rural Asia that have no access to communications facilities. Bhatnagar argues that a proactive policy is needed to encourage investment in infrastructure for rural areas. Such investment can pay off if technology is relevant to the life conditions of the local people and provides value to them. He also suggests that the nature of encouragement for different regions would have to be based on the cost of providing access, the potential for earning revenue and the availability of institutions that can deliver a valuable service in rural areas.

Victor Prochnik and Mauricio Yoshinori Une, in their analysis of the diffusion of the Internet in Brazil (Chapter 3), demonstrate that the development of an ICT infrastructure depends not only on government diffusion programmes but also on how the user community reacts to the expansion of ICT. In the case of Brazil, the Government tried to involve the academic community and private enterprises in an ambitious program to constitute an 'Information Society', but its success has been limited by the characteristics of Brazilian enterprises in the information and telecommunications sector.

In the final chapter of this part of the book (Chapter 4), Shirin Madon questions the explanatory strength of the diffusion perspective of ICT innovation. She examines an example of the policy initiatives of the Kerala state government in India directed at diffusing IT with the aim of providing services to citizens. She argues that the analysis of the social and political biases inherent in the environment, as suggested by diffusion theory, need to be augmented with concepts from the social construction of technology – and thus to pay attention to issues of technology usage, as well as decisions relating to adoption.

I.2.2 Part II: ICT Adoption

The second part of the book focuses on how ICT adoption is conditioned by institutional and economic characteristics, with the authors trying to identify the main concepts that can be used to analyse these aspects.

The part is opened by Renata Lèbre La Rovere (Chapter 5), who draws on a study of Brazilian SMEs to demonstrate that ICT is adopted as a result of a cumulative learning process, and that the innovative character of the activity is a key determinant in ICT adoption.

In their study of e-commerce, Paulo Bastos Tigre and Renata Lèbre La Rovere (Chapter 6) identify the main concepts that are useful to understanding the dynamics of ICT adoption. The fact that these concepts come from different branches of economics research (mainstream, transaction costs theory and evolutionary theory) demonstrates the diversity of economics studies about the impact of ICT innovation on firms, and on the relations between firms.

Abiodun Bada (Chapter 7) presents two descriptive/interpretive case studies of banks implementing ICT and organizational change programmes in response to wider environmental changes within this industry. On the basis of these studies, he argues that organizational actions for the adoption and adaptation of innovations are a function both of management choice as well as institutional forces. An important theoretical implication of this study is that symbolic or ritual actions are not necessarily dysfunctional; technical/rational actions can indeed be supported and enhanced by symbolic and ritual actions.

I.2.3 Part III: Innovation in the Organizational Setting of ICT Use

The third part of the book examines aspects of the innovation process in the settings within which ICT is used.

Chrisanthi Avgerou (Chapter 8) discusses how the understanding of the ICT innovation process in organizations has changed from the days of the first commercial applications of computers to the contemporary setting of packaged software implementation and flexible technologies. She then outlines the emerging theoretical perspectives of information systems research for the understanding of innovation as a situated process in which emphasis shifts from design and technical/rational decision making to improvisation and political actors' behaviour.

In the same vein, Tony Cornford (Chapter 9) elaborates on theories used in information systems to understand how innovation is constituted through the use of ICT in the context of an organization's practices. He identifies the new challenge of IS research as being to investigate the open-ended prospects of change triggered by new ICT at the work place.

In the last chapter of this part (Chapter 10), Rodrigo Magalhães uses theories of management to analyse the significance of organizational context in ICT innovation. He discusses three perspectives of innovation: resource-based business economics; the process of organizational maturity; and IS/IT governance. He puts forward a model for understanding the formation of such desirable aspects of organizational context, based on a learning or knowledge culture drawn mainly from autopoiesis and structuration theories.

REFERENCES

Alchian, A.A. and S. Woodward (1988), 'The Firm is Dead; Long Live the Firm. A Review of Oliver E. Williamson's *The Economic Institutions of Capitalism*', *Journal of Economic Literature* **26** (1), 65–79

Antonelli, C. (1993), *The Diffusion of Technological Systems and Productivity Growth: The Case of Information and Communication Technologies*, Dresden: Germany Herausforderung fur die Informationstechnik Internationale Konferenz.

Archibugi, D. and J. Michie (1997) (eds), *Technology, Globalisation and Economic Performance*, Cambridge: Cambridge University Press.

Archibugi, D., J. Howells and J. Michie (1999) (eds.), *Innovation Policy in a Global Economy*, Cambridge: Cambridge University Press.

Avgerou, C. (1999), 'Information Systems: What Sort of Science is it?', *Omega,* **28**, 567–79

Avgerou, C. and Cornford, T. (1998), *Developing Information Systems*, Basingstoke, UK: Macmillan

Brousseau, E. (1993), *L'Economie de Contrats: Technologies de L'information et Coordination Interentreprises*, Paris: Presses Universitaires de France.

Brynjolfsson, E. (1993), 'The Productivity Paradox of Information Technology', *Communications of the ACM*, **35** (December), 66–77.

Ciborra, C. U. and Associates, (2000) (eds), *From Control to Drift*, Oxford: Oxford University Press.

Coriat, B. and Weinstein, O. (1995), *Les Nouvelles Théories de L'entreprise,* Paris: Le Livre de Poche.

Dosi, G. (1982), Technological Paradigms and Technological Trajectories, *Research Policy*, **11** (3), 147–62.

Dosi, G., C. Freeman, R. Nelson, G. Silverberg and L. Soete (1988) (eds), *Technical Change and Economic Theory*, London: Pinter.

Freeman, C. (1982), *The Economics of Industrial Innovation*, London: Pinter.

Foray, D. and C. Freeman (1993) (eds), *Technology and the Wealth of Nations; The Dynamics of Constructed Advantage*, London: Pinter.

Foray, D. and B.-Å. Lundvall (1996), The Knowledge-based Economy: From the Economics of Knowledge to the Learning Economy, in D. Foray and B.-Å. Lundvall (eds.) *Unemployment and Growth in the Knowledge-Based Economy*, Paris: OECD.

Gillespie, A., R. Richardson and J. Cornford (1995), 'Information Infrastructures and Territorial Development', background paper prepared for the OECD Workshop on Information Infrastructures and Territorial Development, 7–8 November, Paris: OECD.

Hobday, M. (1995), *Innovation in East Asia: The Challenge to Japan*, Cheltenham, UK and Brookfield, US: Edward Elgar.

Hitt, L. and E. Brynjolfsson (1996), 'Productivity, Business Profitability and Consumer Surplus: Three Different Measures of Information Technology Value', *MIS Quarterly*, **20** (2), 121–42.

Landauer, T. K. (1996), *The Trouble with Computers: Usefulness, Usabiliy, and Productivity*, Cambridge, MA: MIT Press.

Lastres, H.M.M. and Ferraz, J., (1999), *Economia da Informação, do Conhecimento e do Aprendizado*, in H.M.M. Lastres and S. Albagli (eds), *Informação e Globalização na Era do Conhecimento*, Rio de Janeiro: Campus

Lundvall, B.-Å., ed. (1992), *National Systems of Innovation: Towards a Theory of Innovation and Interactive Learning*, London: Pinter.

Mansell, R. and U. Wehn (1998) (eds), *Knowledge Societies: Information Technology for Sustainable Development*, Oxford: Oxford University Press.

Nelson, R., (1993) (ed.), *National Innovation Systems*, Oxford: Oxford University Press.

Orlikowski, W.J. (1996), 'Improvising Transformation over Time: A Situated Perspective', *Information Systems Research*, **7** (1), 115–26.

Perez, C. (1983), 'Structural Change and Assimilation of New Technologies in the Economic and Social System', *Futures* **15** (5), 357– 75.

Petit, P. (1998), *L'economie de L'information: Les Enseignements des Theories Economiques*, Paris: La Decouverte.

Schumpeter., J. A. ([1942] 1976), *Capitalism, Socialism and Democracy*, New York: Harper Torchbooks.

Shapiro, C. and H.R. Varian (1999), *Information Rules: A Strategic Guide to the Network Economy*, Boston: Harvard Business School Press.

Walsham, G. (1993), *Interpreting Information Systems in Organizations*, Chichester, UK: Wiley.

Williamson, O.E. (1985), *The Economic Institutions of Capitalism*, New York: The Free Press.

Williamson, O.E. (1990), 'The Firm as a Nexus of Treaties: An Introduction', in M. Aoki, B. Gustaffson and O.E. Williamson (eds), *The Firm as a Nexus of Treaties*, London: Sage Publications.

NOTES

1. The authors who developed evolutionary theories of economic growth are also called neo-Schumpeterians because these theories are based on the ideas developed by economist Joseph Schumpeter. Schumpeter's ([1942] 1976) most famous work was the book *Capitalism, Socialism and Democracy*, first published in 1942. In this, he proposed that the opening up of new markets and the organizational changes of firms illustrate an 'endogenous' process of industrial mutation; that is, a process which incessantly revolutionizes the economic structure from within. Schumpeter called this process 'Creative Destruction', and proposed that the revolutions resulting from this process and the absorption of their results form business cycles. Evolutionary theories of economic growth further developed the idea of endogenous growth by proposing that firms develop routines for operation, investment and decision-making procedures that are eventually challenged and modified by innovation. Innovation is understood as the creation of new products, new processes and new organizational forms.
2. Towards the end of the 1980s, it became apparent that banks which had been investing in the most extensive computerization efforts were not necessarily among the leaders in the banking sector. Moreover, research conducted by economists in the USA challenged the widespread expectation that the diffusion of IT contributes to the growth of productivity as a whole. Such unexpected research findings puzzled the research community, created scepticism among business executives and initiated an on-going debate about the 'real' economic value of IT (Brynjolfsson, 1993; Hitt and Brynjolfsson, 1996; Landauer, 1996)

PART ONE

Infrastructures, awareness building and development of capabilities

1. The Evolution of the Information Society and Regional Development in Europe

James Cornford

1.1 INTRODUCTION

This chapter[1] attempts to set the current debates about ICT and regional development in context by providing a rather stylized account of the linked research and policy agendas concerning the role of ICT in regional development in Europe. This account draws on an argument I have borrowed from Andrew Friedman's (1989) book, *Computer Systems Development.* His account of the evolution of computer systems operates in a dialectical manner, in which a staged series of constraints on development call into being a theoretical critique and programmatic policy response that, over time, loosens or ameliorates the constraint to which they are addressed. However, for Friedman, the very strategies adopted to ameliorate a previous constraint tend to generate a new constraint which, in turn, brings forth a new theoretical critique and policy response. In more concrete terms, Friedman sees the set of constraints in computer systems development evolving as follows.

The first constraint on development took the form of a 'hardware constraint', in which computer systems were limited by the costs of adequate hardware. This was ameliorated by a mixture of programmatic research in the computer industry and moves to capture scale economies in production (resulting in the emergence of Moore's law[2]). However, with the development of ever more powerful and cheap computers, the need came to the fore for ever greater volumes of complex software capable of taking advantage of this new power – 'the software constraint'.

As software became more complex, and its reputation for time and cost overruns and reliability problems became established, the focus of attention moved from hardware to the software development process. A raft of techniques were then developed to attempt to gain greater control over the working methods associated with the development of software, such as formal methods and structured programming (e.g., Sommerville, 2001). The adoption of these techniques slowly ameliorated the 'software constraint' and enabled more complex programs to be produced. Computer systems subsequently grew beyond the Data Processing or IT departments, where they had emerged, began to link together other departments of the organization. As new, and less technically-minded, users came into contact with computer systems, the focus of constraint moved to the 'end user'. This led to the adoption of new methodologies and procedures for 'user needs analysis' and for trying to ensure that end users could 'get what they want'. For Friedman, writing in the late 1980s, this was the current stage. However, he also felt that he could identify the outline of a further stage, based on the emergence of an 'inter-organizational constraint' as computer systems increasingly linked across, rather than simply within, organizations.

It is important to note that Friedman does not see the resolution of each constraint as ever being total or final. For example, the software development process has never been fully 'brought under control'. Rather, his account is one of a shifting focus of attention, research, strategy formulation and policy implementation, in which particular issues are fore-grounded. What is more, these stylized stages do not, of course, correspond to the real histories of computer systems development in any real organization. Their role is strictly analytical.

In this chapter, I borrow from Friedman's schema of 'development-constraint-critique-amelioration-new-constraint' to reconstruct a related evolution: that of thinking about, and policy concerning, ICT in the regional development arena. I will identify four phases, in sections 1.2 to 1.5, each corresponding to a broad notion of the social implications of information and communication technology. Each phase is associated with its own regional research and policy findings, and its own constraint – the overcoming of which leads us onto the next phase.

1.2 SILICON LANDSCAPES

We begin, arbitrarily, in the late 1970s and early 1980s. Technologically, the focus was on the increasing demand for computer hardware, following the emergence of, first, the minicomputer and, later, the microcomputer (culminating in the personal computer). The central concern from the point of view of regional development was the identification of the IT industries as a significant new growth sector in the economy, a *heartland* technology (Perez, 1983). The focus of regional development research was thus on the uneven geography of IT production – the so called 'silicon landscapes', to borrow the title of Hall and Markusen's (1985) book. What I want to emphasize here is the particular focus on the hardware of computing, on the 'silicon' – at this point the focus was very much on IT understood as the production of information *technology*. From a regional development point of view, the focus of academic attention was on the location of IT production activity, while from a regional policy perspective, the focus was on what could be done to attract or stimulate IT production activity.

In the European context, research tended to find that IT production was concentrated in a number of 'islands of innovation', predominantly located in the core regions of the European Union (EU) and forming an archipelago stretching, in a banana shape, from London to Milan. The peripheral and less-favoured regions of the EU generally saw little of this new growth sector, except for low value-added assembly ('screwdriver' plants). The policy response was, crudely, to try to simulate the conditions in the much studied core regions through policies such as the development of science parks and through attempts to attract the plants of IT multinationals to locations in less-favoured regions.

In this first phase, then, the dominant notion was of IT as a specific economic sector of the economy whose expansion created significant regional economic development opportunities. A critique of this emphasis on IT as a sector rapidly emerged. The focus on the production of IT as the principal implication of new technology for regional development was, it was suggested, akin to identifying the manufacture of locomotives and carriages as the principal economic impact of the coming of the railways. This critique sought to elaborate and extend thinking in two directions. First, it saw the significance of IT as principally residing in its application across the whole economy, rather than as a discrete sector. Second, it pointed towards the increasing significance of *communication* technologies, as well as information *processing* technologies – a shift from IT to ICT. Finally, intense inter-regional competition for inward investment in 'high tech', and in particular the provision of large volumes of grant aid to entice multinationals to locate in particular regions, contributed to the development of the EU rules on state aid, which have sought to regulate such inter-regional competition.

1.3 THE CONNECTED REGION

A strong positive correlation between measures of the deployment and uptake of telecommunications and measures of economic development, such as main telephone lines per 100 inhabitants and gross domestic product (GDP), is well established at a national level. A number of studies have also identified the existence of positive relationships of this sort at the regional level (Biehl 1986; Gillespie et al., 1984; Parker and Hudson, 1995). Subsequent studies concluded that causality in this relationship ran both ways (Hardy, 1980; Cronin et al., 1991; 1993); not only do increases in GDP or output lead to increases in telecommunications investment, but the converse is also true: that increases in telecommunications investment stimulate overall economic growth. This finding, coupled with survey evidence from large firms (e.g., Healey and Baker, 1992; Ireland, 1994; DTI, 1994), was enough to 'suggest employing telecommunications-infrastructure investment as a means to stimulate local economic development' (Cronin et al., 1993: 426).

Much research in the late 1980s and early 1990s pointed to a substantial telecommunications gap existing between the prosperous core and the poorer periphery of the EU, despite efforts by the periphery to catch up (CEC, 1994; Nexus Europe et al., 1996). This evidence was used within the EU to justify investing in telecommunications infrastructure 'ahead of demand' in order to stimulate the development of peripheral or remote areas and less-favoured regions. The main expression of this approach was the STAR (Special Telecommunications Action for Regional Development) programme, between 1987 and 1991. Its primary aim was to 'break the cycle by which demand for advanced telecommunications services (ATS) is too low to justify supply on commercial grounds, in which case lack of awareness of the benefits of ATS depresses demand still further' (CEC, 1991). Although the STAR programme included measures to stimulate demand, 80 per cent of the budget was spent on improving infrastructure, with the main thrust being towards network digitalization, public data networks and cellular mobile radio.

According to the evaluation of STAR at a European Community level (Ewbank Preece, 1993), the programme was successful in bringing forward the investment plans of the public telecommunication operators (PTOs), including accelerating network digitalization in Greece by two years and bringing forward the launch of a cellular radio network in Portugal, again by two years. These results are quite impressive when it is realized that the European Regional Development Fund's (ERDF) financing of STAR's infrastructure measures amounted to only 2.2 per cent of the total telecommunications investment in the eligible regions over the 1987–91 period. Evaluating the contribution of STAR's infrastructure measures to regional development proved rather more difficult to achieve. Ewbank Preece was able to conclude only that 'the type of infrastructure supported [by STAR] is important for regional economic development', and that 'our opinion is that, in general, these projects have represented a good use of regional development funds' (Ewbank Preece, 1993: S-17).

By the end of the STAR programme, however, a wave of liberalization, coupled with technological change, was shaping a new uneven geography of telecommunications service supply (Cornford et al., 1996). Although liberalization increased overall investment in telecommunications, that investment was highly unevenly distributed. With the advent of competition in telecommunications markets, commercial considerations come to the fore, creating a pressure on the operator to bring the prices charged for a service into line with the costs of providing that service.

Under these competitive conditions, telecommunications network operators will seek to minimize the costs of provision of new investments, and to maximize the revenues gained from these investments. Therefore, new competitive operators tend to make their investment in the most profitable market segments, that is, services primarily targeted at – or used by – large businesses, such as leased lines, virtual private networks, long distance and international voice telephony and intelligent network functionality. Commercial pressures ensured that established operators were forced to reflect this strategy if they were to meet the competition (see e.g., Beesley and Laidlaw, 1995). The largest and earliest benefits in terms of costs and functionality arising from the liberalization of telecommunications were therefore likely to be seen by large service firms that rely on these services.

Such large business users have a characteristic geographical pattern of location, being concentrated in the Central Business Districts (CBDs) of major cities and in business parks on the periphery of urban areas. From the point of view of the telecommunications operators, targeting such agglomerations of aggregate business demand helps to lower the costs of providing services (as fewer locations need to be serviced) and maximizes the potential revenues received from new investments. Such locations, therefore, tend to receive new investments well in advance of smaller towns, residential urban areas and rural areas. The general pattern, then, has been one of 'hot spots' of intense competition and investment, surrounded by 'warm halos' of duopolistic competition giving way in turn to 'cold shadows' of de facto monopoly (Gillespie and Cornford, 1995). Regions that lack a critical mass of large sophisticated users concentrated in a major CBD have been likely to find that most of their territory will remain in the cold-shadow category. Liberalization has thus ensured that new private investment has been concentrated in core regions, while the take up of new advanced telecoms services in peripheral regions has often been disappointing.

In this context, then, there emerged a critique of the infrastructure-led policies, such as STAR, which pointed out that there was little point in a region having an advanced telecommunications infrastructure if there were no users sophisticated enough to make use of it. As Parker and Hudson (1995: 161) pointed out, regional development 'depends critically on how well individuals, businesses and communities *use* telecommunications networks to improve their economic prospects' (emphasis added). The effectiveness of this critique may be gauged by advice from the European Commission at the end of the 1990s that effectively bans the use of the ERDF for telecommunications infrastructure, in favour of demand-side interventions (CEC, 1999).

1.4 THE INFORMATION-INTENSIVE REGIONS

1.4.1 The Relocation of Service Work

As the focus of regional development policy moved away from telecommunications infrastructure and towards the uses to which that infrastructure could be put, attention naturally moved to the most intensive users of telecommunications: large firms in the increasingly 'industrialized' service sector. The industrialization of services dates back to the early years of the 20th Century, with the progressive simplification, routinization and division of many service activities. Technology has been a key element in this process (Zuboff, 1988). The recent growth of ICT potentially accelerates this process by allowing further codification of information and knowledge, which diminishes the importance of 'substantive knowledge' within the workforce as knowledge becomes systematized and embedded in technology (Richardson, 1994; 1997).

The full routinization of much service work has now penetrated a range of service-sector activities. This 'industrialization of office work' has had important implications for where work takes place: there is a tendency to concentrate these semi-automated functions in a relatively small number of specialist sites in order to gain economies of scale. Changing skills profiles thus make office work more mobile or footloose. Further, ICT can allow firms to enter remote markets cost effectively by trading their service 'over the wire', thereby establishing a 'telepresence' in a region without the necessity of even a temporary physical presence. In doing so, production is separated from consumption and this, in turn, allows organizations greater mobility in seeking production sites where lower costs or higher quality of production inputs (particularly labour) can be obtained. Many firms engaged in service activities are thus able to take advantage of the widespread availability of ICT to (re)discover the basic principles of the (inter)national division of labour (Freeman and Soete, 1994).

Routine back-office work generally deals with 'corporate internal services that require little face-to-face contact with the corporate personnel they support or with the extra-corporate world' (Nelson, 1986: 149), which is usually associated with routine, fairly low-level and often bulk work, most notably data processing work. Traditionally performed in, or close to, the head office, this type of work could now be moved to lower-cost locations. More significantly, the later 1990s saw the rapid growth of a new form of mobile work, generally known as 'teleservices'. Here, face-to-face customer service is replaced, or supplemented, by telephone-based customer service. A number of functions have been 'telemediated' in this way, including sales, banking, marketing, market research, technical support, reservations, appointment setting, order taking, lead generation, membership renewal, insurance and customer enquiries (Richardson, 1997; Richardson et al., 2000). Once the face-to-face link is broken, such service activity no longer needs to be co-located with service consumption, and firms are able to concentrate operations into one or a few 'customer service factories' or 'call centres' (Richardson, 1997).

Although most call centres are relatively footloose workplaces, teleservices are far from homogeneous, with such services ranging from the delivery of simple information (e.g., flight times) to fairly complex technical support (e.g., in computing); different types of call centres, requiring different types of skills, will thus have different locational requirements. Evidence from the UK suggested that teleservice firms which service a national market are tending to locate in large conurbations, such as Greater Manchester, Leeds, Newcastle and Glasgow (Leyshon and Thrift, 1993; Richardson, 1994), where wages are lower and property cheaper than in the south-east of England. Further, grants for training, for property and for capital investment are often available in certain locations within less-favoured city-regions. In Tyne and Wear, for example, around half of all call centres were located in Enterprise Zones[3] (Richardson and Marshall, 1996). The tendency to focus on urban rather than rural areas seems to be explained mainly by the need for a large pool of labour from which firms can cherry-pick staff with particular attributes (Richardson, 1995).

Most high value-added service activities, however, remain in core regions and it is generally the relatively lower value-added activities that are dispersed to less-favoured regions. Where *new* products and processes are developed, face-to-face contact remains crucial for the transmission of ideas and knowledge. ICT serves as a mechanism for enhancing the ability of these central places in core regions to extend their spatial reach, both by controlling less sophisticated parts of the production process and by 'exporting' their own products over the wire. ICT does create opportunities for new growth locations in some non-routine tasks (e.g., treasury and funds management) in areas such as financial services (Warf, 1995; Langdale, 2000). However, this is the exception rather than the rule (Mitchelson and Wheeler, 1994; Castells and Hall, 1994; Sassen, 1991; 1994).

What is more, although much routine work has become more mobile, not all Europe's less-favoured regions have been able to benefit from such mobility. Only those regions that can demonstrate they have a labour force able to perform the required activities to a high quality can expect to attract the newly mobile activities. In addition, many core regions are themselves realizing the importance of these new mobile jobs and are seeking to retain or attract them, thus increasing the competition for these functions. New levels of mobility facilitated by ICT also mean that firms can seek out production locations beyond Europe. So, for example, there has been some evidence to suggest that firms are relocating routine software (and in some cases more complex) activities to the Indian sub-continent, South-East Asia and Eastern Europe (*Computing*, 1993 and 1994; Keen, 1991; Pearson and Mitter, 1993; Wilson, 1995).

Finally, although the volume of information processing is likely to continue to grow, this trend may have only a limited impact on employment growth in less-favoured regions. First, as existing data processing centres are tending to concentrate into even larger sites, fewer regions will attract this form of employment – although those which do will find proportionately greater benefits, at least in the short-run (Gillespie et al., 1995). This trend towards larger centres should exclude the more rural areas without the critical mass of labour. Competition from lower-cost, off-shore locations is also intensifying as ICT becomes more widespread (Pearson and Mitter, 1993; Wilson, 1994; Allan, 1995; Warf, 1995). The introduction of distributed processing means that many processing tasks have been re-integrated into front office operations; meanwhile, processing is likely to become further automated with the development of scanning, bar coding, voice recognition and other technologies (Marshall and Richardson, 1996; Richardson et al., 2000).

1.4.2 SME Networking and Global Reach

Regional development policy did not concentrate only on the externally-led route to regional development based on the new locational freedoms that ICT has opened up to many large service organizations. Another route, which stresses the opportunities for locally-led development, has also been explored. This model emphasizes the way enterprises and entrepreneurs in less-favoured or peripheral regions can use advanced communications networks to gain access to markets, suppliers or sources of specialist information located in core regions (Richardson and Gillespie, 1996).

A succession of infrastructure, service, application and demand-stimulation policies have attempted to facilitate the adoption and use of telecommunications by SMEs in less-favoured regions (Ilbery et al., 1995; Richardson and Gillespie, 1996). However, there has been little evidence so far to suggest that the locally-led model is working. Levels of adoption of ICT in less-favoured regions have lagged those in core regions, particularly amongst SMEs. Perhaps even more disturbingly, the evidence suggests consistently that even when adoption takes place, it is not translated into effective use. Thus, the EU Services and Applications for Rural Business Activities (SARBA) project, which surveyed over 2 000 businesses across a number of rural regions in Europe, concluded that 'there is considerable underuse of equipment and telematics services. This failure to exploit potential suggests that the opportunities offered by telematics, especially for tackling business problems ... are far from being realised' (Ilbery et al., 1995: 66; see also Fuller and Southern, 1999; Mitchell and Clark, 1999; Grimes, 2000). Similarly, a comparative study by Roberta Capello (1994) of the impacts of telecommunications adoption by small firms in the north and south of Italy found that, whereas in the north there was a clear association between adoption of telematics and enhanced competitiveness, in the south no such relationship could be identified. She concluded that 'backward regions ... seem to be quite unable to achieve economic advantages from the use of these technologies' (ibid., 1994: 220).

The evidence suggests that a series of 'translations' need to take place before firms can exploit ICT for competitive advantage. First, infrastructure investment must be translated into the provision of *appropriate services and applications*; users must be made *aware* of what is on offer and what is possible; this awareness must be translated into actual *adoption* of the technologies; adopting firms must reorganize their business processes to ensure *effective usage* of the adopted technologies; and, finally, effective usage must be translated into *competitive advantage*. If any of these translations fail to take place satisfactorily, the assumed causal link from infrastructure investment to regional development will break down (Gillespie et al., 1995; Cornford et al., 2000).

Significantly from a policy perspective, evidence suggests that none of these translations can be relied upon to take place automatically, and that even though they may take place in one regional context, they may well fail in another. Further, it would seem to be questions of skills and organizational and institutional capacities which account for the differing outcomes. Evidence from various European regions for the Advanced Communications for Cohesion and Regional Development in Europe (ACCORDE) project, for example, found that the explanation for why some telematics applications fail while others succeed lay largely in the organizational and institutional contexts within which the applications were situated (Ó Siochrú et al., 1995). In a similar vein, Capello's (1994) study of small firms in the north and south of Italy attributed – on the basis of causal path analysis – the lack of effective use of telecommunications by firms in the south to the absence of various 'micro-conditions', such as the organizational flexibility and innovative capacity necessary for adoption to lead to effective use.

From a slightly different perspective, a study for the European Commission, carried out by Analysys Ltd (Hansen et al., 1990), used econometric modelling techniques to estimate the costs and benefits of stimulating applications of telecommunications and information technologies across Europe. They determined that benefits outweigh costs for most rural areas, and the benefit is reduced for extremely rural areas. They interpreted this finding as supporting a 'threshold hypothesis', such that a certain minimum level of general infrastructure or development is a prerequisite for a sustainable economic take-off. Such a threshold may need to be met across a wide range of infrastructures, both hard (e.g., roads, rail, airports and the availability of suitable commercial and domestic property) and soft (e.g., schools, cultural and leisure facilities), as well as with respect to other issues (e.g., grants and fiscal incentives). Obviously, the precise levels required vary according to the characteristics of the region and the development model being pursued, although basic minima in all fields appears a necessary condition for development. It was concluded that telecommunications alone was unlikely to have particularly beneficial implications for indigenous enterprises – unless these enterprises, and the broader regional contexts within which they are embedded, possess a number of complimentary assets (Ó Siochrú et al., 1995).

Not only is it clear that investing in high-grade information infrastructures is not in itself sufficient to bring about economic development, but even providing services and tailoring them to the (assumed) needs of indigenous enterprises often proves insufficient. In part, this is because the real needs of users are all too often taken for granted or mis-specified in the initiative design process (Gibbs and Leach, 1994; Ilbery et al., 1995; Ó Siochrú et al., 1995; Tanner and Gibbs, 1997; Fuller and Southern, 1999). What is more, the same application, even if designed to meet identical user needs, can have widely differing outcomes in differing organizational and socio-economic contexts. Therefore, it has been argued that, if they are to be effective in meeting economic development goals, policies for both information infrastructure and demand stimulation need to be integrated with policies designed to mobilize and upgrade the other aspects of regional organizational and socio-economic environments.

1.5 THE LEARNING REGION

The information society clearly opens up opportunities for some less-favoured regions to benefit from the increased mobility of routinized and codified work. There are, however, equally clear limits to these opportunities. Some regions have most to gain, in particular those that can offer a large, differentiated and under-utilized labour force at low costs, and which have a reasonably well-developed basic transport and other infrastructure. It is just as clear, however, that there are threats here too: the concentration of service activity in some regions can denude other regions of important service functions and employment; some of these operations could be moved to lower-cost regions beyond the boundaries of the EU; and some of the functions currently undertaken in such 'customer service factories' could be substantially automated in the future. Relying on externally-determined location decisions may provide a short-term fix to some of the problems of unemployment or underemployment in less-favoured regions, but it does not provide the basis for a robust regional economy in the long run (Cornford et al., 2000).

Any attempt by less-favoured regions to pursue a strategy of locally-based development aiming to support a more active form of regional incorporation into the information society faces considerable barriers. While *some* locally-based firms in less-favoured regions are using telematics applications to reach out to new markets and suppliers, or to reconfigure their patterns of operations and enhance their competitiveness, there is little evidence that this is a widespread or systematic development in less-favoured regions or that the new network technologies are supporting successful inter-firm networking within less-favoured regions. If anything, the reverse seems to be the case: take-up of the new technologies is generally lower in the less-favoured regions and much of the adoption that does take place is the result of pressure from suppliers or customers in core regions (e.g., Mitchell and Clark, 1999).

It is increasingly argued that, for high value-added activities, the key regional requirement is not 'information' (codified data) but knowledge; in particular, hard-to-express, or tacit, knowledge – the kind that is resistant to being transformed into information (and thus to manipulation and transfer via information technology). One indicator of this is the slow waning of the notion of the 'information society' as a rubric in regional development and its replacement by the concept of 'the knowledge-based economy' or 'knowledge-based development'. From this perspective, the weaknesses of firms, in particular SMEs, in the less-favoured regions in relation to technology has come to be understood in terms of their failure, individually and collectively, to make effective use of the technologies through complementary process innovations, incorporating both the technologies and the organizational structures and business processes necessary to make use of them. Against the background of this diagnosis, the emphasis in regional-development thinking has moved towards promoting a continuous process of learning and innovation within the regional economy – a 'learning region' strategy.

The concept of a learning region is often little more than a trite application of some fashionable business doctrines into regional development discourse (e.g., Florida, 1995) or a synonym for improvements in the education and training system. Important as individual-level learning is for the acquisition of appropriate skills (Morgan, 1992), or learning associated with innovation within companies and industries (Lundvall and Johnson, 1994; Lundvall 1996), the concept of the learning region implies a focus on the issue of broad *institutional* learning within the regional economy (Storper, 1995, 1997; Morgan, 1997).

Institutional learning is generally understood to be based on dense interaction among regional actors – so-called 'learning by interacting' – including interaction among firms themselves, but also interactions with a diverse range of other bodies, such as universities, regional development and technology transfer agencies and research laboratories. Further, this approach has a strong emphasis on experiential and experimental learning-by-doing as opposed to the adoption of well-standardized and codified routines, leading to the acquisition of tacit knowledge. This focus on tacit knowledge reinforces the need for proximity and a hybrid of technology with older, face-to-face, means of communication. In short, to get the most from *computer* networks (including the Internet), there needs to be a particular form of *social* network in place (Cornford et al., 2000; Storper 1997). To exploit the technological capital represented by ICT, regions need an abundant supply of 'social capital' (Putnam, 1993).

Although the 'learning region' is now perhaps the most sophisticated model of 'information society' oriented to regional development thinking in Europe, it has not gone without criticism (Lovering, 1999; Lagendijk and Cornford, 2000; MacLeod, 2000; Hassink and Lagendijk, 2001; MacKinnon et al., 2002). Here, I want to focus on the practical problems of implementing a strategy based on the 'learning region' diagnosis. The central problem, well identified in an OECD (2001) report, concerns the problems of implementing a 'learning region' policy in the less-favoured regions. As the report's authors argue:

> On the one hand, [the learning region approach] suggests that localised learning policies are required. On the other, it shows that such localised learning policies cannot readily be transposed from one region to another, because ... such learning policies derive their efficacy precisely from the specificities of their regional context (OECD, 2001: 25).

There is, therefore, no 'off the peg' set of policies that can be expected to work in all regional contexts. Rather, policy development needs to be highly sensitive to local economic and social traditions, norms and conditions. Such policy development and implementation require a very different set of competencies – we might even say, a different worldview – from those required by early policy formulations, and it is unclear to what extent regional development agencies are able to rise to this challenge.

1.6 CONCLUSIONS

What is striking, looking back on the above schematic account of the development of regional policy thinking and policy engagement with ICT, is the slow process by which each shift of emphasis has moved the debate further away from a concern with the technologies themselves – understood as silicon and boxes or wires and software applications – and towards a concern with the core economic and social processes of learning and innovation, and the dense networks of face-to-face contact which they appear to require. This increasing focus on the importance of the social context in shaping the degree to which, and the ways in which, ICT is absorbed into, and used within, regional economies and societies helps to explain the resilience of the core regions and their capacity to dominate the supposedly 'weightless', knowledge-based economy. The technologies themselves seem to change almost daily; but if the core determinant of the capacity of regions to utilize those technologies for growth is actually social capital and, as Putnam (1993) has argued, social capital is accumulated over centuries rather than decades, then we should expect no quick fixes and no sudden turnarounds in the economic fortunes of the less-favoured regions.

Will a new chapter in the story emerge from the critique of the 'learning region'? Here, I have been concerned with a retrospective view rather than with any kind of prediction. I would argue that, in one sense at least, there can be no further development of this dialectic, at least in the form in which I have presented it, because the underlying dynamic of this development – the elaboration of technological possibilities and their negation in the embedded social structures and processes – appears to have run its course. What started with the dynamic powers of the 'new' technologies has, therefore, ended with the realization of the resilience of some very old features of regional societies.

REFERENCES

Allan, J. (1995), 'Crossing Borders or Footloose Multinationals?', in J. Allan and C. Hamnett (eds), *A Shrinking World? Global Unevenness and Inequality*, Buckingham, UK: Open University Press, 55–102.

Beesley, M. and B. Laidlaw (1995), 'Development of Telecommunications Policy', in M. Bishop, J. Kay and C. Mayer (eds), *The Regulatory Challenge,* Oxford: OUP, 309–35.

Biehl, D. (1986), *The Contribution of Infrastructure to Regional Development*, Final Report of the Infrastructure Studies Group to the Commission of the European Communities, Luxembourg: Office for Official Publications of the European Communities.

Capello, R. (1994), *Spatial Analysis of Telecommunications Network Externalities,* Aldershot, UK: Avebury.

Castells, M. and P. Hall (1994), *Technopoles of the World: The Making of 21st Century Industrial Complexes,* London: Routledge.

CEC (1991), Commission of the European Communities, *STAR: Programme Report*, Brussels: CEC.

CEC (1994), Commission of the European Communities, *Competitiveness and Cohesion: Trends in the Regions,* Fifth Periodic Report on the Social and Economic Situation and Development of the Regions in the Community, Brussels: CEC.

CEC (1999), Commission of the European Communities, *Information Society and Regional Development: ERDF Interventions 2000/2006, Criteria for Assessment*, Technical Papers for the New Programming Period 2000/2006, No. 2, Brussels: CEC.

Computing (1993), 'Sun Life Finds Success in India', 28 October.

Computing (1994), 'Passage to India Brings Savings for Data Logic', 5 May.

Cornford, J., S. Ó Siochrú and A. Gillespie (1996), *Regulation and the Supplyside: Volume 4 of An Assessment of the Social and Economic Cohesion Aspects of the Development of an Information Society in Europe*, report to DGXIII and DGXVI of the Commission of the European Communities, Dublin: Nexus Europe (see www.iol.ie/nexus/cs.htm for the Summary volume).

Cornford, J., A. Gillespie and R. Richardson (2000), 'Regional Development in the Information Society', in K. Ducatel, J. Webster and W. Hermann (eds.), *Social and Societal Aspects of the Information Society in Europe*, Lanham, MD: Rowman and Littlefield, 21–44.

Cronin, F.J., E.B. Parker, E.K. Colleran and M.A. Gold (1991), 'Telecommunications Infrastructure and Economic Growth: An Analysis of Causality', *Telecommunications Policy,* **15** (6), 529–35.

Cronin, F.J., E.B. Parker, E.K. Colleran and M.A. Gold (1993), 'Telecommunications Infrastructure Investment and Economic Development', *Telecommunications Policy,* **17** (6), 415–30.

DTI (1994), Department of Trade and Industry, *Study of the International Competitiveness of the UK Telecommunications Infrastructure*, report for the DTI, prepared by Robert Harrison, PA Consulting Group, London: DTI.

Ewbank Preece (1993), *STAR – Special Telecommunications Action for Regional Development: Community-level Evaluation, Executive Summary*, Brighton, UK: Ewbank Preece Ltd.

Florida, R. (1995), 'Towards the Learning Region', *Futures,* **27** (5), 527–36.

Freeman, C. and L. Soete (1994), *Work for All or Mass Unemployment: Computerised Technical Change into the 21st Century*, London: Pinter.

Friedman, A. (1989), with D. Cornford, *Computer Systems Development*, Chichester, UK: Wiley.

Fuller, E.C. and A. Southern (1999), 'Small Firms and Information and Communication Technologies: Policy Issues and Some Words of Caution', *Environment and Planning C: Government and Policy*, **17** (3), 287–302.

Gibbs, D. and B. Leach (1994), 'Telematics in Local Economic Development: The Case of Manchester', *Tijdschrift voor Economische en Sociale Geografie*, **85** (3), 209–23.

Gillespie, A. and J. Cornford (1995), 'Network Diversity or Network Fragmentation? The Evolution of European Telecommunications in Competitive Environments', in D. Banister, R. Capello and P. Nijkamp (eds), *European Transport and Communications Networks*, Chichester, UK: Wiley, 319–32.

Gillespie, A.E., J.B. Goddard, J.F. Robinson, I. Smith and A.T. Thwaites (1984), *The Effects of New Information Technology on the Less-Favoured Regions of the Community*, Studies Collection, Regional Policy Series No 23, Brussels: Commission of the European Communities.

Gillespie, A., R. Richardson and J. Cornford (1995), 'Information Infrastructures and Territorial Development', background paper prepared for the OECD Workshop on Information Infrastructures and Territorial Development, 7–8 November, Paris: OECD.

Grimes, S. (2000), 'Rural Areas in the Information Society: Diminishing Distance or Increasing Learning Capacity?', *Journal of Rural Studies*, **16** (1), 13–21.

Hall, P and A. Markusen (1985), *Silicon Landscapes,* Boston, MA: Allen and Unwin.

Hansen, S., D. Cleevely, S. Wadsworth, H. Bailey and O. Bakewell (1990), 'Telecommunications in Rural Europe: Economic Implications', *Telecommunications Policy*, **14** (3), 207–22.

Hardy, A.P. (1980), 'The Role of the Telephone in Economic Development', *Telecommunications Policy*, **4** (4), 278–86.

Hassink, R. and A. Lagendijk (2001), 'The Dilemmas of Interregional Institutional Learning', *Environment and Planning C: Government and Policy*, **19** (1): 65-84.

Healey and Baker (1992), *European Real Estate Monitor*, London: Healey and Baker.

Ilbery B., D. Clark, N. Berkeley and I. Goldman (1995), 'Telematics and Rural Development: Evidence from a Survey of Small Business in the European Union', *European Urban and Regional Studies*, **2** (1), 55–68.

Ireland, J. (1994), *The Importance of Telecommunications to London as an International Financial Centre*, Subject Report XVIII, The City Research Project, London: London Business School and Corporation of London.

Keen, P.G.W. (1991), *Shaping the Future: Business Design through Information Technology,* Cambridge, MA: Harvard Business School Press.

Lagendijk, A. and J. Cornford (2000), 'Regional Institutions and Knowledge – Tracking New Forms of Regional Development Policy', *Geoforum* **31** (2), 209–18.

Langdale, J.V. (2000), 'Telecommunications and 24-hour Trading in the International Securities Business', in M.I. Wilson and K.E. Corey (eds.), *Information Tectonics: Space, Place and Technology in an Electronic Age*, Chichester, UK: Wiley, 89-100.

Leyshon, A. and N. Thrift (1993), 'The Restructuring of the U.K. Financial Services Industry in the 1990s: A Reversal of Fortune?', *Journal of Rural Studies*, **9** (3), 223–41.

Lovering, J. (1999), 'Theory Led by Policy: The Inadequacies of "The New Regionalism"', *International Journal of Urban and Regional Research*, **22** (2), 379–95.

Lundvall, B.-Å. (1996), *The Social Dimension of the Learning Economy*, Working Paper No. 96/1, Copenhagen: Danish Research Unit for Industrial Dynamics (DRUID).

Lundvall, B.-Å. and B. Johnson (1994), 'The Learning Economy', *Journal of Industry Studies*, **1** (2), 23–42.

MacLeod, G. (2000), 'The Learning Region in an Age of Austerity: Capitalizing on Knowledge, Entrepreneurialism and Reflexive Capitalism', *Geoforum*, **31** (2), 219–36.

MacKinnon, D., A. Cumbers and K. Chapman (2002), 'Learning, Innovation and Regional Development: A Critical Appraisal of Recent Debates', *Progress in Human Geography*, **26** (3), 293–311

Marshall, J.N. and R. Richardson (1996), *The Growth, Location and Mobility of Services*, Glasgow: Locate in Scotland.

Mitchell, S. and D. Clark (1999), 'Business Adoption of Information and Communications Technologies in the Two Tier Rural Economy: Some Evidence from the South Midlands', *Journal of Rural Studies*, **15** (4), 447–55.

Mitchelson R.L. and J.O. Wheeler (1994), 'National and International Information Flows: The Role of Major U.S. Metropolitan Centers,' *Annals of the Association of American Geographers*, **84** (1): 87-107.

Moore, G.E. (1965), 'Cramming More Components onto Integrated Circuits', *Electronics*, **38** (8): 114-17.

Morgan, K. (1992), 'Telematics and Regional Development – Conference Report', in *Telematics Conference Proceedings,* Kells, Northern Ireland, 30–31 May, Brussels: Commission of the European Communities.

Morgan, K. (1997), 'The Learning Region: Institutions, Innovation and Regional Renewal', *Regional Studies*, **31** (5), 491–503.

Nelson, K. (1986), 'Labour Demand, Labour Supply and the Suburbanisation of Low Wage Office Work', in A.J. Scott and M. Storper (eds), *Production, Work and Territory: The Geographical Anatomy of Industrial Capitalism*, Boston, MA: Allan and Unwin, 149–67.

Nexus Europe, CURDS and Culture and Communications Studies (1996), *An Assessment of the Social and Economic Cohesion Aspects of the Development of an Information Society in Europe. Volume 5: Synthesis and Recommendations,* final report to DG XIII and DG XVI of the CEC, Dublin: Nexus Europe.

OECD (2001), Organisation for Economic Co-operation and Development, *Cities and Regions in the New Learning Economy*, Paris: OECD.

Ó Siochrú, S., A. Gillespie and L. Qvortrup (1995), *Advanced Communications for Cohesion and Regional Development (ACCORDE),* Final Report to Commission of the European Communities, Dublin: Nexus Europe.

Parker, E. and H. Hudson (1995), *Electronic Byways: State Policies for Rural Development through Telecommunications*, Washington, DC: The Aspen Institute Rural Economic Policy Program.

Pearson, R. and S. Mitter (1993), 'Employment and Working Conditions of Low-skilled Information Processing Workers in Less Developed Countries', *International Labour Review*, **132** (1), 49–64.

Perez, C. (1983), 'Structural Change and Assimilation of New Technologies in Economic and Social Systems', *Futures*, **15** (5), 357–75.

Putnam, R. (1993), with R. Leonardi and R. Nanetti, *Making Democracy Work: Civic Traditions in Modern Italy*, Princeton, NJ: Princeton University Press.

Richardson, R. (1994), 'Back Officing Front Office Functions – Organisational and Locational Implications of New Telemediated Services', in R. Mansell (ed.)

Management of Information and Communication Technologies, London: Aslib, 309–35.

Richardson, R. (1995), *Teleservices and Economic Development: A Case Study of Ireland*, Newcastle-upon-Tyne, UK: Centre for Urban and Regional Development Studies (CURDS), University of Newcastle.

Richardson, R. (1997), 'Network Technologies, Organisational Change and the Location of Employment: The Case of Teleservices', in A. Dumort, T. Fenoulhet and A. Onishi, (eds), *The Economics of the Information Society*, Luxembourg: Office for the Official Publications of the European Communities, 194–200.

Richardson, R. and A. Gillespie (1996), 'Advanced Communications and Employment Creation in Rural and Peripheral Regions: A Case Study of the Highlands and Islands of Scotland', *The Annals of Regional Science*, **30** (1), 91–110.

Richardson, R. and J.N. Marshall (1996), 'The Growth of Telephone Call Centres in Peripheral Areas of Britain: Evidence from Tyne and Wear', *Area* **28** (3), 308–17.

Richardson, R., V. Belt and N. Marshall (2000), 'Taking Calls to Newcastle: The Regional Implications of the Growth in Call Centres', *Regional Studies*, **34** (4), 357–69.

Sassen, S. (1991), *The Global City*, New Jersey: Princeton University Press.

Sassen, S. (1994), *Cities in a World Economy*, Thousand Oaks, CA: Pine Forge Press.

Sommerville, I. (2001), *Software Engineering*, Harlow, UK: Addison-Wesley.

Storper, M. (1995), 'The Resurgence of Regional Economies, Ten Years Later: The Region as a Nexus of Untraded Interdependencies', *European Urban and Regional Studies*, **2** (3), 191–221.

Storper, M. (1997), *The Regional World*, New York: Guildford Press.

Tanner, K. and D. Gibbs (1997), 'Local Economic Development Strategies and Information and Communications Technologies', in J. Simmie (ed.) *Innovation Networks and Learning Regions*, London: Jessica Kingsley, 196–210.

Warf, B. (1995), 'Telecommunications and Knowledge Transmission', *Urban Studies*, **32** (2), 361–78.

Wilson, M.I. (1994), 'Offshore Relocation of Producer Services: The Irish Back Office', paper presented at the Conference of the Association of American Geographers (AAG), Florida, March, Washington, DC: AAG.

Wilson, M.I. (1995), 'Press 1 for Reservations: Information Technology and the Location of Airline Operations', paper presented at the Conference of the Association of American Geographers (AAG), Chicago, March, Washington, DC: AAG.

Zuboff, S. (1988), *In the Age of the Smart Machine: The Future of Work and Power*, New York: Basic Books Inc.

NOTES

1. This paper draws extensively on a great deal of joint work carried out over the past decade and more in the Centre for Urban and Regional Development Studies (CURDS) at the University of Newcastle. I would particularly like to acknowledge the work of Andy Gillespie, Ranald Richardson and Vicki Belt, on which I have drawn freely. Any errors are, of course, my own.
2. What has come to be known as Moore's law is based on the observation made by Gordon E. Moore, one of the founders of Intel Corporation, that the number of transistors which could

be packed into an integrated circuit was doubling every year or so (e.g., Moore, 1965). The law has subsequently come to be associated with the notion that computer hardware in general can be expected to double in nominal power and halve in cost every eighteen months. Some have argued that this has become a self-fulfilling prophecy, as it provides the chip designers and manufacturers with a benchmark for which to aim.

3. Enterprise Zones are areas designated by the British Government for a period of ten years. The aim is to encourage private sector activity in these zones, to create jobs and bring derelict land back into use by removing certain tax burdens and relaxing, or speeding up, the application of statutory or administrative controls.

2. Development and Telecommunications Access: Cases from South Asia

Subhash Bhatnagar

2.1 INTRODUCTION

Case studies of innovative experiments from India and Bangladesh are provided in this chapter, to illustrate the impact of telecom and Internet access on development in rural areas. The first example discussed, Grameen Telecom (GTC), examines the socio-economic impact of providing mobile telephones for community use to villagers in Bangladesh. The second, the Gyandoot project, illustrates how communities in rural areas can be empowered by delivering information and services through the Internet. Another example, from the context of the cooperative dairy movement in India, indicates that rural communities are willing to invest in ICT provided that real value is achieved. Collectively, these examples highlight the potential impact on development of enhanced rural telecom access. However, telecom access across Asia is poor and would require huge investment to cover large parts of rural areas, necessitating a proactive policy that encourages investment in infrastructure for rural areas. The nature of policy encouragement for different regions would have to be based on the cost of providing access, the potential for earning revenue and the availability of institutions that can deliver a valuable service in rural areas. The chapter proposes a framework of micro-analysis for this purpose.

2.2 DEVELOPMENTAL IMPACTS OF ICT: THE CASE STUDIES

The case studies in this section do not view telecom access in isolation from the value-added services that can ride on telecom infrastructure. In fact, many development practitioners recognize the value of enhancing communications reach through whatever media are most appropriate in a specific context. For instance, there are interesting experiments where community radio, telephones and the Internet have been used together to deliver functional knowledge to rural communities in an interactive fashion (Jayaweera, 2001). GTC is one of the few such examples where the results of a survey-based impact analysis conducted by an external agency are available. The two other cases included here are anecdotal in nature and provide a qualitative assessment of the developmental impact of taking Internet access to rural areas.

2.2.1 The Grameen Village Pay-Phone Initiative in Bangladesh

The Grameen Bank of Bangladesh (GB), a non-governmental organization (NGO), introduced Village Pay Phones (VPPs) into villages in Bangladesh by leasing cellular mobile phones to women members of its micro-credit program. The aim was to ensure easy telephone access to all residents in rural areas and to introduce a new income-generating activity for GB members. GB seems to have been prompted to enter the rural telecom sector by the following basic premises:

1. Asymmetry in the realm of information is one of the principal causes of inequality, backwardness and poverty.
2. Telephone services can have a perceptible influence on production, marketing and other important economic decisions confronting rural households.
3. Technology, per se, cannot be the solution to the problems of rural development and poverty reduction unless the issue of 'who controls the technology' can be resolved. Historically, the control of modern technologies wielded by the rural wealthy empowered them to extract rents, for example for modern irrigation or chemical fertilizer in Bangladesh. This experience, and the insight that the poor are indeed creditworthy, indicates that the poor could be given control of the latest ICTs, such as cellular mobile phones.
4. Even if specific individuals are unable to buy a phone, they should have access to phone services as and when they need it. Labour mobility, both inside and outside the country, has increased very fast over the years. The volume of rural-urban migration has outpaced economic growth. All these factors have heightened the demand for VPPs.

In November 1996, licenses to operate cellular mobile phone networks were issued, and GB (as GTC), Telecom Malaysia, International Bangladesh Ltd and Sheba Telecom Ltd entered the market at that time. GTC holds 35 per cent of Grameen Phone Ltd. (GPL), a joint venture of these four partners, which was awarded a nationwide licence for GSM 900 cellular mobile phones. GPL is responsible for network operations throughout Bangladesh, and for providing services to urban subscribers in particular. GTC as the service provider buys airtime in bulk from GPL. The cellular mobile phone is provided by GB under a lease arrangement, where the members have to repay the cost of purchase through weekly instalments within the stipulated period of three years. The telephone costs Tk.18 000 but, with the interest that accrues, the sum to be repaid by the GB member within three years totals Tk.23 050 ($1 = approximately 60 takas [Tks]).

2.2.1.1 Selection of operators and pricing of calls

In a pilot project covering 950 villages and 65 000 people, GB leased cellular phones to women members who had a very good record of repaying GB loans and running a good business (preferably a village grocery store). Operators were required to be able to read and write. Their residences would be located near the centre of their villages. Plans foresaw GTC providing services to 100 million rural inhabitants in 68 000 villages within four years, through the financing of 40 000 VPPs to the two million GB members and other potential customers. GPL's investments totalled $90 million initially, and are expected to reach $500 million within seven years of the company's formation (Richardson et al., 2000).

In order to promote usage, the call charges for VPP operators and their users were set at a very reasonable level. For domestic calls, a bulk-airtime rate is paid by GTC to GPL: Tk.2 and Tk.1 per minute for peak and off-peak hours, respectively. VPP operators pay the bulk-airtime rate plus 13 per cent to cover GTC overhead costs and VPP customers pay the same charges as are fixed for regular GPL subscribers. VPP operators charge their customers Tk.10 per call for all incoming international calls and Tk.2 for each incoming domestic call.

2.2.1.2 Benefits to the rural populace

A study was conducted by the University of Bonn's Centre for Development Research (ZEF) to determine how VPPs affect rural development and poverty reduction. It surveyed 50 phone owners and 356 users from 50 villages. The study reported (Bayes et al., 1999) a growing demand for phone use in rural Bangladesh, as demonstrated by the fact that 76 per cent of the users surveyed had used a telephone within the last year, while 49 per cent had used one within the last five years.

The analysis of 1 060 phone calls made in a week revealed that the combined groups of the poor made 268 calls, thus accounting for about a quarter of all calls. Within the owner/user group, the share of calls made by the poor and the non-poor appear to be more or less evenly distributed (45 per cent vs 55 per cent), while most phone calls among the villagers were found to have been made by non-poor households (roughly 78 per cent vs 22 per cent). It is noteworthy that the intensity of use by the poor is 50 per cent greater than that of the non-poor. A breakdown of the phone calls according to their respective levels of importance indicates that 85 per cent of the calls made by the sample users are 'important' ones. 'Less important' calls constitute about 12 per cent and 'could be avoided' calls 3 per cent.

The study categorized calls on the basis of respondents' specification of the chief purposes of their telephone conversations (see Table 2.1), including groupings such as: economically-related (e.g., concerning employment opportunities, business and the remittance of funds received from relatives working in other countries); social/personal (family- and office-related); and health (emergency and advice).

Table 2.1: Purposes of phone calls made by rural users in Bangladesh

Purpose	**Economic Status***			
	Extremely Poor	*Moderately Poor*	*All Poor*	*Non-poor*
Economic:	34 (53.9)	33 (39.8)	67 (45.9)	429 (46.9)
(a) Market prices of commodities	3 (4.8)	2 (2.4)	5 (3.4)	50 (5.5)
(b) Employment opportunities	4 (6.4)	13 (15.7)	17 (11.6)	50 (5.5)
(c) Land transactions	14 (22.2)	11 (13.2)	25 (17.1)	65 (7.1)
(d) Business-related	13 (20.5)	5 (6.0)	18 (12.4)	231 (25.3)
(e) Remittance	Nil	2 (2.4)	2 (1.4)	33 (3.5)
Social/personal	16 (25.4)	30 (36.1)	46 (31.5)	323 (35.3)
Health-related	11 (17.5)	15 (18.1)	26 (17.8)	94 (10.3)
Other	2 (3.2)	5 (6.0)	7 (4.8)	68 (7.5)
Totals	*63 (100.0)*	*83 (100.0)*	*146 (100.0)*	*914 (100.0)*

* Figures in brackets show percentages of all calls made by each group.

Source: Jahangirnagar University/ZEF Field Survey, 1998.

The poor and non-poor groups accounted for about the same proportion of economic/finance-related calls (almost 46 per cent and 47 per cent, respectively). Within the all-poor group, however, the extremely poor seem to use phones chiefly for economic purposes, making about 54 per cent of all their calls with these purposes in mind. The poor group also makes relatively more phone calls for health-related purposes than the non-poor (around 18 per cent and 10 per cent, respectively). The non-poor group, on the other hand, makes relatively more calls for business-related purposes (approximately 25 per cent vs 12 per cent), remittances (around 4 per cent vs 1 per cent) and for social/personal considerations (about 35 per cent vs 32 per cent). However, even in the extremely poor group, about 21 per cent of calls are for business reasons – showing that even the poorest sections of the village, which are involved in the production of eggs, vegetables and other produce, make phone calls to keep informed.

An assessment of the benefits of VPP use accrued by farmers revealed improved market efficiency as a key outcome (see Table 2.2). For instance, farmers in the target village received 70–75 per cent of the paddy prices paid by the final consumers, discernibly more than the 65–70 per cent of the prices received by control villagers. The price of eggs in target villages was reported to be Tk.13 per hali (four) during the period of the survey, compared to Tk.12 per hali in control villages.

Table 2.2: Assessment of selected benefits of Village Pay Phones

Variable	**Target Village (N=50, averages)**	**Control Village (N=10, averages)**
Prices:		
Paddy (% of final consumer prices)	70-75%	65-70%
Eggs	Tk.13 per hali*	Tk.12/hali*
Cost of information/knowledge	Tk.17	Tk.72
Chickens/ducks	Higher	Lower
Chick feeds	Lower	Higher
Supply of inputs:		
Diesel	Stable	Fluctuating at times
Fertilizer	Regular	Occasional problems
Others:		
Poultry mortality rate	Lower	Higher
Law and order situation	Improved	Same
Communication during disasters	Quick, effective	Slow, less effective
Communication with relatives at home and abroad	Anywhere, any time any day	Anywhere, but fixed time, fixed day
Transmission of new ideas	Improved	Same
Mobility of people	Higher	Lower
Spoilage of perishable products	Less	More
Access to health-care services	Faster/effective	Slower/less effective

* 'Hali' means four.

Source: Case studies and discussions during Jahangirnagar University /ZEF Field Survey, 1998.

The study of VPP benefits assessed that the operation was quite profitable, as the VPP owners earn an average net profit of Tk.277 per week. The profit level ranges from as high as Tk.683 per week to as low as Tk.35 a week. Half of the sample owners reap a net profit of more than Tk.300 per week, and another one-tenth earn more than Tk.500 a week. Data from twelve Subscriber Trunk Dialling (STD) booths in rural areas in India indicated a monthly revenue of Rs.450 to Rs.2500 ($1 = approximately 45 rupees) from local calls, and Rs.2500 to Rs.15000 from STD calls (Jain and Sastry, 1997). These tally with the figures indicated by the Bangladesh study, strengthening the view that many rural service centres can be economically viable.

2.2.1.3 Policy lessons from the Grameen Village experiment

The following lessons for policy makers can be derived from the Grameen Bank experiment with village pay phones, together with another study done in Ahmedabad, India that surveyed women users and non-users of telephones (Bhatnagar and Kedar, 1999):

1. Access to telecommunication capabilities produces a level of economic benefits that enables the beneficiary to pay for such services. The implication of this is that rural telephone services can be priced at rates comparable to urban areas. The pricing needs to support the promotion of services in initial stages.
2. The entrepreneurs providing services through public phones in rural communities can run profitable ventures. Subsidies are not required in all rural areas to provide telephony, provided the selected rural areas thus covered have a minimum critical mass of economic activity and some integration with the economy of the rest of the region.
3. By specifically targeting women as entrepreneurs who could provide the VPP service, government can empower women. This came about not only because the income of rural families increase, but also because the status of women is enhanced both within the family and the rural society.
4. The impact of proactive policies often gets negated through sloppy implementation. Success stories reiterate the importance of detailed planning. For example, GB's success stemmed from the detailed guidelines developed for choosing women pay-phone operators.

2.2.2 Gyandoot: A Community-owned Rural Intranet Project

The Gyandoot project was launched in January 2000 with the objective of establishing a community-owned, innovative and sustainable ICT project in a poverty-stricken, tribal-dominated rural district of Dhar in Madhya Pradesh, a state in central India (Bhatnagar and Vyas, 2001). Dhar has a population of 1.7 million, of which 54 per cent are the tribal population and 60 per cent live below the poverty line. The entire expenditure of Rs.2.5 million for the

Gyandoot network has been borne by 'panchayats' – elected committees constituting local government – which means no expenditure burden was placed on the government. The average cost incurred by the village committee and the community in establishing a single kiosk at the village panchayat buildings was Rs.75,000. Each kiosk caters to about 25 to 30 villages. The entire network of 31 kiosks covers 311 village panchayats, over 600 villages and a population of around half a million (nearly 50 per cent of the entire district).

2.2.2.1 Village information kiosks

Kiosks have dial-up connectivity through local exchanges on optical fibre or Ultra High Frequency links. The server hub is a remote access server housed in the computer room in the District Panchayat. Each kiosk has a computer, modem, printer, uninterrupted power supply (4-hour rating), furniture and stationery. The first 20 kiosks established by the village panchayat have been turned over to a manager/owner of the kiosk, after executing an initial agreement for one year. The village maintains the building and fixtures, while the manager is responsible for all the operational expenses and revenue collection. Managers pay 10 per cent of income as commission to the District Panchayat for maintaining the network. For the 11 centres started as private enterprises, the owner pays $100 as a license fee for one year to District Panchayat.

Funds for the Gyandoot network have come from: existing untied funds available to the village committee; private investment; the annual State Finance Commission share of revenues for village committees; and National Social Aid Programme allotment available to the District Panchayat.

2.2.2.2 Services at the kiosks

During the formation of the Gyandoot project, meetings were held with villagers to understand their felt needs. For example, due to a lack of information on prevailing rates at auction centres, farmers were unable to get the best price for their agricultural produce. To get copies of land records, the villager had to go out in search of the 'patwari' (a village functionary who maintains all land records), who is often unavailable because of extensive travel duties.

Services offered by the kiosks included:

- Relevant online information about activites at agriculture-produce auction centres. Prevailing rates of prominent crops of the district at local and other prominent auction centres of the country are available online at a nominal charge of Rs.5. Other information also provided on demand include the volume of incoming agricultural produce and previous rates.

- Copies of land records. Documents relating to land records are given on the spot at a charge of Rs.15 per extract. All the banks accept these extracts issued from kiosks for banking transactions, and around 200 000 farmers require these extracts at every cropping season to obtain loans from banks for purchasing seeds and fertilisers.
- Online registration of applications. Previously, the villagers had to make several visits to the local revenue court to file applications for obtaining income/caste/domicile certificates. With the kiosks, they can send the application at a cost of only Rs.10; subsequently, in a maximum period of ten days, an indication of the readiness of the certificate is sent back to them through e-mail at the appropriate kiosk. Only one trip is needed to collect the certificate
- Online redress for public grievances. A complaint can be filed and reply received in seven days for a cost of Rs.10. Complaints can be about issues such as drinking water, scholarship sanction/disbursement, quality of seed/fertilizer, employee conditions (like leave or provident- fund sanctions), functioning of schools, the public distribution system, beneficiary-oriented schemes and functioning of the village committee.
- Village auctions. Auction facilities are made available to farmers and villagers for land, agricultural machinery, bullocks, equipment or other durable commodities. Farmers can put on the system information about their commodities on sale, for a charge of Rs.25 for three months. They can also browse the list of saleable commodities for Rs.10.
- Transparency of government information. Kiosks help to make the functioning of the government transparent by making available online information. This includes, for example: the latest information regarding the public distribution system; a list of families below the poverty line; beneficiaries of social security pension and rural development schemes; and government grants to village committees.

2.2.2.3 Back-end processing

Twice every day, the server manager at a kiosk produces a printout of the complaints, applications and e-mails that have been received, and sends them to the appropriate authority. Necessary remedial action is expected to be taken within seven to ten days. A reply received at the server room is forwarded to the kiosk manager. The district collector responds to certain questions, queries or complaints. If a complaint cannot be addressed, a reply is accordingly forwarded to the kiosk manager.

The district is in the process of establishing a Local Area Network connecting major departments to the Gyandoot server. This will eliminate the manual handling of papers.

2.2.2.4 Costs and benefits

Each kiosk was expected to earn a gross income of Rs.4 000 per month (50 per cent from Gyandoot services, 25 per cent from training and the remainder from work services, like typing). The monthly operational costs are Rs.1 000, and the net income of Rs.3 000 must cover investments and profit for the entrepreneur. In practice, the gross income has been Rs.1–5 000 per month.

Nearly 55 000 accesses were made for various services from the 31 kiosks during the first 11 months, during which there was a four-fold increase in the number of transactions per month. The month-by-month numbers from January to November 2000 were: 1 200; 3 455; 6 210; 4 601; 3 530; 6 089; 8 920; 3 005; 6 564; 6 854; and 4 341, totalling 54 904. Rates of agricultural produce, land records and grievance-redress services were the most popular features, accounting for 95 per cent of the usage.

The following examples underscore the potential benefits of kiosks to a rural population.

- Rapid response to a problem with the availability of drinking water. A complaint was made from a kiosk about the drinking water available to 39 households, after the villagers' complaint to local authorities had not yielded results for six months. Unsure of the response to the online message, the complainant was quite reluctant to pay Rs.10 at the kiosk. To the surprise of the villagers, a hand-pump mechanic reached the tribal hamlet within two days of complaint being filed and the pump was repaired within three hours.
- A good price for the sale of a cow by auction. A milk farmer wanting to sell his cow registered it with the auction facility of Gyandoot. He received four trade enquiries and sold his cow to the highest bidder for Rs.3 000.
- 256 milch animals vaccinated in one day. On receiving an e-mail from a kiosk warning that an epidemic had broken out amongst the milch cattle of the village Kot Bhidota, a veterinary rescue team was despatched the same day. The disease of haemorrhage septicaemia was detected. The team promptly started curative treatment and vaccinated the rest of the animals. They also conducted a search and survey operation in the neighbouring villages for the detection of any disease symptoms and carried out preventive vaccination. No deaths were reported.
- Access to market rates leads to better deals. Farmers in Bagadi village were getting a rate of Rs.300 per quintal from local traders for their potato crop. The kiosk enabled access to the prevailing market rate in a town 100 miles away, which were Rs.100 higher. Consequently, the Bagadi potato produce was sold in the distant town. There has been about a 3–5 per cent increase in their profit margins, saving around Rs.200 million from going to middlemen and traders.

2.2.3 Case Study of an IT Application in Milk Collection Societies

India became the largest producer of milk in 1999, largely because of the efforts of the cooperative movement initiated by the National Dairy Development Board (NDDB). The efficient collection of milk and remunerative prices to the producers have been a prime reason for the growth of milk production in India. Both of these have, to some degree, been influenced by the innovative use of ICT at the milk collection centre.

Milk is collected at the cooperative milk collection centres that are located within 5–10 kilometres of the villages supplying the milk. The number of farmers selling milk to these centres varies from 100 to 1 000, and the daily collection varies from 1–10 thousand litres. Farmers drop their plastic identification cards into a box that reads them electronically and transmits the identification number to a personal computer (PC). Then the milk is emptied into a steel trough kept over a weighbridge. The weight of the milk is displayed instantly to the farmers, as well as being communicated to a PC. An operator takes a 5ml. sample of milk; assesses the fat content using a fat-testing machine; and the fat content is displayed to the farmer and communicated to the PC, which calculates the amount due to the farmer using a rate chart based on the fat content. The total value of the milk is printed out and given to the farmer. The payment to the farmer is automatically rounded to the closest rupee and the balance due is stored, to be added to the farmer's pay-out for the next day. At many centres the whole transaction takes about 20 seconds.

The entire system costs around $2 000. Nearly 600 such systems are in operation in Kheda district in Gujarat. Most of these were supplied by two small private companies. There are a total of 70 000 village societies in India, of which about 2 500 have been computerized.

The benefits to the farmers and the local cooperative have been documented by Chakravarty (2000). The farmers benefit from the computerization as their payment is now based on an accurate measurement of fat content and weight. In the previous system, the fat content was calculated a few hours after the milk was received because the process of measurement was cumbersome, which led to malpractice and under-payment to the farmers. Compared to this, the IT system enables prompt, accurate and immediate payment, while the waiting time at the milk collection centres has gone down. Given that 600 such centres receive milk from 60 000 farmers daily, even a ten minutes saving for each farmer every day amounts to a total saving of 30 000 person-days in a month.

A pilot project providing Internet connectivity to one of these computerized societies has been launched. It connects the society to a Dairy Portal (www.iimahd.ernet.in/egov) at the district level, which serves transactional and information needs of all members and staff at various levels in the district cooperative structure.

These centres offer services such as:

- Delivery of information related to dairying, including: best practices in breeding and rearing milch cattle; the schedule of services provided by government and other private sector agencies; and collecting feedback on the quality of service provided to the catchment area.
- Providing access to a multimedia database on the many innovations captured from hundreds of villages by SRISHTI, an NGO working in cooperation with Indian Institute of Management, Ahmedabad. The innovations covered include agricultural practices, medicinal plants, home remedies, tools and implements.
- If Internet telephony were to be permitted, such a centre could also be used as a communication centre offering services like e-mail and fax, in addition to the Internet telephony.
- Internet banking services and automated teller machines (ATMs) would enable the milk societies to credit the payments directly into the banking accounts of the sellers. The plastic-card identifier may then have to be upgraded to 'smart' cards carrying biometric identification, which could be used for withdrawing cash from ATMs.
- The automatic printing of daily payment slips provides a means of communicating with the farmers. For example, a database maintained in the computer for each farmer indicates the number of milch cattle and other details. If cattle require inoculation on a specific day – as indicated by information provided in a veterinary service database – this fact can be printed out on the farmer's payment slip as a reminder

A large amount of detailed historical data on milk production by individual farmers is available in the database at the milk collection centre. This can be utilized for forecasting milk collections and to incorporate seasonality factors. Analysis of seasonal variations in fat content of milk can be useful for the dairy, veterinary services, cattle-feed companies and the milk collection societies. Many interesting decision-support systems can be built to forecast aggregate milk collection statistics and to monitor the produce from individual sellers, based on data about farmers, their milch cattle and the past record of transactions.

This entire project focuses on improving the delivery of artificial insemination, veterinary services, education and the purchase and sale of milk for achieving increased productivity and collection.

2.3 PROVIDING ACCESS TO INFORMATION AND COMMUNICATION TECHNOLOGIES IN RURAL ASIA

There were about 3.7 million telephone lines in rural India in March 2000, putting the 'tele-density' at around only 0.33 per thousand. Of the 600 000 villages, only 55 per cent had a telephone. A target was not met to extend coverage by 2002 to 25 per cent of the villages yet to have telephone links. Even in urban areas, the private service providers have not been able to meet their commitments.

The Indian landscape is dotted with sparsely populated villages spread far and wide, as almost 91 per cent of the 600 000 villages have a population of less than 2 000. This has implications for the cost of building infrastructure to take telephony to rural areas, as well as for demand for services and revenue generation.

Accurate figures of Internet penetration in India are difficult to find. The Indian Parliament was informed that there were 1.4 million subscribers on 30 June 2000 (*The Times of India*, 2000). In 2002, the Internet subscriber base was estimated to be around 3 million. A study by Nielson in 2002 reported that 7 per cent of households with a phone were connected to the Internet (McDonald, 2002). The National Association of Software Companies (NASSCOM, 2002) reported that the growth in Internet subscribers has been much slower than expected, indicating the total of *active* subscribers was 1.5 million in March 2002. About 29 nine per cent of the surfers access the net from a cyber cafe, 31 per cent from the workplace and 22 per cent from home. In comparison to the 1 million PCs sold currently, it is expected that 7 million PCs will be sold in 2004.

However, what might be disturbing to the policy makers is the 'digital divide' in India created by inequalities in access to the Internet. As in the case of telephones, the divide is acute between urban and rural areas. Nearly 55 per cent of Internet use takes place in Mumbai, Delhi, Chennai, Bangalore and Calcutta, the five metropolitan towns. Just three of the 26 states (Maharashtra, Tamil Nadu and Delhi) account for 60 per cent of the Internet subscription base. More than 77 per cent of Internet access is accounted for by 25 state capitals (large cities of population more than 1–2 million). According to a NASSCOM survey (*The Times of India*, 2000), 92 per cent of net access come from 68 cities and towns, while 200 cities account for more than 98 per cent. A clarification in the Indian Parliament recorded that the north-east of India had fewer than 1 000 Internet connections (*The Times of India*, 2000).

The story is similar in Bangladesh, where only 0.25 per cent of GDP is invested in the Telecommunication Sector, as against 4–6 per cent in neighbouring countries, resulting in less than five telephones per 1 000 population. In rural areas of Bangladesh – where more than 80 per cent of the population live – there are only three telephones per 10 000 inhabitants (compared to 644 in the USA). The Internet came late to Bangladesh, with e-mail in 1993 and full Internet connectivity in 1996. By July 1997, there were an estimated 5 500 accounts. In 1999, there were 22 000 accounts and an estimated 100 000 users (Rao et al., 1999). The line quality is poor, as 60 per cent of them are analogue, resulting in a connectivity rate of only 30 per cent (see www.american.edu/carmel/ap1579a/about.htm).

2.4 KEY ISSUES IN THE PROVISION OF RURAL TELECOM ACCESS

To provide telecom access in rural areas, infrastructure must be built up in terms of exchanges/Remote Terminal Units (RTUs) and copper-paired cable connections to the terminal equipment for fixed lines. One key issue for a new service provider operating in a small area is the interconnection with the rest of the network.

In discussing access to ICT by a rural population, key issues relate to the nature of demand, investment and revenue potential and organizational mechanisms to ensure reliable service are important. These are discussed in the following subsections.

2.4.1 Nature of the Demand for Telecom Services

The felt need for improved communication systems should be examined carefully, as well as the types of communications the system support, e.g.. voice telephony, e-mail, fax, paging and two-way radio links. The technologies to be used also require serious consideration. Some studies have shown that real economic benefit can arise if a rural population can receive calls (Bhatnagar and Kedar, 1999). Calls coming from migrant labourers could increase if a direct contact can be established between migrant labourers and their family members. One of the disadvantages of a community call centre is its inability to pipe-in telephone calls to individual homes. Cellular phones can, perhaps, offer such advantages.

2.4.2 Investment and Revenue Potential

The investment in telecom capabilities will be high irrespective of whether technologies are used to provide these services separately or through convergence via a single medium. But will a rural population be able to pay for the services at rates that justify the investment, and will sufficient revenues be generated? There has been a considerable debate in India on whether rural telephones can generate adequate revenue. Some evidence suggests that private telephones in the rural areas do not contribute significant revenues to the service provider.

For example, a study of telephone traffic in India by ICICI (1998) found that nearly 70 per cent of the outgoing traffic from rural areas is meant for a destination within the district. Of this, 40 per cent remained within the Taluka (sub unit of a district). Only 20 per cent traffic goes to another district and barely 10 per cent to another state in India. International calls represented less than 1 per cent of the traffic. The revenue potential from rural areas is therefore small and large operators do not stand to benefit. In fact, a large proportion of private telephones in urban areas also do not generate adequate revenue that would justify investment (Manikutty, 1999).

The ability to afford an individual connection in rural areas is poor. In 1997, revenue per telephone was 1.4 times the per capita income in India, compared to 0.05 in industrialized countries, making the service appear 28 times less affordable in India. Any approach to rural telecom access therefore needs to be based on community access. Although there may generally be a need for subsidy to rural telephony, there are pockets of rural areas with economical activity which can easily support telephones with a normal tariff charge. In a survey in India, it was found that some public call offices (PCOs) in rural areas were generating monthly revenues of as much as Rs. 14 000 (Jain and Sastry, 1997). Similarly, studies of Bangladesh's Grameen Telephone have shown that women entrepreneurs could pay the lease amount for the handset and air-time charges – and still make profits of Tk.300–400 per week.

For most rural areas there is need to look for opportunities to add value. The Internet kiosk is one such opportunity, where the variety of services offered could include access to public and market information and the delivery of news, education and telecom services. NGOs and dairy/agricultural cooperatives can provide such services and content for the benefit of the rural population. If these kinds of kiosks were to be established, it would be reasonable to expect that all sectors and organizations which can deliver services through them would participate in making the necessary investment.

2.4.3 Organizational Mechanisms for Supplying Reliable Community Telecom Services

In India, the discussion on rural telephony has been confined to examining technological solutions to the problem of extending coverage to areas with low subscriber density. The utilization aspect of the problem has been largely ignored. Yet, it has been widely observed that mere provision of access does not ensure its use; many social and economic factors intervene.

For a community access approach, an important consideration is ensuring access to different castes and communities The performance record of Village Panchayat Telephones (VPT) in most villages is very poor (Das, 1998). Large numbers of them are out of order and many are disconnected, due to the non-payment of bills as villagers often perceive it as a free service provided by the government. VPTs that function normally operate only for limited hours of the day, as they may be housed in Post Offices and non-commercial establishments.

Initiatives such as Grameen Telecom are proving that micro-credit programmes tied to the development of micro-enterprises like the VPP significantly increase rural access to telecommunication systems. In many regions of developing countries, however, the challenges of acquiring service and equipment prevent rural entrepreneurs from establishing locally-owned and managed PCO operations. Also, operators of existing rural telecommunication systems may be reluctant to expand, due to the challenges of revenue collection, equipment maintenance, vandalism and providing customer support. The solution, perhaps, lies in linking existing and successful micro-credit organizations with rural telecom operators (fixed line and/or wireless) to expand PCO coverage in rural areas. Small loans to rural entrepreneurs (perhaps targeted to women and youth) can enable entrepreneurs to establish PCOs providing a range of communication services. A franchise programme of this sort would also establish consistency of service across a region that would, in turn, support the social and economic development of the region.

2.5 PROPOSAL FOR A FRAMEWORK BASED ON A MICRO UNDERSTANDING OF RURAL AREAS

The discussion above suggests that no single approach to providing community services will succeed in all rural areas. Perhaps rural areas could be segmented in a 2x2 matrix, as shown in Table 2.3. One dimension to be considered is the level of economic activity and the consequent size of demand, whether large or small. The other dimension is the kind of investment that would be required to provide telephone access to a specific rural area. This depends on the existing infrastructure and the kinds of technologies that may be usable. There are villages to which telephone access can be provided with limited investment because they are within easy reach of existing rural exchanges. On the other hand, some villages are remote, so considerable new investment would be required in fixed lines or radio transmission to cover these areas. The investment can therefore be seen as low or high.

Table 2.3: Providing community telecom services in rural areas

		Revenue Potential	
		High	*Low*
Investment	*High*	Allow small private telecom operators to run level 1 exchanges and to offer telecom services independently, or as an exclusive franchise of large operators. Encourage telecom companies and the operators through a 'no tax' regime. Financing institutions may need to be created to provide funding to such operators.	Subsidize the operators on the basis of least-subsidy needs. Encourage NGOs, cooperatives and other developmental organizations to form rural telecom firms. Interconnection to existing networks is mandated. Encourage community services through developmental agencies.
	Low	Enable small private companies to manage rural telecom infrastructure and provide service. Encourage local entrepreneurs to open community telecom service centres and information kiosks	Encourage cooperatives and NGOs to take the lead in the establishment of multiple-service community communication centres, which can also be useful for the primary tasks of such organizations.

The cost estimates for providing a village public telephone can vary considerably, depending on the technology used and the closeness of the village to the current infrastructure. Some estimates from Tamil Nadu, Uttar Pradesh, Kerala, Punjab and Rajasthan vary around Rs.154 000 per line when Multiple Access Radio Relay (MARR) is used (Das and Jain, 2000). The required investments range from Rs.32–55 thousand or more for wired line connections. Typically, planners have used three cost estimates at varying levels from Rs.50–100 thousand. In Bangladesh, Grameen Telecom is using cellular technology for its VPP project. This has cost GT less than half of the fixed line cost, but the coverage is restricted to a narrow corridor around the urban infrastructure.

An approach could be identified that is most suitable for each of the four boxes in the matrix in Table 2.3. Where demand is high and investments are low, emphasis should be on delivering reliable service through small private local entrepreneurs. They can be encouraged by facilitating the establishment of PCOs and kiosks through reduced paper work and the provision of loan assistance to establish ventures such as shops.

In cases where the existing demand is poor, other services should be bundled-in with telecom services. The best way to do that is to allow cooperatives and NGOs to take the lead, so that telecom access could be useful for the primary tasks of such organizations. Since a relatively small investment is required, such organizations can create the infrastructure on their own. In the long run they would not be losers, as the total value of the bundled services might still outweigh the cost of investment and operational expenses. The principle of the workability of this proposition has been established by examples like that of Gyandoot and the use of computers in thousands of rural milk collection societies cited above, as well as the work by the Swaminathan Foundation in India in establishing information kiosks in Pondicherry (www.mssrf.org).

For areas that will require high investment and have a substantial potential demand, large operators should be allowed to franchise the operations at a village exchange level to a few private telecom operators, on an exclusive basis. Small private companies could manage the infrastructure from the last level at the exchange up to the end-user's instrument. These companies would be responsible for revenue collection, providing new connections and maintenance. Since the potential demand is large, a subsidy may not be required; however, the operators may need encouragement through a no-tax regime. Financing institutions may need to be created to provide funding to such operators, as they are likely to be small in size with limited facilities. Government and non-government development agencies need to identify areas with high revenue potential and make business plans for partnerships with existing and/or new operators to create infrastructure.

Subsidies would be required in the most difficult areas: those requiring high investment, but likely to have poor revenue potential. However, to minimize the impact on the exchequer, such areas could be auctioned to small operators on the basis of least-subsidy requirements. Cooperatives and NGOs can be encouraged to form telecom companies (Handerson, 2000). However, the statutes covering the cooperatives usually prevent them from diversifying into related activities. On the other hand, rural areas do not offer space for a multiplicity of organizations to operate. It is therefore more viable to allow a single agency to provide the entire range of services needed in rural areas. These would also include telecom services.

The government/public sector has been unable to deliver telecom or information services in rural areas, as there are problems in providing new connections, maintenance of lines and collection of revenues. Also, there is a large amount of revenue leakage through corruption. In fact, it seems the government is best suited for creating and maintaining an appropriate telecom infrastructure. Provision of services to the end consumers should be left to private entrepreneurs and other organizations that have gained experience in dealing with clients and providing services. A subsidy from a fund created by a 'universal service' levy on rural service providers would act as an incentive for them to provide reliable service.

The subsidy for universal-service provision could also be targeted specifically at building interconnect arrangements. License conditions must mandate an obligation to provide interconnections to all operators who venture into high-investment or low-revenue potential areas. Details of such a scheme in India are being worked out by the Government in consultation with the Telecom Regulatory Authority of India.

2.6 CONCLUSIONS

The evidence linking access to ICTs and development is growing, but is largely anecdotal. Successful deployment of technology for development represents the work of a few development entrepreneurs. The challenge is to scale-up so that a countrywide impact can be realized. One of the major bottlenecks in such scaling-up is telecom access.

Simple access to telephony can produce value, as in the case of the Grameen Village experiment, but the impact can be greater if meaningful content can be delivered via the Internet. Any effort seeking to scale-up such a service should understand both the needs of rural communities and why the delivery of Internet content in a local language and idiom is a large undertaking. Even if this kind of effort could be mounted, the issue of the digital divide must also be confronted.

Telecommunication investors, financial institutions providing telecom loans, urban telecom operators and telecom equipment vendors are generally reluctant to undertake rural operations because they perceive telecom ventures in rural areas – especially those in developing countries and emerging markets – as high-risk, troublesome or not worth significant effort. One potential solution is to target un-served and under-served regions, and to provide support for the acquisition of high-quality market appraisal knowledge and market data through market research in the field. This would help to prove the business case, attract investment capital and reduce the effort required by investors and operators.

Telecom operators and equipment vendors typically have the technical resources and operational expertise necessary to leverage profitable rural telecom opportunities. If they are presented with a solid business case, the operators are relieved of the burden of researching rural markets themselves. For example, in the case of Grameen Telecom, it was business case interventions on behalf of Grameen Bank that attracted external investment from a qualified foreign operator.

There is so much happening on the technology front that it is difficult to suggest robust approaches for taking telecom to rural areas. Considering the case of India, the policy around the turn of the Century focused on imposing a universal service obligation on fixed-line basic service providers. However, experience suggests that such service providers are not interested in expanding their network, as their strategy revolves around corporate users. Compared to the 0.2 million lines that basic providers added in urban India in the three years between 1999 and 2002, hand-held cellular telephony grew to a subscriber base of 2.1 million. Thus, it seems that the future of rural telephony in India may ride on wireless technology such as cellular, wireless-in-the-local-loop and corDECT (developed by the Indian Institute of Technology, Madras). The current limitations of low data bandwidth on wireless may also be overcome in due course.

Rural areas need to be serviced through low-cost, low-bandwidth solutions that have high reliability. This means that technology solutions will have to be adapted to local terrain and conditions. Demand for information services would have to be generated through aggressive marketing, and overheads kept low to serve a cost-sensitive market. Large organizations in the public or private sector are unlikely to be able to operate in this manner. Perhaps the rural telecom environment would have to be less regulated than it is in the urban and metropolitan towns. For example, cable operation has been considerably less regulated and this has enabled a large number of small players to spread the network.

REFERENCES

Bayes. A., J. von Braun and R. Akhter (1999), 'Village Pay Phones and Poverty Reduction: Insights from a Grameen Bank Initiative in Bangladesh', *Information and Communication Technologies and Economic Development*, **8** (May–June).

Bhatnagar, S.C. and S. Kedar (1999), 'Do Gender Issues Have a Place in Indian Telecom Policy?' *Voices: A Journal of Communication for Development*, **3** (3).

Bhatnagar S.C. and N. Vyas (2001), 'Gyandoot: Community-Owned Rural Internet Kiosks', www1.worldbank.org/publicsector/egov

Chakravarty, R. (2000), 'IT at Milk Collection Centres in Cooperative Dairies: The National Dairy Development Board Experience', in S.C. Bhatnagar and R. Schware (eds), *Information and Communication Technology in Development: Cases from India*, New Delhi: Sage Publications, 65–75.

Das, P. (1998), 'Rural Telephony: Telecommunications Development in Rural India', in *Connectworld India Annual*, Mumbai, India: ICICI Ltd, 42–5.

Das, P. and R. Jain, (2000), 'Assessment of Universal Service Obligations', presented at the Workshop on Next Generation Reforms in Telecom, 13–14 October,

Ahmedabad, India: Centre for Telecom Policy Studies, Indian Institute of Management.

Handerson, B. (2000), 'A Historical Perspective of Rural Telecom Policies for India', Emerging Market Forum Round Table on Telecom in India, 28–9 August, Stanford, CA: Stanford University.

ICICI (1998), *The Village Public Telephone and the Poverty of Universal Service Coverage – A Study of Telecommunications Development in Rural India*, Mumbai, India: ICICI Ltd.

Jain, R. and T. Sastry (1997), 'Rural Telecommunication Services', Workshop on Telecom Policy Research, Ahmedabad, 28 February–1 March, Ahmedabad, India: Indian Institute of Management.

Jayaweera, W. (2001), 'Kothamale Radio/Internet Project: Expanding the Knowledge Base', www1.worldbank.org/publicsector/egov/kothmale_cs.htm, June.

McDonald T. (2002), 'Home Internet Access Tops Record 500 Million', News Factor Network, www.newsfactor.com/perl/story/16664.html, March.

NASSCOM (2002), 'India Underutilizing Net Bandwidth', www.nasscom.org, February.

Manikutty, S. (1999), 'The Nineties: A Lost Decade for India in Telecom', presented at the Workshop 'Telecom Policy Initiatives: The Road Ahead', August, Ahmedabad, India: Indian Institute of Management, Centre for Telecom Policy Studies.

Rao M., I. Rashid, H. Rizvi and R. Subba (1999), 'Online Content in South Asia, Opportunities and Realities', *Economic and Political Weekly*, 20 November.

Richardson D., R. Ramirez and M. Haq (2000), 'Grameen Telecom's Village Phone Programme in Rural Bangladesh: A Multi-Media Case Study', www.telecommons.com/villagephone/contents.html, March, Hull, Quebec: Canadian International Development Agency.

The Times of India (2000), 'Only 900 Subscribers in North-East', 5 August, 7.

3. The Computer Sciences Academic Community and the Diffusion of the Internet in Brazil

Victor Prochnik and Maurício Yoshinori Une

3.1 INTRODUCTION

This chapter[1] deals with the development and diffusion of the Internet in Brazil. In particular, it describes the increasing participation of the Brazilian computer science and software engineering academic community (CSSAC)[2] in the introduction and growth of the Internet. It also seeks to demonstrate the important participation of this community in the decision-making process for regulating the commercial Internet, and in government projects for expanding this network.

In this respect, the chapter divides the history of the participation of the CSSAC in the evolution of the Internet in Brazil into three phases:

1. Phase I (1988–94) saw the setting up of an Internet capability through the creation of the first national network 'backbone'. This was based on the National Research Network (RNP), a cooperative research project undertaken by the main CSSAC centres and administered by members of this community.
2. Phase II (1995–98) corresponds to the introduction and growth of the commercial Internet in Brazil. when prominent members of the CSSAC become the managers of the Brazilian Internet Supervisory Committee.
3. Phase III (1999 onwards) marks the implementation of the Brazilian programme for the Information Society (SocInfo), which is being carried out by the Ministry of Science and Technology (MCT).

In the first phase, the use of the Internet was almost exclusively academic. The cooperative work experience between the CSSAC centres, the efforts of some of their leading figures and the interests of this community in absorbing and using these technologies played a part in this initiative. The establishment of the RNP as the Internet backbone benefited every Brazilian university, which had an additional work tool at its disposal. However, the RNP was much more than an isolated project.

The introduction and management of the Internet was one of three parallel initiatives in a broader CSSAC plan, called the Strategic Development of Information Technology (DESI). This also covered two other programmes: the funding of cooperative research between computer science centres all over Brazil and support for the national software industry. Accordingly, the DESI plan laid great emphasis on the creation of technology in Brazil, particularly inside the universities, and its transfer to the productive sector. For this reason, it differs from the decidedly neo-liberal orientation adopted by the Brazilian government.

The implementation of DESI was made possible not only through the participation of prominent members of the CSSAC who held strategic posts in research-funding agencies, but also through the cooperation and participation of other government agencies and programmes, which were greatly enthused by the expected impacts of DESI on the creation and diffusion of ICTs in Brazil. However, as explained in Section 3.2, financial constraints led to the project having less of an impact than expected in some of the targeted areas.

In the second phase, from 1995–98, responsibility for this task was given to Embratel, the enterprise owned by the Federal Government that was responsible for interstate and international telecommunications (at the time, telecommunications services were a state monopoly). However, as discussed in Section 3.3, there was enormous resistance throughout the country to Embratel's practices. Due to the climate of animosity which ensued, the Federal Government then decided to transfer the coordination of the commercial Internet to the RNP. In practice, the CSSAC became responsible for managing the whole Internet in Brazil.

From the very start, the commercial Internet grew exponentially and academic research continued developing new initiatives. The CSSAC launched a project to set up in Brazil something on the lines of the American Internet2 project, also known as a high-speed Internet, which allows for large-scale interactive applications. Once again, the paucity of funding delayed the CSSAC project.

The third phase, starting in 1999, focuses on an MCT programme. The activities in this phase are a continuation, on the one hand, of CSSAC's research work, insofar as its main objective is to set up in Brazil an equivalent project to that of Internet2 in the USA (and thus called RNP2) and to develop applications to run on this network. On the other hand, the SocInfo Programme provides an important guideline for CSSAC's research work, directing it towards the major needs of national economic development. This time, greater financial resources have been pledged. The way the Programme is being planned and overseen by prominent members of the CSSAC is examined later in this chapter. Should it achieve its goals, this community's efforts might finally make a significant impact on Brazilian society.

Overall, this chapter therefore traces how the project of implementing the Internet in Brazil started initially as an academic network, then became the origin of the commercial Internet and is now being upgraded in the context of a broad Information Society Programme. It highlights how the academic community managed to achieve considerable technical and political success in the technological policy area by occupying the space left vacant by an increasingly neo-liberal State, and by the IT and telecommunications industry after it was acquired largely by multinational companies that show little interest in Brazilian technological policy.

3.2 PHASE I: EVOLUTION OF THE NATIONAL RESEARCH NETWORK

This section outlines the role of the CSSAC during the setting up of the Internet in Brazil, covering the period 1988–94. It was at the end of the 1980s and beginning of the 1990s that the Internet became widespread in the universities and technological centres, through the CSSAC's RNP project, supported by Brazilian institutions that sponsor science and technology. The RNP provided enormous benefits to the scientific community in Brazil, as one of three initiatives in the much broader DESI scientific and technological development programme that had been put forward and implemented by the CSSAC.

3.2.1 DESI: The Brazilian Strategic Development of Information Technology Programme

Compared to its regional neighbours, Brazil had well-developed important scientific capabilities in the IT field in the decades prior to the 1990s, especially in computers and telecommunications. The analysis of university-firm relationship in the 1970s and 1980s by Prochnik (1988a, b) showed both the great importance of university–firm technology flows and the way that, when students and professors were hired by firms, the leading Brazilian IT companies maintained continuous cooperation and technological development programmes with major university IT departments[3].

Also of extreme importance was the participation of renowned members of the academic computer science community in the decision-making process for formulating industrial and technology policies in the 1970s, and the National Information Policy in the 1980s. The tendencies towards university/firm interaction and the participation of CSSAC members in government decision making not only grew stronger in the 1990s, but acquired their own dynamic. In fact, it was through an initiative in the 1990s led by academics from this field – who were also members of the federal executive power structure – that the Federal Government undertook the broad DESI research programme, which was comprised of three National Priority Programmes:

1. ProTeM-CC, the Multi-institutional Thematic Programme in Computer Sciences. This aimed to amplify the technological potential of the country by means of cooperative research, fostering partnerships between enterprises and universities and research institutes, as well as intensifying high-level personnel training for the growing demands of the industrial sector.
2. SOFTEX 2000, the National Software Export Programme, which targeted the development of 'export software' (see Prochnik, 1998 for a detailed analysis of this programme).
3. RNP, the National Research Network set up with the objective of diffusing the Internet use throughout the Brazilian scientific community.

Thus, DESI's mission was to realign National Information Policy (Lucena, 1992) by the establishment of a broad process of national scientific and technological training (ProTeM-CC), the creation of a solid national infrastructure of digital communication (RNP) and the building of a high-technology software exporting base (SOFTEX 2000). DESI was conducted by the academic centres, which involved the participation of prominent members of the community and other institutions sympathetic to the views and programmes of the CSSAC. Among these other institutions, special mention is deserved for the Department of Scientific, Technical and Technological Cooperation of the Ministry of Foreign Affairs and FINEP, an MCT agency for financing private technological projects.

DESI's three programmes were managed by the Special Programmes Board of the National Council of Scientific and Technological Development (known as CNPq[4]). The director was Professor Ivan de Moura Campos, a Ph.D. in computer sciences from the University of California and full professor and former head of the Department of Computer Sciences of the Federal University of Minas Gerais (UFMG).

Finally, it should be stressed that one important feature of DESI, and of each of its three programmes, was the way it was conceived and conducted: strongly based on fostering cooperative activities between the various agents. Another key feature was the scale of resources, which were very small for national needs. The project as a whole was budgeted at $28 million over four years for the three programmes. In the case of SOFTEX 2000, for example, the final funding that the affiliated companies received added up to little more than support for hiring a few staff members (who were paid a salary equal to academic research scholarships), a few microcomputers and access to collective services (Prochnik, 1998).

In view of the small sum that firms were entitled to receive, the Municipality of São Paulo declined to participate at the start of the project. Afterwards, other sources of funding were added, including a contribution from the National Bank of Economic and Social Development. Nevertheless, the total amount of resources allocated by this and other institutions was very small, due to various causes, such as the small size of the software companies requiring resources and their lack of capacity to meet even the limited demands for guarantees. Venture-capital mechanisms were also tried, but the high rates of interest in force in the country, among other factors, also hampered the development of this source of financing.

3.2.2 The ProTeM-CC Multi-institutional Programme

The ProTeM-CC initiative within DESI resulted in greater financial support for the computer sciences departments of universities, and also helped to bring universities and companies closer together (Table 3.1).

Table 3.1: Projects submitted to ProTeM-CC (1992–98)

Phase	Projects Submitted	Institutions Involved	Projects Selected
1992/94	167	55	43
1994/96	47	80 (25 companies)	21
1996/98	56	139 (43 companies)	22

Source: Ribeiro Filho and Simões (1999).

ProTeM-CC consisted of multi-institutional thematic projects and was perceived to be an innovative programme:

> ProTeM, on being created in CNPq, inaugurated, in fact, a new paradigm of support in the Agency. Through Public Notices, focussing on issues/problems of national interest, support for medium to large scale *cooperative* projects (in the US$100 000 to US$1 million range) was launched which, by definition and/or out of necessity, became progressively and increasingly committed to results (or at least were expected to achieve them) (Lucena, 1996: 9).

In a country like Brazil, which covers a huge area with a dearth of specialist personnel and R&D activities and a limited number of academic groups, ProTeM-CC's emphasis on cooperation has been described as 'revolutionary':

> According to Claudia Medeiros, of Unicamp [Campinas State University], this revolution occurred principally in two ways: incentives to intra- and inter-institutional cooperative work, supporting emerging centres and using a new process of managing projects, in which the focus on germinating a process of formative assessment and follow-up were pioneering (CESAR, 1999).

Later, this organizational innovation was also adopted in CNPq programmes for other areas.

3.2.3 The SOFTEX 2000 Software Export Programme

SOFTEX 2000 was the productive arm of DESI. Its goal was to win a 1 per cent share of the world software market. According to a projection made at the time, this represented $2 billion of annual exports in 2000. If this target was reached, software would become Brazil's main export product. The rationale behind the 1 per cent number was the following (Lucena, 1993): Brazil produced about 1 per cent of the scientific articles in the area of software engineering; given that technical capacity is the main input of software production, Brazilian exports would be able, if supported, to reach the country's level of scientific production.

However, this expectation did not materialize. Optimistic estimates of Brazilian software exports in 2002 were around $100 million dollars (www.softex.br). Among the reasons for this failure to achieve expectations are the limited resources received by the programme, the anti-exporter bias of national macro-economic policy (e.g., an overvalued exchange rate and high interest) and the small size of national firms and their difficulty in raising additional resources.

It should be noted that although SOFTEX 2000 aimed at providing support for the software industry, it was also managed by CNPq. An alternative hypothesis would have been for it to have been managed by the MCT's FINEP agency. There are many differences between CNPq and FINEP, the most significant being that the latter financially supports private expenditure on R&D technology in a very substantial way and its management seems to have no defined role for the academic community.

University professors and their respective centres played major roles in SOFTEX 2000, helping to boost the number of software enterprises in Brazil and the geographical diversification of the industry. For instance, the central management of the programme was for many years under the guiding hand of the programme's first proponent, Eduardo Costa, a researcher in the area, together with other colleagues. In the local nuclei, scattered all over the country, academia participated intensely. In several cases, the different state nuclei of the programme were founded in academic departments. New links between the academic community and the programme have continued to be forged, and SOFTEX 2000 has earned itself a reputation for providing strong support and creating new enterprises though the use of technological incubators.

3.2.4 The RNP: Introduction and Evolution of the Internet in Brazil

In the second half of the 1980s, a number of Brazilian scientific institutions began to connect themselves to the academic telecommunications network BITNET. Observing this tendency, the MCT finally set up a Working Group in 1988 to discuss a similar national information network initiative. In 1989, RNP[5] was formally launched as an MCT priority programme focused on the Brazilian National Information Infrastructure, to be executed by the CNPq. In practice, CNPq's Board of Special Programmes exercised both the political and the budgetary coordination of the project.

In 1992, Professor Tadao Takahashi of Campinas State University (Unicamp) took over the coordination of the RNP; in 2002, he was responsible for the Brazilian programme for the information society. The model adopted to define the National Information Infrastructure was based on similar past experiences in developed countries, bearing in mind the reality of the situation in Brazil at the time. This analysis led to the division of RNP's infrastructure into three levels:

1. Individual institutional level: each institution sets up one internal network, so that its different units can communicate with each other directly and share one external communication point.
2. Regional and state level: regional or state agencies, preferably agencies connected to science and technology, plan and implement an information network of regional or state scope.
3. National and international level: the Federal Government, through RNP, plans and implements network infrastructure and services at a national level to link and integrate the efforts of the different states, while also executing the link-up of the national infrastructure to international networks in Latin America, USA, Canada and Europe.

It should be noted that achieving a closer working relationship between universities, industry and government was one of the explicit goals of the programme. In practice, however, the project was limited to creating a national network of university research.

From 1991 to 1993, the RNP Backbone Phase 1 was implemented, with the preliminary objective of interconnecting different states of Brazil. In

1993, this basic backbone was already interconnecting eleven Brazilian state capitals using dedicated connections, at speeds varying between 9.6 and 64 Kbps. Besides implementing the backbone, RNP also turned its attention to consolidating the Brazilian Internet through seminars to the academic community, personnel training and the implementation of Internet services – for example, e-mail, remote access to data bases and dial-a-network – and other activities that helped to increase awareness of the strategic importance of the Internet to the country.

This experience proved to be so successful that more financial support was guaranteed for RNP activities by CNPq and the United Nations Development Programme (UNDP). According to Stanton (1998): 'by 1993, [Brazil] had already reached thirtieth position in order of activity in the world, with around 2,000 registered computer names in the '.br' domain of the Domain Name System (DNS)'.

By the end of this first phase, Brazil already had a national network at its disposal. In 1994, due to the great number of institutions already connected to RNP, especially in the Rio de Janeiro/São Paulo corridor, it was found that increased demand was already overloading the backbone installed in Phase I. Furthermore, for speeds below 64 Kbps, it was not viable to maintain interactive applications. Other problems, according to Takahashi (1994)[6], were: lack of financial resources for acquiring certain equipment, such as routers[7]; little involvement from the states; shortage of human resources; and a decision to opt for isolated Points-of-Presence (PoPs) inside universities, where entire networks or individual equipment are connected to a larger network or backbone.

However, the RNP brought the Internet within reach of the academic community and 'allowed a substantial amount of experience in engineering and operating networks' (Lucena, 1996: 88). By 1996, the Internet reached 600 institutions, 60 000 academic users and a growing non-academic public.

3.3 PHASE II: INTRODUCTION AND GROWTH OF THE COMMERCIAL INTERNET IN BRAZIL

Phase II in the diffusion of the Internet in Brazil was marked by significant moves to develop commercial Internet use.

3.3.1 Role of the CSSAC in Developing the Commercial Internet

All the developments in the first stage of forming the RNP were subsequently strongly influenced by the events of 1995, which marked the start of Phase II:

when the commercial Internet began to be managed by a committee in which the academic computer science community predominated. However, the commercial Internet in Brazil started out taking a different route.

The Federal Government had initially transferred the task of administering this network to the Embratel telecommunications company, within the Ministry of Telecommunications. At the end of 1994, Embratel began to offer commercial Internet services directly to the final consumer. The Government's aim was to verticalize services, but the effective control of the Internet by Embratel came in for strong criticism at the time because:

- the prices that were charged were excessive;
- the centralizing philosophy was contrary to the conception of the Internet as an open network;
- the decentralization of aggregate-value services would no longer be possible; and
- there would be a possibility that the supply of new services of greater scope could be restricted, as could freedom of access and expression at some future date.

After some delays and countless political disputes, the Department of Telecommunications and the Department of Science and Technology announced in May 1995 an important change. Administration of the project for expanding the Internet in Brazil was transferred from Embratel to RNP, which therefore became the institution responsible for constructing the backbone, coordinating expansion of the network – including opening up the network up to private suppliers of access and information – and disseminating the 'Internet culture'. To perform this task, the Ministers of Communication and of Science and Technology created another agency, the Brazil Internet Supervisory Committee (CG/InternetBr)[8]. Its main objectives are to:

1. foster Internet service development in Brazil;
2. recommend technical and operational standards and procedures for the Internet in Brazil;
3. coordinate the assignment of Internet addresses, registration of domain names and the interconnection of backbones; and
4. collect, organize and disseminate information on Internet services.

The members of the first Supervisory Committee were unashamedly associated with the interests of the CSSAC. Of the nine members, the majority were distinguished scientists in the computer science area, such as: the IT and Automation Policy Secretary at MCT, Professor Campos, with a deciding vote on the Committee as an MCT representative; Carlos José

Pereira de Lucena, representing the scientific community; Sílvio Romero de Lemos Meira, representing end-users; and Demi Getschko, network consultant for the Supervisory Committee. In addition, the CNPq representative was the researcher Eduardo Moreira da Costa, general coordinator of the SOFTEX 2000 programme, and the representative of the access providers, Carlos Alberto Afonso, came from a non-governmental organization involved in social action work (which had its own Internet provider, Alternex).

It was in this way that the academic community, with a strong presence in the MCT, became the Internet supervisor in Brazil, to the detriment of the Ministry of Telecommunications, which had only two seats on this committee. Thus, from May 1995 on, with the opening of the commercial Internet in Brazil, the RNP was no longer an exclusively academic backbone and started providing a service to the whole of Brazilian society. The RNP acted as a guide to non-academic Brazilian society at this time, by providing an Information Centre (CI/RNP), sharing information on network operations and supporting not only the network's commercial development but also the emergence of private information and service providers.

It is interesting to note the success the Internet had obtained in Brazil by this time. End users promptly adopted the Internet idea, and the commercial use of the Internet through the RNP proved to be a great success regardless of Brazil's poor IT indicators[9] compared even with other developing countries. The number of Brazilian hosts leapt from around 800 in January 1995 to 1 644 575 in January 2002, placing Brazil in 11th position in the world ranking, third in the Americas and first in Latin America, in terms of the number of computers connected to the Web[10]. In October 2001, the number of Internet subscribers was put at between 12 and 16 million[11]. Table 3.2 shows data concerning the rapid evolution of the number of Brazilian hosts.

Table 3.2: Internet hosts with a Brazilian '.br' domain name (1995–2002)

Period	No. of Hosts*
1995	800
1996	20 113
1997	77 148
1998	117 200
1999	215 086
2000	446 444
2001	876 596
2002	1 644 575

* In January of the year shown.

Source: www.isc.org/ds/

Undoubtedly, the Internet in Brazil – an academic-community initiative through RNP – boosted economic welfare in the country and generated thousands of jobs. The mission of RNP was seen in 1995 as temporary; its objective, in the words of its coordinator, Professor Takahashi, was 'to catapult the use of the network' (Takahashi, 1995). But the outcome was somewhat different than expected. Having won a new institutional role through the commercial Internet, RNP pursued an expansion strategy, now with access to more ample resources.

After 1995, 'countless IT manufacturers, such as Compaq, Equitel, IBM, Philips, began to offer concrete support to RNP, supplying equipment, software and, even, financing direct activities in the project' (Sobre a RNP/Histórico section at www.rnp.br). This support was given in exchange for fiscal incentives. In Brazil, private IT companies who invested at least 5 per cent of their revenues in R&D, with at least 2 per cent associated with universities, research institutes or the so-called Priority Programmes of Information Technology, would be entitled to a series of fiscal incentives (MCT, 1998).

However, the direct investments of the MCT in RNP declined in the following years: $12.5 million in 1996, $9.8 million in 1997 and $8.0 million in 1998. The network, however, continued to grow. From 1996 until 1998, RNP began improving its infrastructure by means of expanding its connections and speed. That success led to the implementation of the RNP2 project to provide a qualitative leap in increasing the transmission capacity of the Internet. This also represents RNP's return to its initial functions of serving the academic community.

3.3.2 RNP2: The Brazilian Initiative to Implement Internet2

RNP2 is linked with the US proposal for developing the 'next-generation Internet', also known as Internet2. Due to its advanced infrastructure – based on ATM technology applied to its fibre-optic cables to allow much greater capacity and faster connections – RNP2 supports advanced highly-interactive multidisciplinary applications. The formal objectives of RNP2 are to:

1. facilitate and coordinate the development, deployment, operation and transfer process of advanced network application and service technology;
2. promote the introduction and development of applications making intensive use of interactive and multimedia resources, especially for education and research purposes; and
3. prepare the Brazilian infrastructure to meet the demand created by next-generation Internet2-type applications.

The RNP2 project was strategically divided into three basic stages:

1. installation of High Speed Metropolitan Area Networks (REMAVs) to promote the creation of consortia to put together REMAVs all over the country;
2. development of the National Backbone to interconnect all the REMAVs; and
3. Internet2 collaboration through active participation in the Internet2 project.

The RNP2 backbone is being established in a similar way to the initial RNP backbone. That is to say, firstly REMAVs are to be installed in isolated PoPs. However, RNP2 and other new Internet2-like infrastructure projects will employ GigaPoPs, which operate with higher speeds and capability than the type of PoP used in the first-generation RNP network. RNP2's REMAVs will then be interconnected, so that this new infrastructure will eventually be linked to other national infrastructures.

The initial step for the first stage of this development was taken in October 1997, when RNP together with ProTeM-CC invited proposals for setting up the REMAVs. In all, 25 proposals from 110 institutions were received. Eventually, out of the analysed proposals, 14 consortia were selected from different cities: Belo Horizonte, Brasília, Campina Grande, Campinas, Curitiba, Florianópolis, Fortaleza, Goiânia, Natal, Porto Alegre, Recife, Rio de Janeiro, Salvador and São Paulo.

Among the dispersed consortia members, there are 79 research and education institutions, apart from government agencies and telecommunications operators. Contributions are distributed mainly as follows: the telecommunications operators provide the technology; the Federal Government the hardware and scholarships; and the higher education institutions provide qualified personnel and capabilities.

The consortia are expected, in their respective areas, to develop, prototype and test new network applications, exchange experiences and undertake training activities. Some were also chosen for the availability of line and fibre optic infrastructure between the academic participants and the local telecommunications operators. According to José Luiz Ribeiro Filho (1998), the RNP general coordinator, the main opportunities for these consortia are:

1. partnerships between universities and telecommunications and private service technology network corporations;
2. resources provided by the telecommunications funds and the new National IT Policy Law of fiscal incentives[12]; and
3. institutionalization of the GigaPoPs in the REMAVs .

After the institutionalization of the GigaPoPs, the new national backbone is to be implemented, interconnecting all the REMAVs and linking them to Internet2. Implementation of RNP2 eventually became an integral part of Phase III Internet development and diffusion in Brazil (see Section 3.4).

The implementation of the RNP2 infrastructure process does not differ greatly from the implementation of the RNP infrastructure. In both cases, University and Government institutions initiate the process of network architecturing through R&D investment, move on to the experimentation and implementation stages and then pass on the responsibility for commercialization. In fact, during the 1990s both these institutions were very much one and the same in Brazil. However, the attitude of the computer industry, and possibly its role, changed dramatically in the final half of the 1990s.

With the privatization of telecommunications, the bulk of the sector was de-nationalized. This raises an additional question: the extent to which multinational companies will participate in the project. By acquiring national enterprises, these firms inherited their commitments. However, keeping them to such commitments is quite another matter, and there was little evidence of this by 2002.

3.4 RNP2 AND THE BRAZILIAN PROGRAMME FOR THE INFORMATION SOCIETY

The success of RNP was important not only in economic terms but also politically. The massive attachment of civil society and the business community to this academically-initiated project encouraged the computer science academic community to lay the groundwork in 1996 for implementing a project of broader scope, the formalization of the SocInfo Information Society Programme in Brazil (MCT, 1999 a, b, c).

In this respect, the Internet Management Committee of Brazil put together a preliminary study suggesting to the National Council for Science and Technology (CCT)[13] – an agency which directly advises the President – that a proposal be made for a Brazilian information society programme. The plan subsequently produced by CCT was approved by the government, which gave rise to the SocInfo Programme, instituted through Presidential Decree in December 1999[14].

The SocInfo Programme concentrates activities previously conducted in other sectors of the government, including the concession of fiscal exemption that constitutes the greatest stimulus to establishing the IT industry in Brazil. According to both the recommendations of the Management Committee and a proposal made by the CCT, the main activity of this Programme would be to develop and implement both an advanced Internet2-type telecommunications network, in the form of RNP2, and applications that such a network would allow:

> The implementation of the programme and above all the development and prototyping of strategic applications will take place parallel to the construction of an advance network infrastructure involving Universities, research centres and companies in the telecommunications and IT sector, with a strong human resource training component (MCT, 1999c).

The curriculum vitae of the coordinator of the SocInfo Programme, Professor Takahashi – a former professor of the University of Campinas who had coordinated the CNPq team that set up the initial RNP network – shows the extreme importance of this task and the key role it plays in the collective efforts of the CSSAC, as described in this chapter. Subsequently, he was also coordinator of the Network Engineering Task Force and RNP Representative on the Brazilian Internet Management Committee.

The development of the RNP2 project has been included in the SocInfo Programme's initiatives, together with the funding of the latest RNP backbone. The organizational mechanism for developing the network is ProTeM-CC, that is, the research and development of the network and its applications are being undertaken with the full participation of the CSSAC.

The implementation of the RNP2 backbone began in 2000, when the fibre-optic network had been extended throughout the country. In February 2002, the backbone consisted of 27 PoPs, four connected at 155 Mbps, nine at 34 Mbps and the others at lower speeds. From 2001, a new connection to the Internet in the USA was established through a 155 Mbps line and a 45 Mbps line, replacing the four previous connections of 2 Mbps each. In August 2001, the first of these two new Internet connections also became linked to the Internet2 network.

Thus, the Information Society Programme is essentially an R&D programme in information and telecommunications technology. This puts it in opposition to another possible approach for regulating economic activity, typified by the economic policy put into effect in the second half of the 1990s by the Brazilian Federal Government for the telecommunications sector. During this period, the state telecommunications companies were privatized and sold off, almost all to foreign-owned companies. In this process, there was almost no concern about the adverse effects on domestic R&D activities.

Interest in designing a programme to generate or adapt new technologies is evident in various documents, including the original proposal that was made for the National Council of Technology to discuss the theme 'information society' (Lucena et al., 1997). This stated[15]:

It is of special importance for this proposal and the subsequent action of the CCT concerning this theme that the major part of international discussion about the Information Society has concentrated on the infrastructure and service level and the various regulatory aspects, at the expense of a whole series of equally important questions, particularly for developing countries.

3.5 CONCLUSIONS

This chapter has shown the importance in the 1990s of the mobilization of the Brazilian computer science and software engineering academic community in formulating and executing national scientific and technological policy for these fields. This community coordinated various initiatives, initially encompassing a support programme for the software industry, the introduction of the Internet in Brazil – which at the time was nothing but an academic research network – and a project to re-equip computer science departments.

Such initiatives represented both technical and political victories for this community, which at that time occupied various high ranking positions in the Ministry of Science and Technology. When the Internet was opened to public use, this community obtained another political victory, by maintaining control over the coordination activities of the network. With these notable successes, the responsibilities of the academic community were enlarged in 2002 to lead the Brazilian project for the Information Society, with particular responsibility for the RNP2 upgrade of the Internet in Brazil.

However, it seems that the response and participation of private agents has not corresponded to the model's expectations. In the case of the software export programme SOFTEX 2000, performance was still very weak in 2002, with the sector composed mainly of small firms, of which almost all are not at the leading edge of technology. In the case of the networks, the telecommunications companies operating in Brazil, although large enterprises, are foreign owned, except for one. The externally-owned companies usually concentrate the bulk of their R&D activities in their country of origin. Thus, there has been little sign of any motivation to participate in the CCSAC's efforts.

On one hand, this case of telecommunications development can be generalized for other sectors. With the widespread de-nationalization of companies witnessed in the 1990s, the participation of private firms in projects such as those described here has perhaps been less than was originally desired by the formulators of the proposals. On the other hand, Brazilian legislation regulating R&D incentives is being steadily improved and, in particular, funding support for such activities is beginning to appear.

The fiscal incentive law, for example, induces companies to invest in technology in Brazil. There is also a telecommunications universalization fund that imposes a levy on the billing of telecommunications service operators. It is expected that part of this fund will be invested in the Information Society Programme.

The final outcome of the interplay between the many different actors involved in the development and diffusion of the Internet in Brazil will take time to emerge and cannot be predicted because it depends on many variables.

REFERENCES

Cavalcanti (1997), 'A Internet, o Modelo Nacional e uma Proposta de Enfoque para uma Política de Tarifas em sua Operação no País', *Revista de Economia Política*, **17** (2), April–June, 130–44.

CESAR (1999), Centro de Estudos e Sistemas Avançados do Recife, 'A História dos Programas Prioritários', *Informática Brasileira em Análise*, **2** (27), online at www.cesar.org.br

Coelho, A.J.J. and L. McKnight (1997), 'Brazil: Is The World Ready for When Information Highways Cross the Amazon?', in B. Kahin and E.J. Wilson III (eds), *National Information Infrastructure Initiatives: Vision and Policy Design*, Cambridge, MA: MIT Press, 122–47.

Cornford, J., A. Gillespie and R. Richardson (1995), 'Information Infrastructures and Territorial Development', paper prepared for the OECD Joint ICCP-TDS Workshop on Information Infrastructures and Territorial Development, Paris, November, Newcastle-upon-Tyne, UK: Centre for Urban and Regional Development Studies (CURDS), University of Newcastle.

de Montalvo, U.W., R. Mansell and E.W. Steinmueller (1999), 'Opportunities for Knowledge-Based Development: Capabilities, Infrastructure, Investment and Policy', *Science and Public Policy Letters*, **26** (2), 91-100.

Lucena, C. J. (1992), 'O Projeto Desi: Desenvolvimento Estratégico Da Informática do Conselho Nacional de Pesquisas do Ministério da Ciência e Tecnologia - Resumo Executivo', *SOFTEX 2000 Document 14*, Campinas, São Paulo: SOFTEX.

Lucena, C. J., (1993), 'A Situação Atual e o Potencial da Área de Computação', part of the research report of the Escola de Administração de Empresas of the Fundação Getúlio Vargas to the Programa de Apoio ao Desenvolvimento Científico e Tecnológico (PADCT II), Rio de Janeiro: Ministry of Science and Technology (MCT) , November.

Lucena, C. (1996), 'O Balanço do ProTeM-CC: O Que foi Feito e o Que Falta Fazer?', position paper presented to the XXVI SECOMU Seminario de Computacao na Universidade, part of XVI Congress of Sociedade Brasileira de Computação (SBC), Recife, 4–9 August,, Porto Alegre, Brazil: Sociedade Brasileira de Computação.

Lucena, C.J.P., I. de M. Campos, and S. Meira (1997), 'A Construção da Sociedade da Informação no Brasil: O Papel do Conselho Nacional de Ciência e Tecnologia', proposal presented to the National Council for Science and Technology (CCT), Brasília: CCT, November.

MCT (1998), Ministry of Science and Technology, *Resultados da Lei, no. 8.248/91*, Brasília: Secretaria de Política de Informática e Automação/Setor de Tecnologias da Informação, Brasília: MCT, December.

MCT (1999a), Ministry of Science and Technology, *Ciência E Tecnologia para A Construção da Sociedade da Informação*, Brasília: MCT/CCT.

MCT (1999b), Ministry of Science and Technology, *Bases de Um Programa Brasileiro Para A Sociedade da Informação*, Brasília: MCT/CCT.

MCT (1999c), Ministry of Science and Technology, *Programa Sociedade da Informação*, Brasília: MCT/CCT.

Prochnik, V. (1988a), 'A Cooperação Universidade/Empresa: Tendências Internacionais Recentes no Setor de Informática', *Revista de Administração de Empresas*, **28** (1), 27–38

Prochnik, V. (1988b), 'A Contribuição da Universidade para o Desenvolvimento da Informática no Brasília', *Revista de Administração de Empresas*, **28** (3), 36–49.

Prochnik, V. (1998), 'Cooperation between Universities, Companies and Government in the National Export Software Program', Documents of reference, www.idrc.ca/lacro/smmeit/innovacion/docs_e.html, July 2002, Ottawa: International Development Research Centre (IDRC).

Ribeiro Filho, J.L. (1998), *Formação de Redes e Cooperação Interinstitucional A Experiência da RNP*, Brasília: MCT, April

Ribeiro Filho, J.L. and Simões, N. (1999), *RNP: Situação Atual e Perspectivas*, Rio de Janeiro: Rede Nacional de Pesquisas (RNP), January.

Stanton, M. (1998), 'A Evolução das Redes Acadêmicas no Brasil: Parte 1 – da BITNET À Internet (1987 a 1993)', *News Generation* **2** (6), Rio de Janeiro: Rede Nacional de Pesquisas (RNP), 10 July.

Takahashi, T. (1994), 'RNP – Situação das Redes nos Estados: Uma Visão Preliminar', working document, Rio de Janeiro: Rede Nacional de Pesquisas (RNP).

Takahashi, T. (1995), *RNP Planejamento Geral '95 Parte I'*, document RNP/ORG/0080, Rio de Janeiro: Rede Nacional de Pesquisas (RNP), February.

NOTES

1. An earlier version of this chapter was presented to the Third Triple Helix III International Conference, Rio de Janeiro, April, 2000.
2. Lucena (1993) defines the computation area '... by enumerating the groups of interest of the SBC (Brazilian Society of Computation). These are: computation theory, data banks, computer architecture, computer networks, graphic computation and image processing, artificial intelligence, computers and education and software engineering.' For the same author, information technology has a wider meaning, including 'at least, micro-electronics, industrial automation and computation mathematics'.
3. In one extreme case, in the mid-1980s, a Brazilian company hired at one and the same time all twelve teachers from the Computer Science Department of the important Federal University in the same state, forcing this department to be closed for a considerable time.
4. CNPq is an MCT agency traditionally responsible for distributing scholarships and resources for university research, and where the allocation of such resources within each scientific area is decided by senior professors from these areas.
5. The name RNP came into use only after 1990.

6. Cited in Cavalcanti (1997).
7. Routers are devices that find the best path for a 'packet' digital data to be sent electronically from one network to another).
8. The Committee was created by Interministerial Ordinance No. 147 of 31 May 1995, and its members were nominated by the Interministerial Ordinance Number 183 of 3 July 1995.
9. For references on Brazilian IT indicators, see Coelho and McKnight (1997) and MCT (1998). For other IT indicators, see Cornford et al. (1995) and de Montalvo et al. (1999).
10. Source: www.isc.org/ds/, January 2002.
11. Source: the Web site (www.estadao.com.br/agestado) of the news agency, Agência Estado, of the newspaper *Estado de São Paulo*, 13 August 2001.
12. Law No. 8.248/91.
13. CCT is a high level advisory board to the President of Brazil. It is composed of prominent members of the Brazilian scientific and technological communities and meets regularly to debate priority programs in science and technology. It should not be confused with CNPq, an executive agency of the Ministry of Science and Technology (see Note 4).
14. Decree No. 3.294 of 15 December 1999.
15. This quote was obtained from the document as presented in January 2002 on the CCT Web site www.cct.gov.br (subsequently www.mct.gov.br/cct, but with that document no longer available online in July 2002).

4. IT Diffusion for Public Service Delivery: Looking for Plausible Theoretical Approaches

Shirin Madon

4.1 INTRODUCTION

The promise of an information society is increasingly being used as a guide for policy initiatives to transform the way government is run. Numerous programmes were launched in the late 1980s in governments around the world in order to replace existing manual systems and improve the efficiency of operations and the delivery of public services through computerization (Heeks, 1999). In popular parlance, these initiatives have been captured under the heading of 'e-governance'. This is usually taken to represent a continuum of initiatives, ranging from IT automation in individual government department, to the use of IT to promote intra-governmental coordination, to the electronic delivery of government services to the public, to the use of IT for enabling citizens to participate in governmental decision-making (Ranerup, 1999).

Considerable attention has been focused on the electronic delivery of government services to the public as a key e-governance application – a trend which has been as noticeable in developing countries as in advanced industrialized nations. There is increasing recognition of the need for citizens to interact with government departments through public information kiosks for a whole range of routine transactions. Among the many functions that can be carried out at such kiosks is the possibility of automatic modification of existing records and the downloading/uploading of application forms for benefits (Dutton, 1999; Heeks, 1999). This kind of approach has been particularly popular in developing countries, where the sheer volume of transactions has always been a serious obstacle for the delivery of public services, causing citizens to endure hardship.

This chapter focuses on such needs in developing countries through a study of the FRIENDS (Fast Reliable Instant Effective Network for

Disbursement of Services) experiment in the south Indian state of Kerala, which was part of a proactive programme to enhance public service delivery by promoting IT applications with a high level of public interface. There are many examples of such initiatives being started in developing countries, with the goal of providing a fast and effective government service to citizens in the payment of household and personal taxes and bills. For instance, in Malaysia a network was established in the late 1990s to enable government agencies to offer their counter-based services to the public using the online computer and network facilities of local post offices (Heeks, 1999). Applications like these are often considered successful in creating a climate of acceptance of technology and perhaps, in a subtle way, of encouraging administration to usher in more fundamental and long-awaited changes.

As is well-documented in the literature, the majority of programmes to computerize the automation of individual government departments – in both industrialized and developing countries – have suffered from serious deficiencies in the way they were planned and implemented, resulting in no significant improvement in the efficiency of operations (Committee of Public Accounts, 2000). For example, Madon and Bhatnagar's (2000) study of the impact of the computerization of district administration functions in India over a period of years concluded that these efforts had resulted in no significant impact on the overall efficiency or effectiveness of government programmes. The underlying reason for the poor impact of these projects was understood to be the need for more radical structural reform within the administration in terms of work processes and internal coordination. This has been difficult to achieve and, while conscious of the need for more substantial reform within the public sector, a spate of policy initiatives have been undertaken by governments around the world aimed at diffusing IT to provide services to citizens. The idea has been to emulate in the public sector techniques that have been well proven in the private sector for a wide range of high-volume transactions.

Although many initiatives in developing countries have been heralded as success stories in terms of the interest shown by citizen groups, there has been little systematic analysis of the reasons for this success. For example, the Electronic Government Centre at Ahmedabad in India, sponsored by the World Bank, has its own web site that acts as a repository of experiences of electronic public service delivery in developing countries[1]. The 'diffusion model of innovation' subscribed to by this web site sees technologies as originating from developed countries according to a certain logic, before spreading out to developing countries. While this model is the approach often adopted by international aid agencies, it does not do adequate justice to improving our understanding of the different networks and contextual circumstances that exist in a particular environment and which changes over time. The Ahmedabad Centre's web site provides little contextual background information to help understand why these systems have seemingly been successful. This lacuna has precluded any serious attempt at trying to replicate experiences across countries.

In this chapter, we seek to overcome this gap by attempting to analyse within its historical context the successful FRIENDS project. We discuss the interaction between this context and the process of technology diffusion in the light of relevant approaches from studies of IT diffusion and information systems. Before examining findings from the FRIENDS study in the remainder of the chapter, we consider in the next section some plausible theories of the IT diffusion process that can be useful in analysing the impact of such policy initiatives aimed at transforming the way services are provided to citizens.

4.2 INTERPRETING THE PROCESS OF IT INNOVATION

4.2.1 The 'S' Curve Theory of Technology Diffusion

Despite the various policy initiatives undertaken to diffuse IT for the delivery of public services, great uncertainty continues to surround the impact of these initiatives (Dutton, 1999; Castells, 2001). One way to think about the scope of the tremendous changes these initiatives have brought about is to draw on classical theories of technology diffusion developed by sociologists in the 19th Century and early 20th Century, which have also been advanced more recently by communication scholars, most notably Everett Rogers ([1962] 1995). He suggested that the adoption of many successful innovations have commonly followed an S-shaped pattern: experiencing a slow rate of initial adoption, followed by a substantial surge that peaks when penetration levels reach saturation point as demand slows down.

There are two variants of Rogers' theory of technology diffusion. First, the more optimistic 'normalization' thesis predicts that the social profile of the digital community will gradually broaden over time, like the early audiences for radio and television, until eventually it comes to mirror society as a whole (Norris, 2001). Perhaps in countries at the forefront of the information revolution, like the USA, Australia and Britain, it is legitimate to argue that Internet use has rippled out since the 1990s from an information source for networking scholars and scientists at elite research institutions to become a medium of mass communications for the delivery of news, music, video and audio programming, as well as e-commerce and home shopping.

Yet, even in these countries, cross-national evidence on this issue remains scattered and inconclusive. Some reports emphasize that in terms of educational, income and racial inequalities, the digital divide between those with access to new technologies and those without actually widened – not narrowed – from the mid to late 1990s (NTIA, 1999). In developing countries, there is far more evidence to support the notion that the introduction of IT is creating a more polarized society. Wresch (1996) illustrates this in terms of a story of two men living in Namibia, one a businessman connected to global and local networks of information, the other a poor labourer who is completely ostracized from modern information services because of a lack of money and skills.

The second variant on Rogers' theory is the more pessimistic 'stratification' thesis, which predicts that groups already well networked via traditional forms of information and communication technology will maintain their edge in the digital economy. This thesis seems to offer a more plausible theoretical account of IT's societal impact to date. The traditional model put forward by Rogers was essentially supplier-focused, in that it aimed at helping technology suppliers to promote more rapid diffusion of predefined best-practice innovations to communities of potential adopters (Rogers, [1962] 1995). One of the model's predictions was that the more radical the innovation, the slower would be its diffusion into society. This came to be challenged with the emergence of business process re-engineering which, although complex and requiring substantial organizational change, appeared to diffuse rapidly. Rogers argued that his model maintained its explanatory power if the defining characteristics of IT are not taken as given and permanent but are perceived – and therefore influenced by – social, political and cognitive processes.

Rogers referred to these processes as 'change agents'. He drew on case studies of technological innovations that ranged from the spread of new crops, studied by rural sociologists, to the implementation of new teaching techniques, studied by educational psychologists, in order to demonstrate that all early adopters of new innovations were drawn from groups with higher socio-economic status. In this way, one of the most important suggestions from diffusion theory was that the adoption of successful new technologies often reinforced socio-economic advantages. Historically, there is evidence to support this claim, when we consider the fact that very little realizable benefit for the average person has been delivered by technological innovations that date back from the Green Revolution of the 1960s to the modern application of computers in government. For instance, out of a population in India in the early 21st Century of around 1 billion, about 920 million cannot use a PC because popular operating systems are not available in any official Indian language. When taken together with other important issues like low purchasing power, poor PC penetration and telephone density and the minuscule number of Internet users, it is easy to see why the majority of the

Indian population are left out of the digital age and from the promise of improvements in public service delivery through the use of IT (Hariharan, 1999).

4.2.2 The Active Role of Users in Innovation Diffusion

While diffusion theory focuses our attention on the diffusion process of an information system innovation and on the influence of wider societal factors on this process, it almost assumes that these wider societal forces and biases will inevitably negatively influence usage of technology. This view is socially deterministic and underestimates the role of users in seeking and creating knowledge relevant to the innovation,. through a wide range of social networks (Swan et al., 1996). The active role of users in innovation diffusion is discussed by many writers in the information systems field (Clark et al., 1992; MacDonald and Williams, 1993; Fleck, 1994; Swanson and Ramiller, 1997) under the guise of the 'social shaping' or 'social constructivist' perspective (Edge, 1995; Williams, 1999).

Social constructivism has constituted a major development in the social studies of technology since the mid-1980s, due primarily to Pinch and Bijker (1984). This perspective emerged partly from critiques of technological and social determinism, which uses simplified linear models to argue that technology determines the outcome, or that the outcome was determined by the existing socio-economic and political biases in society. In contrast, social constructivists argue that technology continues to be shaped and reconfigured beyond its design according to the circumstances of the context where it is implemented. They try to show that technology is patterned by the way in which it is used, rather than solely according to an inner technical logic or 'best practice'. The social constructivist argument goes further by arguing that the impact of the technology introduced is eventually a matter of interpretation by human actors according to their social conditions. The focus of social constructivist studies is on the 'interpretive flexibility' of technology, whereby different groups of people involved with a technology can have very different understandings of that technology in terms of what the artefact represents and whether it is useful.

4.2.3 Information Systems Perspectives on Innovation

Perspectives from the information systems field have offered insights into the mechanisms surrounding the diffusion process, particularly recognizing the need to study both the macro context within which an innovation takes place, and the functioning and dynamics of the local context as it interacts with its macro environment. Yet, the analytical capacity of information systems research to consider the social context of IS innovation remains limited. This is more apparent in efforts to study IT innovation in developing country settings where, in order to study the outcome of innovations, it becomes necessary to trace the roots of the outcome of innovation in the economic, cultural and political domains of the social context (Madon, 1993; Avgerou and Walsham, 2000). Increasingly, the flow of people, technology, capital, media and ideologies to different parts of the world creates a hybridization of identities (Appadurai, 1990). For example, Nelson (1996) relates how Mayan activists in Guatemala described how this community appears to be refusing modernization while, on the other hand, appropriating modern technology and knowledge.

A growing body of research in information systems seeks to examine critically the limitations of IS theory in accounting for the context of IS innovation. On the one hand, universalistic perspectives pursued in IS studies assume that IS innovation is driven by a particular general logic or universal validity. On the other hand, situated studies tend to be preoccupied with the 'here and now' actions and interactions comprising IS innovation, producing a detailed description about behaviour and actions but without being able to answer why certain behaviour or actions are made manifest. The need is for situated approaches to be enhanced by studying the logic of actions observed in IS innovation. This can be achieved through current research in the field that aims to justify observed behaviour in IS innovation processes in terms of its historical and social setting by expanding the focus of study across social and institutional space.

4.3 THE FRIENDS PROJECT

4.3.1 The Context within Kerala and India

Kerala has a population of approximately 32 million people and is one of the most densely populated states in India. It was a poor state in the mid-1950s, but more recently has become well known for its social development indices and sustained public action (Kannan, 2000). With regard to basic educational provision, one of the legacies of this period of over half a century of mobilization has been the establishment of village libraries throughout the state. These libraries are now an established part of village life in Kerala, being used as centres for adult literacy and the venue for political meetings and youth events. Education has played a larger role in the evolution of Kerala's society by encouraging the growth of the print media and communication industry, most notably IT diffusion.

The initial e-governance mandate of the Kerala state government in 1998 was to identify government departments with a high level of public interface. Around 34 departments were identified, but studies revealed that substantial reform was needed before e-governance applications could be implemented. This was due to a combination of bad work procedures, poor infrastructure and the poor image of government held by citizens and by government administrators themselves. As a result, Kerala decided to implement a long-term programme of reform within government, including computerization of individual departments and integration across departments. This programme has been ongoing since 1996 with funding from the Asian Development Bank. Kerala also decided to implement a medium-term programme of introducing front-end computerization of high visibility 'people-oriented projects', one of which is FRIENDS.

FRIENDS was launched in Thiruvananthapuram Corporation as a pilot project in June 2000, and was rolled out to all fourteen district headquarters in Kerala by late 2001. As in all other Indian states, Kerala has seven or eight departments collecting taxes and utility bill payments, which citizens are expected to pay at the office of the department or agency concerned. This means that every citizen has to visit at least seven offices personally, then stand in queues waiting their turn to pay whatever is due to government. Some earlier efforts to facilitate payments through the banking network led to delayed collection and reconciliation problems, since many banks and government departments were not computerized. Moreover, only 2 to 5 per cent of the population used this facility. A similar project was implemented in one ward of the municipal corporation of Hyderabad in the Indian state of Andhra Pradesh in February 2000. For this, a comprehensive database of every citizen was built up. In order to sustain such a system over a period of time, it was obvious that there needed to be processes in place to update the database automatically. This required a fully-fledged computerization of all the departments concerned, which was at best a medium-term project.

The FRIENDS project is conceptually different from these experiments and it has become the subject of much interest around the country and region. Our findings are based on fieldwork carried out by the author in August 2001 with members of the IT Secretariat in the city of Thiruvananthapuram and with user departments at the FRIENDS counter in the city.

4.3.2 The FRIENDS Implementation Strategy

A State Level Implementation Committee was constituted to facilitate the speedy implementation of FRIENDS. The Kerala State IT Department was awarded the lead role in implementation and was designated as the nodal agency for all activities related to this project. It is the main driver of the project, coordinating with a nodal officer from each government department to develop a software prototype and a logistical plan for information transfer. The participating departments were asked to designate a nodal officer, and detailed interactions were held with each nodal officer to identify the nature and procedure involved in each transaction.

Government departments were initially sceptical of FRIENDS. This is perhaps not surprising for a state full of militant unions who feared job losses. However, no additional recruitment was made and staff were deployed from participating government departments and given the common designation of 'service' officers. Ten officers at the junior level in each of the participating departments were identified for staffing the counters, after the individuals involved had been interviewed to assess their suitability. Most of these officers came forward on a voluntary basis. Three areas of training were identified: public relations and personality development training; computerization; and motivation and self-esteem.

4.3.3 FRIENDS Capabilities and Outcomes

Each FRIENDS centre offers a one-stop, IT-enabled payment counter where citizens can pay all their bills due to government in one go. These are located in modern air-conditioned environments within which citizens can pay their utility bills from 9 a.m. until 7 p.m., seven days a week. Each centre operates on an 'any service, any counter' basis, with each counter run by a service officer who deals with all transactions of all departments. Seven departments participated. About 1 000 types of bills in various combinations were accommodated by 2001 (see Table 4.1). Citizens present only the demand notice they receive by post from the utility company and pay using cash, draft and, planned for 2003, by credit cards. Each counter prints receipts that are honoured by departments as legitimate evidence of payment. If there is a query with the bill, the citizen can go to the help-desk staff at the FRIENDS centre, who liase with departmental staff at the centre or communicate with the relevant department via telephone to sort out difficult queries.

A collection centre of the State Bank of Travancore functions at the premises of FRIENDS. Soon after the end of the shift, the money collected is passed on to the Bank, which ensures the payment and details about it are passed to the relevant departments. Departmental registers are updated daily by a system in which daily collection scrolls are printed out, with two copies signed by the project manager being sent to the offices specified by the departmental staff and another signed copy filed at the FRIENDS centre. A floppy disk is physically delivered each day to each of the seven departments, which pastes a printout of new transactions into existing departmental registers. Some departments have experimented with online data transfer from the FRIENDS centres as part of longer-term plans.

Table 4.1: Departments represented and types of bills handled by FRIENDS counters in 2001

Department	Types of Bills
Utilities	KSEB (power) bill payments
	KWA (water) bill payments
Local bodies	Property tax
	Professional tax
	Traders License fee
Revenue Department	Building tax
	Basic tax
	Revenue recovery
Civil Supplies	Fee for new ration card
	Fee for trade licenses (11 types)
Motor vehicles	One time vehicle tax
	Motor vehicle tax (105 types)
	Fee for licenses from motor vehicles department (20 types)
	Fee for permits from motor vehicles department (142 types)
	Registration fee for motor vehicles (37 types)
	Fee for fitness certificate of motor vehicles
University	University exam fee (352 types)
	General fee for university (96 types)
BSNL	Telephone bills

FRIENDS has become a popular example of how computers can be used to improve the lives of citizens. To appreciate the difference, one needs to contrast the FRIENDS facility with the situation that prevailed before in Kerala, and that still prevails in other states: where the citizen has to go to different offices, then stand in queues in the sun or rain without any clue to when her or his turn will come.

At the same time, there remain serious questions regarding the long-term sustainability of the project. In mid-2002, around 40 per cent of the population of Kerala used the FRIENDS centres. While this appears good in absolute terms, the government is planning to survey users and non-users from different socio-economic classes to study their levels of satisfaction with the centres and why certain categories of citizens are not users. The evaluation will also study the attitudes of service officers and participating government departments.

4.4 DISCUSSION

Although the FRIENDS project has been popularized both in India and in international fora, there has been little analysis of the long-term sustainability of the project. The scope of this section is to discuss the utility of theory from innovation-diffusion and social-constructivist literature.

Both diffusion theory and social constructivism recognize the importance of understanding the context within which IT innovation takes place. Fundamental to this context in the case of FRIENDS is the historical legacy of vocal citizen groups and workforce militancy in government. FRIENDS has been fundamentally demand-led with a strong pull from citizens, which offset even initial resistance from government departments to the idea of FRIENDS.

In Kerala, departmental compartmentalization is very high and there is a strong history of unions and militancy that makes lower levels of administration generally unresponsive in their work. For instance, research undertaken by the author in Kerala in the early 1990s to study the impact of government-sponsored IT projects in the state found that Kerala was unique in the country, in that hardly any government-sponsored computer applications had been implemented at the time. Indeed, during the late 1970s and 1980s, government staff had led a series of agitations against computerization, fearing that this would result in a loss of jobs. Most staff from government departments had very little computer knowledge because of the strong and militant anti-technology bias of government workers.

Analysing the outcome of an IT innovation using the theoretical lens of diffusion theory would involve an empirical study of how a particular technology is designed and developed in one setting and rolled out in another. In the case of FRIENDS, a key research question would be to study how the electronic utility payment system designed and developed by a small group of government-sponsored computer scientists fits into the existing social fabric in the state of Kerala. Of importance in such a study would be the degree to which the technology influences social change. For example, the way in which the electronic utility payment system improved the efficiency of routine interactions between government and citizens. Of equal interest in such a diffusion theory approach would be an attempt to identify deep-rooted socio-political and cultural characteristics of Keralan society that influence technology adoption.

The brief review here of the unique historical socio-political context of the region is a start in this direction. However, we would argue that such an approach to studying FRIENDS is limited because it is inherently deterministic, implying that technology impacts social change or that social factors impact technology. Therefore, we advocate social constructivism as a more useful approach to study an IT innovation such as the FRIENDS project. A key question posed by this approach is the extent to which FRIENDS, once designed and implemented, is amenable to further shaping according to the circumstances of the context of Kerala.

Earlier, we identified four main social groups involved with the FRIENDS project: the state government; government departments; service officers; and citizen groups. Let us revisit the latter two. By doing so, we focus on the way in which these different groups of people involved with the technological artefact can have different interpretations of the value of the technology. Service officers and citizens are perhaps the most crucial groups in shaping long-term change. With FRIENDS, many critics have called into question whether it will lead to lasting reform because its single-minded focus on public service delivery applications has not been associated with creating other more fundamental changes in the structure and systems of public administration. We believe this question can be answered only by studying the changing perceptions of these two social groups in terms of how the technological artefact incrementally implies different roles for the actors around it.

4.4.1 Service Officers

A unique element of FRIENDS is the human 'front end' established by the service officers in each centre. Government functionaries from different departments are working together in the same physical location to service citizens in an integrated fashion. This activity is changing attitudes of government administrators, who earlier suffered from apathy and low morale in their work. It was extremely important for the success of the project that staff became emotionally involved with the project. The strategy was to send home the message that the individuals selected for FRIENDS have a very special responsibility on them – that of taking the state to the next millennium. Staff were clearly told about the importance of the project in terms of how it is going to benefit the citizen and how each one of them is going to make a difference to the lives of so many other fellow citizens. Individually, most of the staff could also realize how useful the project would be as they themselves had been facing difficulties in effecting these kinds of payments. Moreover, the working environment and ambience provided was much superior to normal work settings. The point was driven home that this ambience has been created not just to impress customers, but because the staff themselves are special. Self-esteem of the workers went up substantially, as they could perceive themselves as computer professionals working in an excellent environment.

4.4.2 Citizen Groups

Citizen attitudes towards government are also changing as a result of FRIENDS because, for the first time, the government is seen as being capable of providing a reasonable level of service without corruption. This attitudinal change is very important. Despite initial resistance from participating departments, right from the start a strong citizen-pull for the FRIENDS project was manifested through the many vocal citizen groups in the state. It is interesting to note that FRIENDS was not aggressively marketed in the state. The project stabilized within a period of five months, after which a limited publicity of the facility was done through the local cable network for a period of one month. The main lobbying was done through citizen-based organizations that encouraged people by word of mouth to use the services of the FRIENDS centres.

The social constructivist theoretical perspective that has done most to sensitize the field to this issue is called 'actor-network theory'. It was developed by several scholars, such as Bruno Latour, Michel Callon, Madeline Akrich and John Law (Latour, 1987; Callon, 1991, Akrich, 1992). The theory proposes that both society and technology are made of networks that link humans and non-human entities. The fundamental idea is that human and non-human actors interact to form heterogeneous networks. In the case of FRIENDS, such a heterogeneous network consists of the payment and utilities system, computer consultants, IT trainers and support staff, the citizens, service officers, the state government, central government and international agencies.

Not only is each FRIENDS counter a conglomerate of heterogeneous actors, but it is also an actor itself. This can be seen, for example, by contrasting it with earlier manual forms of utility payment to government that have been substituted by modern e-government applications like FRIENDS. This comparison can lead to a discussion of the issue of 'technology transfer'. In many academic discussions, the term is taken to mean the transfer of an artefact from the 'north' to the 'south'. Viewed from this perspective, arguments are made about the incompatibility of western management methods and techniques that inscribe assumptions of rationality different from those of a developing country like India. Such a perspective favours the diffusion model of innovation adopted by international aid agencies and national governments, which views technologies as originating from one point and then spreading out. However, we argue that this is an adequate approach to improving our understanding of the different networks that get formed in the course of the transfer process, which in turn may give rise to different effects (Akrich, 1992).

In the case of FRIENDS, the diffusion model would imply that the innovation was conceived by the Kerala state government, with influence from the international community, and then rolled out to the districts of Kerala for statewide implementation. Actor-network theory would encourage us to trace the negotiations that take place as the software for FRIENDS is transferred from the development team to the districts. As the technology is transferred, it necessarily implies different roles for the actors around it – for example the service officers and citizens. FRIENDS illustrates how various transformations can occur in the process of government with the introduction of modern electronic utility payment systems that begin to treat citizens as 'customers' whose satisfaction has to be maximized, rather than as objects who need to comply with government regulations. This shifting perception creates a new basis for the relationship between citizens and government, with the latter gradually trying to align the interests of the citizens with priorities of revenue collection, honesty and transparency. These are indeed new virtues as compared to the past.

4.5 CONCLUSIONS

To summarize, the creation of a plausible theoretical approach to the study of IT diffusion for public service delivery will combine elements from diffusion theory and the social construction of information systems. From diffusion theory, we are able to relate the outcome of an IS innovation directly to the social and political biases inherent in the environment that directly influence the diffusion of the technology. We are able to augment this approach using concepts from the social construction of technology, which focuses our attention on issues of technology usage – although how far the two theories are compatible still remains a matter for further discussion. According to the social constructivist argument, actors are capable of shaping the way in which a technology innovation is used through various subtle processes of interaction and negotiation over a period of time.

A final addition to the creation of a framework for the study of IT diffusion comes from our earlier discussion of research in information systems. Within its first year of implementation, FRIENDS was deemed a success and the project has received a lot of publicity worldwide. The state government of Kerala has been measuring success in terms of certain indicators, such as the amount of funds transferred from citizens to government via the centres and the number of people who have visited the centres. However, there has been little qualitative analysis undertaken to study why the system has been so successful and how this success may trigger more substantial long-lasting administrative reform. The author is planning to attempt a more appropriate framing of the research context through an extended period of study in Kerala that will focus on identifying the perspectives of key actors in the state government, FRIENDS centres and among a sample of citizens, some of whom are users and others who are non-users of the centres.

REFERENCES

Akrich, M. (1992), 'The De-Scription of Technical Objects', in W.E. Bijker and J. Law (eds), *Shaping Technology/Building Society: Studies in Sociotechnical Change*, Cambridge, MA: MIT Press.

Appadurai, A. (1990), 'Disjuncture and Difference in the Global Economy', in M. Featherstone (ed.), *Global Culture: Nationalism, Globalisation and Modernity,* London: Sage. 295–310.

Avgerou, C. and Walsham, G. (2000) (eds), *Information Technology in Context: Implementing Systems in the Developing World*, Aldershot, UK: Ashgate Publishers.

Callon, M. (1991), 'Techno-economic Networks and Irreversibility', in J. Law (ed.), *A Sociology of Monsters: Essays on Power, Technology and Domination,* London: Routledge.

Castells, M. (2001), *The Internet Galaxy,* Oxford: Oxford University Press.

Clark, P., S. Newell, P. Burcher, D. Bennett, S. Sharifi and J. Swan (1992), 'The Decision-episode Framework and Computer-aided Production Management (CAPM)', *International Studies of Management and Organisation*, **22**, 69–80.

Committee of Public Accounts (2000), *Improving the Delivery of Government IT Projects*, London: The Stationery Office.

Dutton, W.H. (1999), *Society on the Line: Information Politics in the Digital Age*, Oxford: Oxford University Press.

Edge, D. (1995), 'The Social Shaping of Technology', in N. Heap, R. Thomas, G. Einon, R. Mason and H. MacKay, *Information Technology: A Reader*, Milton Keynes, UK: Open University, 14–33.

Fleck, J. (1994), 'Learning by Trying: The Implementation of Configurational Technology', *Research Policy*, **23**, 637–52.

Hariharan, V. (1999), 'Information Poverty: India's New Challenge', *Information Technology in Developing Countries*, Newsletter of IFIP Working Group 9.4 and Commonwealth Network for Information Technology, **9** (2), available online at www.iimahd.ernet.in/egov/ifip/wg.htm

Heeks, R. (1999), 'Reinventing Government in the Information Age', in R. Heeks (ed.), *Reinventing Government in the Information Age*, London: Routledge, 9–22.

Kannan, K.P. (2000), 'Poverty Alleviation as Advancing Basic Human Capabilities: Kerala's Achievements Compared', in G. Parayil (ed.), *Kerala: The Development Experience*, London: Zed Books, 40–66.

Latour, B. (1987), *Science in Action,* Cambridge, MA: Harvard University Press.

MacDonald, S. and C. Williams (1993), 'The Informal Network in an Age of Advanced Communications', *Human Systems Management*, **11**, 77–87.

Madon, S. (1993), 'Introducing Administrative Reform Through the Application of Computer-based Information Systems: A Case Study in India', *Public Administration and Development,* **13,** 37–48.

Madon, S. and S.C. Bhatnagar (2000), 'Institutionalising Decentralised Information Systems for Local Level Planning: Comparing Approaches Across Two States in India', *Journal of Global Information Technology Management,* **3** (4), 45–59.

Nelson, D. (1996), 'Maya Hackers and the Cyberspatialised Nation State: Modernity, Ethnostalgia, and a Lizard Queen in Guatemala', *Cultural Anthropology,* **11** (3), 287–308.

Norris, P. (2001), *Digital Divide: Civic Engagement, Information Poverty, and the Internet Worldwide*, Cambridge: Cambridge University Press.

NTIA (1999), National Telecommunications and Information Administration, *Falling Through the Net*, Washington, DC: US Department of Commerce.

Pinch, T. and W. Bijker (1984), 'The Social Construction of Facts and Artefacts', *Social Studies of Science*, **14**, 399–441.

Ranerup, A. (1999), 'Internet-enabled Applications for Local Government Democratisation', in R. Heeks (ed.), *Reinventing Government in the Information Age,* London: Routledge, 177–94.

Rogers, E.M. ([1962] 1995), *Diffusion of Innovations*, New York: Free Press.

Swan, J.A., S. Newell and M. Robertson (1996), 'The Illusion of "Best Practice" in Information Systems for Production Management', in *Proceedings of the 4th European Conference on Information Systems*, Lisbon: New University of Lisbon, 1031–7.

Swanson, E.B. and N.C. Ramiller (1997), 'The Organising Vision in Information Systems Innovation', *Organisation Science,* **8**, 458–74.

Williams, R. (1999), 'The Social Shaping of Technology', in W.H. Dutton (ed.), *Society on the Line: Information Politics in the Digital Age*, Oxford: Oxford University Press, 41–3.

Wresch, W. (1996), *Disconnected: Haves and Have-nots in the Information Age,* New Brunswick, NJ: Rutgers University Press.

NOTES

1. See www.developmentgateway.org/topic/index?page_id=3647 on the web site of the Centre for Electronic Governance, Indian Institute of Management, Ahmedabad.

PART TWO

ICT adoption

5. ICT Adoption in Small and Medium-Sized Enterprises: Lessons from Case Studies

Renata Lèbre La Rovere

5.1 INTRODUCTION

This chapter explores the relationship between innovation, competitiveness and ICT adoption in small and medium-sized enterprises (SMEs). In starts with a discussion of how the sectoral position of SMEs affects their competitiveness and ability to innovate. The main issue for these enterprises is that their size leads to a strong vulnerability to changes in the competitive environment. SMEs can overcome this vulnerability if they organize their information flows in ways that support their ability to define their competitive strategies and increase their innovative activities.

The study of the adoption of ICT by firms can provide insights into how enterprises create appropriate information flows and an organizational learning process that establishes the conditions for innovation. Therefore, we then present some lessons of a study conducted among SMEs in Rio de Janeiro, which asked questions related to ICT use and competitiveness. The definition we use of SMEs encompasses micro (up to 20 employees), small (20 to 100 employees) and medium-sized (up to 500 employees) enterprises. The study's findings show that when firms have a short-term vision to compete they are not able to identify the importance of the creation of knowledge and of cooperation links. As a result, they use ICT in a very limited way, with no effects on competitiveness. In the concluding section of the chapter, possible strategies for SMEs are discussed.

5.2 INNOVATION, COMPETITIVENESS AND ICT ADOPTION IN SMES

The economist Joseph Schumpeter defined innovation as the creation and adoption of new products, new processes and new ways of organizing production[1]. From this Schumpeterian perspective, we can observe a debate in the literature about SMEs' innovative capacities. This debate arises because an SME's ability to innovate actually depends on several factors related to the sector and the innovation system within which the firms belong. As observed by Rothwell and Dodgson (1993), both SMEs and large enterprises have advantages they can exploit in creating and adopting innovations. While large firms have material advantages related to the R&D capacity needed to assist innovation, SMEs have behavioural advantages in terms of their flexibility. Most SMEs have diversified activities and flexible structures that favour fast answers to changes in the market. SMEs may also operate in market niches with high innovation rates and have a business culture where teamwork favours learning and the diffusion of tacit knowledge (Julien, 1993; La Rovere et al., 2000).

However, small enterprises are not necessarily more innovative than large ones. SMEs usually have less access to technological information and, therefore, can be less prone to innovation (OECD, 1995). SMEs also have less favourable credit conditions than large enterprises (Acs and Audrestch, 1992), so are more sensitive to economic cycles. Large companies have greater access to credit and can have scale economies in R&D. Thus, they have a greater chance of developing something that becomes the dominant design of an industry. In addition, large enterprises have greater political power, which enables them to influence the direction of innovation policies (Marcum, 1992). Finally, in the new techno-economic paradigm[2], large enterprises are enhancing their learning and flexibility capabilities (La Rovere et al., 2000).

The innovation capacity of small and medium-sized enterprises depends on several elements related to their culture, to the organization of the sector they belong to and to their institutional environment. SMEs in general are not aware of possible competitive gains brought about by innovation. Most SMEs develop innovations only when they perceive clearly the related business opportunities (Gagnon and Toulouse, 1996), or because they are under pressure from clients or suppliers. This is because of the specific characteristics of the learning process of SMEs, where the search and selection of information is affected by time and human-resource limitations (European Commission, 1996).

The obstacles to innovation in SMEs may be overcome if the enterprises constitute networks or establish cooperation links in R&D, marketing and the acquisition of inputs. However, SMEs normally prefer to operate on a stand-alone basis. Their resistance to cooperation stems from the fact that they are generally family-owned and are therefore managed in a traditional (reactive) way. The short-term horizon of planning that is typical of most SMEs is another obstacle to innovation because this does not cope with the uncertainties related to cooperation in the innovative process. As SMEs are more sensitive to economic downturns, they attribute a high value to short-term gains that may be reduced with the establishment of cooperation. Also, the limited access SMEs have to technological and marketing information means they may not be able to develop an innovation successfully.

Fostering the organization of information flows in SMEs is an important way of stimulating innovation in these enterprises. When firms organize their internal information flows, they set the basis for the creation of tacit and codified knowledge that spur the innovation process. And when firms organize their information with suppliers, clients and R&D organizations, they are establishing cooperation links that contribute to the diffusion of tacit and codified knowledge and feed the innovation process.

In the context of the new techno-economic paradigm, the ability to transform information into knowledge is essential for the enterprise. This requires a process of interactive learning that includes the activities of learning-by-doing, learning-by-using, learning-by-searching and learning-by-interacting. Generated knowledge may be codified or tacit. For example, Capello (1999) made an empirical analysis of Italian high-tech enterprises and observed three types of learning processes: learning based on external knowhow; knowledge based in internal competencies; and collective learning based on cooperation links. The more innovative firms were those where collective learning dominated.

This result confirms the suggestion of Lundvall (1999) that product innovations generate information problems, since producers must have feedback from the users – and those users must have information about the new product. The collective learning process helps to solve these problems because it allows enterprises to exchange information about the product collected by users and to make joint efforts to diffuse the new product.

The means by which information circulates inside the enterprise is also essential for the learning process required for obtaining sustainable competitive advantages. Cavalcanti et. al. (2001) suggest that the management of information in the knowledge society must be oriented towards problem-solving processes. The definition of a firm's competitive strategy requires the definition of production and commercialization goals that may be translated into problems: how, how much and in what time the enterprise will attain its goals. The flexible enterprise uses different combinations of resources to solve problems: workers can form a group at one moment and a different one at another.

Information systems are therefore strategic for the firm because they enable it to assess its competitive environment and define a competitive strategy that includes appropriate innovation. Information systems are also important to the integration of the enterprise with its users and suppliers, and in setting the framework for cooperation. Although the ability to innovate depends on organizing information so that learning processes can be developed, SMEs sometimes fail to recognize the importance of information systems to their innovative activity. Therefore, SMEs may not grasp the benefits of organizing their information flows in information systems, even if they are under strong competitive pressure.

The study of ICT adoption by SMEs can give us clues to how the firms organize their information flows, and how they can use these flows to spur their competitiveness. ICT can mediate the organizational changes required to enhance the competitiveness of the firm (Agrasso and Abreu, 2000). This is why the literature suggests that firms will gain competitive advantage with ICT only if they align their information systems with their competitive strategy or if they implement organizational changes (Baile and Sole, 1995; Bielli, 1998; Agrasso and Abreu, 2000). However, when adopting new technologies, SMEs generally prefer ready-made solutions because of their own lack of competence in evaluating the benefits of the new technologies for their business. If this happens in the case of ICT adoption, there will be no positive effects on competitiveness. The survey described in the next section provides some evidence of the relation between ICT adoption, innovation and the competitiveness of SMEs.

5.3 SMES AND ICT ADOPTION: CASE STUDIES FROM BRAZIL

In Brazil, SMEs account for about 66 per cent of registered jobs. However, until the late 1990s there were few studies on how these firms adopt ICT, and whether ICT use has implications on the competitiveness of SMEs. Since 1997, I have therefore been developing case studies to explore these issues. The case studies described here were part of a research project funded by the Brazilian national council of research (CNPq) and were conducted between 1997 and 2000 by myself with the help of undergraduate students[3]. The choice of the cases was derived from a review of the literature on ICT and SMEs in developed countries (OECD 1995). These were selected to examine two main hypotheses.

The first hypothesis is that ICT is adopted as a result of a cumulative learning process, where adoption of one technology leads to the adoption of others. If this hypothesis is true, then firms in sectors where the use of information is intensive will have a pattern of adoption more intense and diversified than firms in sectors that are not information intensive. Therefore, the cases were chosen to include those in: one sector that is intensive both in the use and provision of information (software); a sector intensive in the provision of information but not so intensive in its use (tourism agencies); and a sector with low information use (garment industry).

The second hypothesis is that the innovative character of the activity is a determining factor in ICT adoption. This hypothesis can be verified by comparing the results related to the software industry with those from the garment industry. Finally, a comparison between the three sectors will lead to the identification of problems related to ICT and competitiveness among SMEs from different sectors.

We started with the study of the software sector in 1997. A questionnaire was sent to all enterprises associated to Rio de Janeiro's trade association of software and informatics services companies – SERPRORJ. At that time, SERPRORJ had 335 associates and the questionnaire was answered by 10 per cent of them (33 enterprises). The questionnaire asked about ICT patterns of use, reasons for ICT adoption, benefits and obstacles to ICT use, main sources of competitiveness and the learning process.

We then surveyed the tourism sector, about a year later. A questionnaire was sent to all enterprises associated to Rio de Janeiro's trade association of travel agencies – ABAV. At the time, ABAV had 575 associates, and the questionnaire was answered by 8 per cent of the companies (46 enterprises). The questionnaire had the same questions as that sent to the software companies, plus some items specific to this sector; for instance, in the competitive-performance question, we asked about the importance of offering closed tourist packages in understanding the relationships of the firms with their suppliers[4].

When we came to the study of the garment sector, it was not possible to proceed with the same methodology because the trade association of garment producers of Rio de Janeiro (SINDIROUPAS) did not have an updated list of all associates. The sector had suffered a severe shock with the devaluation of the Brazilian currency in 1999 and many companies had subsequently gone out of business. Given this background, we decided to undertake in-depth interviews instead of sending questionnaires. After an interview with the director of SINDIROUPAS, we focused the survey among 11 representative firms of the sector.

Due to the changes in the methodology for the garment industry, I will first compare and discuss the results from the software and tourism enterprises, before comparing them with the findings from interviews with the garment small and medium-sized enterprises.

5.3.1 ICT in Software and Tourism SMEs

The pattern of ICT adoption in SMEs in the software and tourism industries in Brazil confirmed the hypothesis that more information-intensive firms have a pattern of adoption more intense and diversified than other firms (Table 5.1). As the survey among software firms was done a year before the survey with tourism enterprises, the software figures are probably lower than they would have been if both surveys were done at the same time.

Table 5.1: Use of ICT services

Services	Software*	Tourism*
Internet	90.0	78.2
E-mail	75.7	67.1
Online data banks	45.4	32.3
EDI	24.2	4.1

* Percentage of positive answers.

For software companies, the main reason for adopting ICT was the fact that their clients use these technologies and their use makes it possible to win new clients (Table 5.2). ICT adoption gives the firm a positive image, which was also considered very important by travel agencies. The main difference among software and tourism companies is related to the importance attributed to clients. This indicates that the software sector is more aware of the importance of stable relations with clients, which are essential for a firm's competitiveness.

Table 5.2: Main reasons for adopting ICT

Motive	Software*	Tourism*
Clients use these technologies	1	3
Use of these technologies has a positive image	2	1
Low costs of use	3	2
Low costs of implementation	4	5
Suppliers use these technologies	5	4

* Ranked by importance (1 represents most important, 5 least important).

The main sources of competitiveness for software companies are the quality of services, efficiency of production and development of new products

(Table 5.3). For tourism, low prices are more important than developing new products. In both sectors, the main sources of learning are specialized literature and information obtained from suppliers and at industrial fairs[5].

Table 5.3: Main sources of competitiveness for firms

Source[a]	Software[b]	Tourism[b]
Quality of services	1	1
Production efficiency	2	2
Product development	3	4
Low prices	4	3
Proximity of clients	5	5
Distribution channels	6	6
Proximity of suppliers	7	7
Low salaries	8	8

Notes
(a) Within the tourism sector, for travel agencies we considered velocity of information as a proxy for production efficiency and tourism operators as a proxy for suppliers.
(b) Ranked by importance (1 represents most important, 8 least important).

With regard to obstacles to ICT use by firms (Table 5.4), the answers from software companies in Rio de Janeiro emphasized the cost and quality of telecommunications infrastructure, organizational changes related to these technologies and new training requirements associated with these technologies. The tourism companies had similar results, except for the high costs of implementation, which were considered more important. It must be noted that both surveys were made while the Brazilian telecommunications infrastructure was in a transition process from public to private ownership. By the early 21st Century, the infrastructure had improved considerably and is probably not such a serious problem for companies anymore.

Table 5.4: Main problems in the adoption of ICT

Problem	Software*	Tourism*
Telecommunication problems	1	1
Use of ICT requires organizational changes	2	3
Use of ICT requires workforce training	3	4
High costs of use	4	5
Clients do not use these technologies	5	7
Lack of information concerning ICT	6	6
High costs of implementation	7	2
Suppliers do not use these technologies	8	8

* Ranked by importance (1 represents most important, 8 least important).

The fact that tourism companies considered high costs of implementation more important than software companies suggests that sectoral conditions do affect the pattern of ICT implementation. Being ICT companies themselves, the software enterprises had less costs to implement ICT than their counterparts in other sectors. The interviews in the garment sector confirmed that implementation of ICT is costly for SMEs in traditional sectors, and this cost sometimes delays adoption of these technologies.

Survey results concerning the obstacles to competitive performance were quite different among the sectors (Table 5.5). For travel agencies, equipment costs are a severe obstacle to performance but training is not so important. The opposite is true for software companies. This suggests that training is perceived as more important by companies that are more information intensive and, therefore, require higher expertise. The importance attributed by the software companies to training suggests that they view learning and organizational conditions as essential for their competitiveness, while the travel agencies have a more traditional view of competition, centred on costs and prices.

Table 5.5: Main obstacles to competitive performance

Obstacle	**Software***	**Tourism***
Deficiencies in telecommunications	1	3
Difficulties in training workforce	2	6
Lower prices from competitors	3	4
Lack of credit from public institutions	4	5
Lack of credit from private institutions	5	7
Lack of demand	6	1
Costs of equipment	7	2

* Ranked by importance (1 represents most important, 7 least important).

The survey's results suggest that software companies and travel agencies are aware of the benefits of ICT for their competitiveness, and adoption of ICT is made accordingly. The findings also show that firms from different sectors have similar views about benefits and obstacles of ICT adoption, as well as about sources of competitiveness. This indicates that the techno-economic paradigm of ICT is well diffused among SMEs, which means they are aware that ICT adoption is important in helping to cope in a competitive environment by enhancing the speed and flexibility of doing business.

The obstacles to competitive performance depend on sectoral conditions. Therefore, although ICT may enable competitiveness, its use to gain competitive advantage requires a further step. The literature suggests that firms will gain competitive advantage with ICT only if they align their information systems with their competitive strategy (Baile and Sole, 1995) or if they implement organizational changes (Bielli, 1998). The survey showed that software companies are more aware of this fact than travel agencies, so they attributed more importance to training.

5.3.2 ICT Adoption by SMEs in the Garment Sector

The interviews with SMEs from the garment sector were used primarily to explore the relations between competitive performance and sectoral conditions. This was because it was clear from the interview with the director of the trade association of garment producers that the widespread use of ICT among companies was limited to simple tasks, like accounting and stock management.

We introduced questions about training to this study because it was a sensitive issue for SMEs in the other sectors (software and tourism) we had surveyed. Basically, the garment firms train their workforce at the workplace, and half of them also used training courses offered by Government institutions. However, the use of these external courses was sporadic and was not integrated into firms' long-term strategies. The firms that used training more intensively were also those with higher use of plant equipment.

As in the other sectors, the garment companies considered quality of products essential for their competitiveness. This quality was reached essentially by trying to maintain a stable workforce (which is not usual among Brazilian SMEs) and by training within the workplace. Clients were considered very important to the development of product innovations. However, for most companies, the innovative process was limited to copying and adapting existing models; innovations in the production process were not adopted. The learning process of managers was based in specialized literature and information collected at industrial fairs, as for the other sectors surveyed.

The obstacles to competitiveness felt most among garment companies were high taxes, lack of credit (from public and private institutions alike) and lower prices from competitors. The garment sector has a serious problem with competition from non-registered firms, unlike the other sectors that were surveyed. Although the managers/owners of the garment enterprises we interviewed were aware of possible ICT benefits for competitive performance, most said they did not have sufficient knowledge of computers to assess real benefits for their enterprises. The interviews suggested most entrepreneurs have a short-term planning horizon, and their competitive strategy basically consists of reacting to market oscillations.

5.4 CONCLUSIONS

The aim of this chapter has been to examine the relationship between innovation, competitiveness and ICT adoption in SMEs. In this regard, I observed in Section 5.2 that SMEs are not necessarily more innovative than large enterprises, and they face obstacles to innovative activity due to limitations in their material conditions and the nature of their reactive competitive strategies. As observed by Kozul-Wright (1995), the development of innovation is not encouraged by a competitive environment in which economic agents merely react to information on relative prices and act in isolation. ICT adoption can spur innovation in SMEs by allowing them to surpass material limitations through the establishment of cooperation links that generate scale and scope economies. ICT adoption is also important in overcoming the limitations of a reactive competitive strategy, by supporting the organization of information flows inside the firm that enable sustained learning and innovation to occur.

The results presented here from the survey of three sectors in Brazil demonstrate that SMEs regard innovation as a way to differentiate products and gain new clients. Although these firms consider innovation important, their innovative activities are not regular and are undertaken more to survive in existing markets than to conquer new ones. This is not sufficient to generate competitive advantages, because innovative activities are not incorporated in the learning and innovation process within the firm.

The comparison between the three sectors studied suggests that ICT is adopted as a result of a cumulative learning process and the innovative character of the activity is a determining factor in ICT adoption. Enterprises in the software sector had a more intense and diversified pattern of ICT adoption than enterprises from other sectors. The fact that SMEs in the tourism sector used more ICT than enterprises in the garment sector suggests that the importance of information to the activity is a determining factor on decisions about ICT adoption. To all firms surveyed, ICT adoption is related to a positive image that is considered very important.

In addition, the study suggests that the importance of training is higher for companies that are more information intensive and therefore require higher expertise. As training affects the learning process and this process is essential for firms in the new techno-economic paradigm of ICT, information-intensive SMEs have more chances to develop and sustain innovations that will support competitiveness.

Finally, the survey also demonstrated that SMEs in different sectors have similar views about ICT and sources of competitiveness. Therefore, the techno-economic paradigm of ICT is well diffused among SMEs. However, as competition depends on the specific sector conditions, the results of ICT adoption on competitiveness are not predetermined. This finding is important. As ICT provides the infrastructure of the knowledge-based society, many policy-makers act as if the diffusion of ICT will be sufficient to improve the competitiveness of firms. In my view, ICT policies must be included in more general innovation policies, tackling not only conditions of infrastructure but also issues such as learning, organization of information inside firms and the creation of networks that support cooperation.

REFERENCES

Acs, Z.J. and D.B. Audrestch (1992), *Small Firms and Entrepreneurship: An East-West Perspective*, Cambridge: Cambridge University Press.

Agrasso N.M. and A.F. Abreu (2000), *Tecnologia da Informação – Manual de Sobrevivência da Nova Empresa,* São Paulo: Editora Arte&Ciência-Villipress.

Baile, S. and I. Sole (1995), 'PME et Investissements en Technologies de l'Information', *Deuxième Congrès International de la PME – Proceedings,* Paris, 25–27 October, Paris: Ecole Nationale Superieure des Telecommunications (ENST), 221–40.

Bielli, P. (1998), 'Virtual Enterprises and Information Technology: An Ambiguous Relationship', in M. Khosrowpour (ed.), *Effective Utilization and Management of Emerging Information Technologies*, Proceedings of the 1998 Information Resources Management Association, Boston, Hershey, PA: Idea Group Publishing, 89–94.

Capello, R. (1999), 'A Measurement of Collective Learning Effects in Italian High-Tech Milieus', *Révue d'Économie Régionale et Urbaine*, **3**, 449–68.

Cavalcanti, M., E. Gomes and A. Pereira (2001), *Gestão de Empresas na Sociedade do Conhecimento*, Rio de Janeiro: Campus.

European Commission (1996), *Electronic Information as a Strategic Tool to Increase the Competitiveness of European Small and Medium-Sized Enterprises – Report of the European Commission Workshop*, Brussels: European Commission, DG XIII/E.

Gagnon, Y.C. and J.M. Toulouse (1996), 'The Behavior of Business Managers when Adopting New Technologies', *Technological Forecasting and Social Change,* **52**, 58–73.

Julien, P. (1993), 'Small Businesses as a Research Subject: Some Reflections on Knowledge of Small Businesses and its Effects on Economic Theory', *Small Business Economics*, **5**, 157–66.

Kozul-Wright, Z. (1995), *The Role of the Firm in the Innovation Process*, UNCTAD Discussion Paper 98, April.

La Rovere, R.L. (1999), 'Difusão de Tecnologias da Informação e Desempenho Competitivo em Pequenas e Médias Empresas: Dois Estudos de Caso', *Proceedings of Primeiro Workshop Brasileiro de Inteligência Competitiva & Gestão do Conhecimento*, Rio de Janeiro, 22 October, Rio de Janeiro: FINEP, 1–20.

La Rovere, R.L. and M.V.R. Pereira (2000), 'Adoption of ICT and Competitiveness in the Tourism Sector: The Case of Brazilian Travel Agencies', in *Proceedings of International Federation for Information Processing WG 9.4 Conference 2000,*

Cape Town, 24–26 May, Cape Town: SBS Conferences and Computer Society of South Africa, in association with International Federation for Information Processing (IFIP) Working Group 9.4, 127–41.

La Rovere, R.L., F. Erber and L. Hasenclever (2000), 'Industrial and Technology Policy and Regional Development: Promoting Clusters', in *Proceedings of the Triple Helix III Conference*, Rio de Janeiro, Brazil, 26–29 April, Rio de Janeiro: Microservice, 1–10.

Lastres, H.M.M. and J.C. Ferraz (1999), 'Economia da Informação, do Conhecimento e do Aprendizado', in H.M.M Lastres and S. Albagli (eds), *Informação e Globalização na Era do Conhecimento*, Rio de Janeiro: Campus.

Lundvall, B.-Å. (1999), 'Spatial Division of Labour and Interactive Learning', *Révue d'Économie Régionale et Urbaine*, **3**, 470–88.

Marcum, J. (1992), 'Centralized Versus Decentralized Policy Towards Small and Medium Enterprises', in A.S. Bhalla (ed.), *Small and Medium Enterprises: Technology Policies and Options,* Croton-on-Hudson, NY: Intermediate Technology Publications, 19–28.

Nelson, R.R. (1995), 'Recent Evolutionary Theorizing About Economic Change', *Journal of Economic Literature*, **33** (1), 48–90

OECD (1995), Organization for Economic Cooperation and Development, *Information Technology (IT) Diffusion Policies for Small and Medium-Sized Enterprises*, Paris: OECD.

Rothwell, R. and M. Dodgson (1993), *Technology-based SMEs: Their Role in Industrial and Economic Change*, Olney, UK: Inderscience Enterprises.

NOTES

1. For a detailed review of evolutionary ideas and related literature, see Nelson (1995).
2. We define techno-economic paradigm as an ensemble of organizational, technical and institutional innovations that transform and shape the competitive environment. Some authors call the current techno-economic paradigm as the techno-economic paradigm of ICT (see Lastres and Ferraz, 1999).
3. I take this opportunity to thank Marcus Vinicius Rodrigues Pereira, Jussiê Ricardo de Medeiros e Rafael Marco Pereira for their work in this research.
4. For a detailed discussion of the case of the tourism sector, see La Rovere and Pereira (2000).
5. These characteristics of software companies' reasons for ICT adoption, sources of competitiveness and the learning process were also found in another survey that was made among software companies from Germany, described by La Rovere (1999).

6. Understanding the Adoption of E-commerce

Paulo Bastos Tigre and Renata Lèbre La Rovere

6.1 INTRODUCTION

Innovations in ICT have been radically altering the way enterprises are organized and their relationship with the market, creating a new growth model that has been linked to a global movement of market liberalization and expansion of tradable services. This movement, coupled with the strengthening of intellectual property rights in industry, is requiring a deep rearrangement of institutions. These changes can be analysed with the help of economic theory and the past experience of service industries, especially ICT industries.

Much discussion around the turn of the century examined the ability of economic theory to explain how the digital economy works. Economists identified with institutionalist and evolutionary theories pointed out that new theoretical and analytical approaches must be proposed to deal with an economy based on information and knowledge[1]. Shapiro and Varian (1999) and other authors propose that although technology may change, the laws of economics do not – suggesting that some concepts from orthodox economic theory are durable enough to explain the economics of information.

Most key concepts that explain the economics of information were developed in the field of Industrial Organization. These include scale and scope economies (Bain, [1956] 1993), externalities (Marshall, [1890] 1997), switching costs (Klemperer, 1995) and transaction costs (Coase, 1937; Williamson, 1975). Other more recently developed ideas that explain the role of learning in economic growth were based on the work of evolutionary authors. These emphasize innovation's role in economic dynamics[2].

The aim of this chapter is to present six of these economic concepts: economies of scale and scope; transaction costs; network externalities; lock-in and switching costs; de-intermediation and re-intermediation; and cumulative learning. They are of particular help in understanding the economics of information and analysing the behaviour of enterprises operating in the new environment created by the diffusion of ICT. The focus for this exploration is the adoption of e-commerce as a way of doing business using the Internet.

6.2 SCALE AND SCOPE ECONOMIES IN INFORMATION PRODUCTION AND DISTRIBUTION

The principle of scale economies is that there will be a decrease in the marginal cost of production as a firm's outputs increase. Scope economies occur when enterprises dilute costs by increasing the range of products and services produced. Both concepts can be applied to reveal valuable insights into activities in the digital economy.

For example, the Internet supports scale economies because it has allowed activities with decreasing returns of scale to be replaced by activities that have increasing returns of scale. As information is costly to produce but very cheap to reproduce, the cost of information is dominated by the costs of the first copy. For instance, software production may require a high investment but its distribution costs can be very low. In the language of economists, the fixed costs of information and of the ICT infrastructure are high, but their marginal costs are low (Shapiro and Varian, 1999).

High fixed costs and low marginal costs are typical of all products of the information industry, including books, newspapers, CDs and movies. These products have low costs of reproduction compared to their production costs. Distribution of these products via the Internet reduces even more their distribution and reproduction costs, increasing the opportunities to benefit from scale economies This tendency for marginal costs to be reduced has important implications for the calculation of prices. Traditional methods of price determination based on variable costs are not relevant for digital products. Prices are determined according to their value to the user, not according to costs. The variables that allow for price differentiation are: the composition of the market; the consumer group; and the time taken to deliver services and products.

Scope economies occur when the enterprise dilutes costs by increasing the range of products and services produced. Synergy effects between the nature of the required investment and the capabilities to produce and distribute different products with common inputs allow for scope economies. Information goods offer several opportunities to obtain scope economies because they can be packaged in many ways and they can share infrastructure, files, equipment, technological knowhow and distribution channels.

As an enterprise develops e-commerce, it can identify new opportunities to use its infrastructure. Amazon.com, for instance, started by selling books; but as its site won clients, it was able to diversify the scope of products it offers over the web. The geographically-dispersed 'virtual' user community created by customers of such e-commerce services can therefore buy a wide range of products and services from the same online site. Enterprises that succeed in the formation of this kind of virtual community tend to transform themselves into horizontal virtual shopping centres, so that they can obtain scope economies.

In addition to the diversification of new products and services available from the same site and infrastructure, the exploitation of scope economies can also be achieved in the digital economy through the creation of new versions of information products developed to capture the interest of specific users or specific groups that have common characteristics. These information services are differentiated according to the value attributed by clients to certain characteristics of the services.

This differentiation can occur in content, quality of resolution, velocity of access and degree of specialization of the information. Therefore, differentiation avoids transforming information into a commodity. For instance, provision of information about price indexes at financial markets can be differentiated according to the delay between generation and provision of information. Financial institutions will pay more for an online service than clients, such as research institutions, that can wait longer to have the same information. Differentiation does not necessarily depend on the cost of providing the service. Instead, it takes place because different clients attribute different values to the service.

The information economy offers new opportunities to small enterprises, while also encouraging large scales of operation. The marginal cost to add a new client to a network is usually very low, whereas the benefits that clients have with the expansion of the network can be significant. The successful examples of Microsoft, Yahoo and AOL (America Online) illustrate this point. This does not mean that there are no opportunities for small enterprises to enter electronic commerce. Such opportunities do exist in market niches, especially on specific sectors or regions. However, it is necessary to recognize the nature of scale and scope economies in defining a strategy compatible with the potential for investment of each enterprise.

6.3 TRANSACTION COSTS

The concept of transaction costs in economics is used to refer to the costs of negotiation and contracting, as well as costs related to the risk of non-compliance to the terms of a contract. Contracts cannot foresee all situations, which can lead to opportunistic behaviour by economic agents involved in a transaction.

There are two ways to reduce transaction costs on the Internet. First, negotiation costs can be cut by the establishment of collective contracts in transactions such as software licensing, sales, acquisitions and services. The web eases access to users, reducing costs through specific contracts and negotiations. Clear rules established before the transaction takes place can include: what downloads are allowed; delivery timescales; payment processes available; product-return conditions; product and service guarantees; and technical support provided. In some cases, especially when the product or service to be acquired has higher value, specific negotiations can be undertaken using e-mail or call centres. Even in those cases, sellers on the web can reduce significantly the costs and hassles of traditional negotiation practices, where normally sellers have to offer customers discounts, longer periods for payment and other advantages.

From the point of view of the customer, transaction costs are important because the risks of the transaction and of opportunistic behaviour are more visible. The reputation of the enterprise on the web is very important, as unsatisfied customers often report their bad experiences in chat services, user forums or by e-mail. Companies that are on the web tend to avoid conflicts with their customers and thus reduce the risks for the user.

A second way of reducing transaction costs results from increased access to information. The asymmetry of information between economic agents in relation to prices, stocks, quotes, supply conditions and other variables is an important source of transaction costs. Easy access via the Internet to information and analysis about markets reduces opportunities for opportunistic behaviour. A typical form of opportunism is to charge high prices to clients that do not have comparative information on prices. On the web, customers can easily get information on prices, by comparing different sites or using automatic search tools. Some sites allow the user to define the maximum price he or she is willing to pay for a product, then try to find a seller able to accept the customer's conditions.

6.4 NETWORK EXTERNALITIES

The significant role of external economies has been recognized since the 19th century as being essential to the success of industrial districts, such as Manchester in the UK. External economies are related to the availability of low-cost production factors in the market, and not from a better use of productive resources inside the firm. The concentration of qualified human resources, physical infrastructure and productive capacity in a given region guarantees the collective efficiency of individual enterprises. The growth of the whole industry allows for the dilution of fixed costs already invested in the economy through a larger volume of production. External economies are also known in the economic literature as 'demand scale economies'.

The principle of externalities is highly relevant to the understanding of contemporary economic dynamics. The ease of communication introduced by ICT brings benefits to economic agents derived from access to information, products and services. This has allowed the diffusion of a horizontal model of the firm among large enterprises, where the firm is more concentrated on its core competencies and more intensive in transactions with external partners.

Virtual networks present significant positive externalities since innovative products and services can be rapidly made known to, and acquired by, other enterprises. However, here we must distinguish between products that are mostly based on codified knowledge and can be easily transferred, and those based on tacit knowledge that depends on specific experience and the organizational learning process. Tacit knowledge is difficult to transfer because it is not formalized in manuals and explicit rules, but is embedded in people and operational procedures. Enterprises try to overcome this barrier by hiring consultants and experienced technicians from other organizations. Nevertheless, sometimes this practice is not successful due to institutional and cultural differences and the intrinsic characteristics of tacit knowledge. Technical qualification and experience are essential to transform information into knowledge. Information by itself, especially non-proprietary information, is highly transferable but requires tacit knowledge to constitute useful tools for production.

Virtual networks present positive externalities when the value of a product or service grows as the number of users increases. Therefore, as new users join a communication network, the size of the network increases and also the possibilities of communication between the network's users. As a result, the utility of the network will increase, thereby increasing its capacity to attract new users. This characteristic is common to material networks, such as transportation networks. The more destinations a transportation network has, the higher the value of the network for their users. This benefit is frequently cited as an example of demand scale economies.

The concept of positive externalities is also important to an understanding of the Internet world. The higher the number of users, the larger the size of the market and the potential of the Internet as a strategic commercial tool. Successful sites, software and protocols are stronger because they attract an increasing number of users, which is of great interest to users as it gives them access to the highest number of other users. All things being equal, as Shapiro and Varian (1999) observed, it is better to connect to a large network than to a small one.

The principle of positive externalities explains why, for instance, Microsoft's operating systems, such as Windows, were more successful than other equivalent systems. Most users of personal computers adopt MS Windows not because this system is technologically superior to its competitors (most users acknowledge it is not), but because it is the system that has become widely used in this market. In addition, the existence of protocols and technical standards officially defined by regulatory agencies, by agreements between companies or by the leader of the market is essential for the success of networks. When adopted by all users, such standards are very important to the consolidation of a network.

The main implication of strong network externalities for competitiveness is the positive feedback effect: when a technology or service is perceived as the winner, it becomes stronger. Success leads to more success, creating a virtuous cycle. The fight for initial success explains the wave of free Internet access around the turn of the century. After mergers and acquisitions, large enterprises had to conquer new clients to establish a critical mass and create a positive feedback.

6.5 LOCK-IN AND SWITCHING COSTS

Lock-in of users is a consequence of the switching costs that users have when they change from a system to another. Switching costs include the costs of making software, files and equipment compatible and of adapting and training users of the new system. Therefore, the use of a new standard requires investment in specific assets that would be avoided when maintaining the existing standard. Lock-in may be a source of problems for users, but it is strategic for providers.

The lock-in of users to given brands and standards is typical of the information economy. When the diffusion of ICT began in the 1960s and 1970s, mainframes and minicomputers had different proprietary architectures and software, making the user dependent on a single provider. The development of IBM-compatible computers when IBM was dominant in the computer marketplace was a tentative step by independent manufacturers to free users from such lock-in. The diffusion of open standards in personal computers reduced switching costs significantly, but most users are still locked into Microsoft and Intel standards. Enterprises that insisted on having their own standard, such as Apple Mac, have been fighting against the negative feedback that results from the fact that its standard has a low diffusion among users, despite any recognized quality and ease of use.

The issue of lock-in in e-commerce has been discussed by sectoral and international organizations. Standards and protocols are very important for the diffusion of electronic commerce and the distribution of its benefits. More open standards for e-commerce mean lower barriers to entry to the information community and a lessening of the power over others of influential members of this community.

For example, until the 1980s Electronic Data Interchange (EDI)[3] proprietary standards were typical of hierarchical enterprise networks, like that of General Motors. The typically sectoral character of EDI networks led to the establishment of standards based on the needs of specific market sectors. These were proposed by industry organizations that aimed to integrate industries with intensive commercial exchanges, such as automobiles, electronics and pharmaceuticals. The movement to standardize EDI on a wider basis became stronger with the effort of international organizations, such as the United Nations, to harmonize and facilitate universal access to information networks.

The main result of this effort is the EDIFACT standard, recommended by the United Nations and defined as the official standard for EDI in 80 countries. In Brazil, for instance, EDIFACT is recommended by the national technical standards organization, and is the basis for the definition of sectoral standards, including Edifarma for pharmaceutical companies.

In contrast to EDI, the Internet has a standard that is totally 'open', being based on standard protocols and services providing e-mail, file transfer, connections and interfaces that allow the interconnection of diverse systems. The universal character of the Internet explains why it won the title of 'network of networks'. Compared to EDI, the Internet has low switching costs because new users have no need to acquire special software.

Nevertheless, Internet providers have several opportunities to strengthen relations with their customers, and thus reinforce lock-in. The practice in this sector shows that small switching costs can lead to larger indirect switching costs. For instance, changing an e-mail address can have no immediate costs to the customer if he or she chooses a free Internet provider. However, at the same time, it can imply high switching costs to the customer if he or she has a large list of correspondents and subsequently wishes to change the address again. The provider can increase these costs by refusing to forward e-mails received to the new address. This problem is also present in telephony, but in this case the national regulatory agency can impose rules to ensure that customers maintain their telephone numbers when they change operators. Electronic addresses are an important asset in the Internet sector, just as the sale of web 'domain' names already constitutes a market. Some names are sold for millions of dollars, like trademarks.

The onset of free Internet access demonstrates how lock-in is important as a competitive strategy for Internet providers. The customer base is a very valuable asset for the provider and the real value of capturing a customer can be higher than the price charged to use the service. The customer base will also define the price the provider can charge for 'banner' on-screen advertising from web sites, as well as the viability of providing multiple services to customers. Most Internet users are loyal to particular sites and tend to concentrate their shopping and search for information to few sites. AOL, for instance, estimates that 70 per cent of its customers navigate the web through sites linked to its pages.

Electronic commerce cannot be characterized as a closed market in the way it currently operates. Even EDI, with its sectorally-defined standards, has relatively low switching costs, according to research on customer loyalty among automobile and electronic enterprises (Pensel, 1996). This research also concluded that partnership relations are not much affected by EDI because they are generally defined before EDI is used and are based on quality criteria, depending on the strategy of the buyer. The cost of change to providers is not affected because investment in EDI is relatively low. Given the tendency with the Internet to standardize applications, the technological cost of breaking commercial relationships tends to zero.

Such research results suggest that lock-in on the web has a contradictory character. On one side, providers fight to lock-in their customers, even if they have to subsidize their switching costs. On the other hand, the customer has more freedom to search for new product and service providers. A simple click of the mouse allows sites and providers to be changed. The ease of communication with the market allowed by the web therefore increases freedom and makes the market more volatile.

The opportunity to increase competition and possible collaboration through EDI implementation was demonstrated by a study on automobile chains in Brazil (Tigre and Sarti, 1997). Before the introduction of EDI, the companies had price quotes from three to five suppliers. With the end of the use of paper proposals brought about by all-electronic EDI processes, the firms began to check the prices of ten to 15 suppliers.

The opening up of possible access to a greater number of suppliers increases the buyer's power to bargain. As a result, companies can avoid long-term contracts with suppliers that set limits to new business opportunities. Thus, technology enhances the buying power of companies, allowing them to compare international prices, to synchronize their processes and to make changes in delivery time. This transfers more responsibility in financing inventories to suppliers.

6.6 DE-INTERMEDIATION AND RE-INTERMEDIATION

One of the most discussed issues about the impacts of e-commerce in the economy is the elimination of intermediaries by the establishment of direct connections between producers and final users. Several analysts argue that the web is a menace to traditional commerce, because transactions are redirected from real physical shops to virtual shops on the Internet.

There are two types of intermediaries that help producers to sell to customers. The first consists of companies that distribute physical products, such as wholesale traders, retailers and transport companies. According to the US Department of Commerce[4], in 1999 distributors in the USA added on average 15.6 per cent to the final price of products: 0.6 per cent of this relates to transportation, 3.8 per cent to wholesale margins and 11.2 per cent to retail margins. Therefore, retail margins are the strongest stimulus to substitute automated transactions for human intermediaries, but in practice the margins vary a lot according to the service. In other countries, such as Brazil, transport, wholesale and retail margins can be considerably higher, because they depend on the size of the market, on distribution costs and on competitive practices. Thus, the value of distributors' margins and the ease of making deals over the web indicate the potential of e-commerce in a country.

The products that have a higher margin of commercialization generally require specialized sellers. For instance, optical and orthopaedic products need sellers that are able to discuss technical aspects with buyers. In these cases, the seller is not a simple 'human modem' – simply relaying communications automatically – and the margin is defined by the aggregation of value to sales. Other products, such as jewellery, watches and fine clothes, require the physical contact of the client. The choice and selection of these kinds of exclusive products is based on subjective decisions that can be stimulated by the physical presence of the seller. In these cases, margins are high but the potential of 'de-intermediation' – the removal of an intermediary – is generally lower than more standardized products that can be sold by themselves, such as books, CDs, software and electronic equipment.

The second group of intermediaries are service providers that act as intermediaries of other services, like travel agents or financial market dealers. These agents operate with lower margins than retailers, but they are more vulnerable to the development of commerce based on Internet. These companies normally act as 'human modems', simply referring information from producers to customers without adding much value. For instance, financial market operators have suffered from a reduction in their commissions. Even those intermediaries who add value by counselling clients have difficulties in competing with electronic sites that work 24 hours a day and offer online information and market-analysis services. In these cases, the survival of service-provider companies depends on their ability to add value to the service and benefit customers by the provision of personalized services.

In contrast to de-intermediation, this leads to new 're-intermediation' requirements opened up because the growing importance of some intermediaries on the Internet creates new intermediation functions. These 'infomediaries' aggregate value by providing qualified information that is easy to understand and to access. For users, owning information may have a quantifiable economic value. Information strengthens the decision process by enabling the user to reduce transaction costs, to obtain better prices, to select more adequate products and to access surveys and product evaluations. Table 6.1 highlights just a few examples of web intermediaries. Opportunities for new services are growing and such 'infomediaries' are assuming great influence in the market by winning over loyal customers on the Internet.

Table 6.1: Web intermediaries

Type of Intermediary	Service characteristics	Examples
Search services	Software that searches for information in web sites and databases using keywords.	Yahoo Altavista
Vertical portals	Portals that assemble a range of interest communities, such as health, tourism, children, law, industrial sectors, economics.	www.verticalnet.com
Generic portals	Virtual shopping centres linked to other information, products and services.	UOL Terra Starmedia
Information providers	Content of interest to consumers who pay fees or subscriptions.	*Wired* magazine news services
Virtual re-sellers	Infrastructure for buying and selling transactions, such as auctions.	Ebazar ForSale Freelance
Web evaluators	Advice to users on evaluating clients and suppliers on the web, e.g. with 'best site' prizes.	Point Communications www.epinions.com I-best
Financial intermediaries	Payment systems using credit card, electronic transfer and other payment forms.	Visanet Mastercard Interchange
'Intelligent' intermediaries	Software that searches for best prices or finds best solutions by learning from past behaviour.	Shopping Pot

6.7 CUMULATIVE LEARNING

The learning process can be defined as one where repetition and experimentation over time allows tasks to be done faster and better. The learning process also involves the definition of, and experimentation with, new operating procedures. Learning is a cumulative process and depends basically on organizational routines, tacit or codified. Routines are the determinant element of the behaviour of firms. Once they are established, they replace the need for rigid hierarchical coordination, as they enable individuals who know their tasks to interpret and answer correctly their messages and take coherent decisions. It is important to differentiate static routines – which simply repeat previous procedures – from dynamic routines that allow the incorporation of new knowledge. Tacit knowledge is more difficult to acquire and transfer, and is therefore a specific asset of the firm that establishes the basis for competitive differentiation.

Electronic commerce depends essentially on dynamic learning in the incorporation of new hardware and software tools, new partners and constant alteration of routines and procedures. From the point of view of enterprises, the sometimes new and adaptable character of ICT requires experimentation and training, which implies a need to establish a collective learning environment.

The evolution of the firm is not necessarily slow and gradual, but it is also not randomly defined. The firm has its evolution conditioned by its accumulated competencies and by the nature of its specific assets. Based on this idea, evolutionary economists propose a theory of the transformation of the firm that explains its entrance in new markets because of endogenous[5] elements. The core competencies of a firm are determined by the technological opportunities it faces. The history of the firm is important, because its accumulation process is based on knowledge previously acquired and its trajectory will change successfully according to changes in the economic environment or in technology.

The development of complementary assets in ICT allows firms to enter into new businesses. For instance, a large bank can enter the web to provide financial services, but it can diversify the web services offered once its site is consolidated. Therefore, the Internet can be perceived as a technological opportunity that opens the way for new growth strategies, such as specialization, vertical integration, diversification, conglomeration and participation in networks and subcontracting activities.

6.8 CONCLUSIONS

In this chapter, we present six key economic concepts that are useful to understanding the dynamics of ICT adoption and diffusion. Coming from industrial organization and evolutionary studies, these ideas refer to the way a firm faces the challenges posed by its competitive environment and the importance of the learning process in enabling the firm to build core competencies that will set the basis for its competitive strategies.

The first two concepts presented are important to understanding how ICT adoption and diffusion alter the costs of firms. The first was that of scale and scope economies. These allow information producers to reduce costs of production and distribution significantly, and to define a strategy compatible with their investment opportunities. Then, the concept of transaction costs was discussed in order to explain why the use of e-commerce and Internet applications reduces the costs of the firm by decreasing negotiation costs and increasing access to information.

The concepts of network externalities, lock-in, de-intermediation and re-intermediation are useful in illuminating how firms define their competitive strategies and answer the challenges and opportunities created by the information economy. The presence of positive externalities creates positive feedback effects that consolidate the leadership of an information product or service. In addition, firms may have a strategy of lock-in to consolidate their leadership. Aware of the fact that customers have costs when changing from one information system to another, information producers try to develop a wide range of associated products and services that will make customers loyal to their brand. ICT applications such as e-commerce and the Internet also eliminate the need for some types of intermediaries and create a demand for other types. In these ways, e-commerce and the Internet alter the organization of production and commercialization flows. This opens several new opportunities, as well as new challenges for all firms.

Finally, the concept of cumulative learning is shown to be essential to understanding why some firms react better than others to the challenges posed by the information economy. The accumulation process of the firm is based on knowledge previously acquired, which conditions its reaction to changes in the economic environment.

REFERENCES

Bain, J.S. ([1956] 1993), *Barriers to New Competition*, New York: Augustus M. Kelley Publishers.

Coase, R.H. (1937), 'The Nature of the Firm', *Economica*, Special Edition, **4** (November), 386–405

Coriat, B. and O. Weinstein (1995), *Les Nouvelles Théories de l'Entreprise*, Paris: Le Livre de Poche.

Klemperer, P., (1995), 'Competition when Consumers have Switching Costs; an Overview with Applications to Industrial Organization, Macroeconomics, and International Trade', *Review of Economic Studies*, **62** (4), 515–39.

Lastres, H.M.M., and J.C. Ferraz (1999), 'Economia da Informação, do Conhecimento e do Aprendizado', in H.M.M Lastres and S. Abagli (eds), *Informação e Globalização na Era do Conhecimento*, Rio de Janeiro: Campus.

Marshall, A. ([1890] 1997), *Principles*, New York: Prometheus Books.

Pensel, J. (1996), *L' impact de l'échange de Données Informatisé sur les Relations Clients-fournisseurs: les cas des Automobile et Électronique*, Rennes, France: Université de Rennes 1, Laboratoire de Recherches en Gestion des Organisations (LARGOR).

Shapiro, C. and H.R. Varian (1999), *Information Rules – A Strategic Guide to the Network Economy,* Boston: Harvard Business School Press.

Tigre, P.B. and F. Sarti (1997), *Tecnologia da Informação, Mudanças Organizacionais e Impactos sobre o Trabalho: Difusão de Electronic Data Interchange*, Rio de Janeiro: CIET/SENAI.

Williamson, O.E. (1975), *Markets and Hierachies: Analysis and Antitrust Implications,* New York: The Free Press.

NOTES

1. For a review of recent non-orthodox approaches to the information economy, see Lastres and Ferraz (1999).
2. For a review of these concepts, see Coriat and Weinstein (1995).
3. Electronic Data Interchange is a technology for electronically exchanging documents from one organization to another. It was conceived originally (in the 1970s) as a proprietary system to support business-to-business transactions. Current EDI systems support transactions between enterprises in both proprietary and non-proprietary forms.
4. Source: Department of Commerce web site (www.doc.gov).
5. A process of industrial mutation that incessantly revolutionizes the economic structure from within.

7. Institutional and Resource-based Perspectives of IT and Organizational Change: Cases from the Nigerian Banking Industry

Abiodun O. Bada

7.1 INTRODUCTION

An important perspective in the study of organizational change has focused on the interaction between the organization and its environment, particularly the significance of the environment in the welfare of organizations. Its central message has been that organizations affect, and are affected to varying degrees by, the environment within which they operate (Goodman, 1982). Key to this perspective are the twin issues of choice and determinism (Astley and Van de Ven, 1983; Hrebiniak and Joyce, 1985). From the 'choice' viewpoint, organizations, and particularly management, are seen as having autonomy in deciding how they deal with the environment; the deterministic perspective, however, believes that much of this choice is constrained by environmental forces. This has suggested that organizational actions can be seen either as a process of rational choice and selection that assumes organizational behaviour is deliberate and systematic, or as a symbolic process of complying with mandatory institutional demands based on the belief that organizational behaviour is compliant, habitual, unreflective and socially justified (Oliver, 1997a).

This chapter highlights recent research evidence that reveals organizational actions as being a much more complex function of both rational (economic) choices and social or political (institutional) environmental prescriptions (Oliver, 1991, 1997a, b; Dacin, 1997; Hung and Whittington, 1997). It is argued, therefore, that autonomy and determinism are complementary elements in understanding the complexity of organizational actions, and so should not be seen as an either/or dilemma. This demonstrates that the institutional contexts within which managers make rational choices have an important influence on such choices. Seemingly rational decisions of management are steeped in established norms of practice and rituals (symbolic actions) within the organization's institutional context. An important implication is that symbolic or ritual actions are not necessarily dysfunctional; rational decisions and choice can indeed be supported by symbolic and ritual actions.

The chapter draws on a study of IT adoption in two banks within the Nigerian banking industry that combines concepts and ideas from both institutional theory and the resource-based model. Such an approach allows for an examination of both rational and symbolic pressures that influence the process of implementing technology-based organizational change initiatives at various organizational levels. The aim is to contribute to the growing body of knowledge that combines both rational and symbolic views to explain organizational phenomena (Oliver, 1997a, b; Dacin, 1997).

The significance of adopting these views in this study lies in the somewhat different conceptions of the interaction between organizations and the environment that the two theories hold: highlighting the rational on one hand and the symbolic on the other. Each theory elaborates on important aspects of the interaction, but the full complexity of issues involved in ICT innovations in organizations is not captured by either theory on its own. A combined model that focuses on both the rational and symbolic factors influencing organizational change seems to have the potential to aid better understanding.

The resource-based view emphasizes objective factors and conditions, such as the resources and capabilities made use of by management in interacting with the environment. The institutional theory, on the other hand, aims to explain symbolic and cultural features of the environment, such as traditions, conventions, norms and taken-for-granted elements of organizational behaviour that tend to influence and constrain decision-making in organizations.

Although much has been made in IS of the interactive model of IT and organizational change, studies that combine two seemingly contrasting views – such as the resource-based and institutional perspectives – are not common. In IS, the benefit of a combined theoretical approach to the study undertaken here was well summarized by Kling et al. (1992):

> Research in the information systems field has demonstrated that parochial theoretical research perspectives often produce little research of lasting value. We suspect that good theories of IT and organizational change are unlikely to be built from discrete intellectual perspectives which rest on narrow disciplinary and ideological assumptions. Our objective must be to study technology in the context of organizational and institutional practices, informed by robust economic and sociological theories (ibid.: 39).

7.2 INSTITUTIONAL AND RESOURCE-BASED APPROACHES TO IT AND ORGANIZATIONAL CHANGE

IT-enabled organizational change has often been studied as a case of strategic change (DeCock, 1996). To exploit changes in the environment, the strategic management school posits that organizations are endowed with a number of resources, which they can successfully deploy to achieve a change programme. These resources, controlled or owned by the firm (Wernerfelt, 1984; Prahalad and Hamel, 1990), are seen as enabling the organization to conceive, choose and implement change strategies (Barney, 1986, 1991). This resource-based approach has been strongly associated with the works of Penrose (1959) and Wernerfelt (1984). As it views firms as a bundle of resources and capabilities owned or controlled by the organization (Barney, 1991; Mehra, 1996; Magalhães, Chapter 10 in this book), this approach argues that rational selection and deployment of these resources will allow the management of an organization to conceive of, and to implement, innovative and sustainable strategies to transform the organization. For example, Oliver (1997a: 697) has noted: 'According to the [resource-based] view, it is the rational identification and use of resources that are valuable, rare, difficult to copy and non-substitutable which lead to enduring firm variation.'

Rumelt (1984) refers to the factors that protect organizations from having their resources copied or imitated by other organizations as isolating mechanisms. Such factors affecting imitability imply that, for a resource to lead to competitive advantage, it must not be readily copied by an organization's competitors (Dierickx and Cool, 1989; Barney, 1991). Another related factor is causal ambiguity (Lippman and Rumelt, 1982), which implies the difficulty – for potential imitators – of knowing exactly what to imitate or ways of carrying out an imitation. 'Immobility' is another important characteristic that a resource must possess in order to engender variations in organizational structures. Immobile resources are those which cannot be bought and/or sold (Peteraf, 1993). Examples of these are idiosyncratic resources that are of little or no use outside the context of the organization owning it.

By implication, when organizations implement strategies to change they should exploit their resources which are imitable, immobile and idiosyncratic. Consequently, organizations would change in different ways, as they are fundamentally heterogeneous in terms of their resources and internal capabilities. However, the sources of these resources are important, so should be taken into account. If all organizations within an industry sector use the same or similar resource providers, such as consultants and software vendors, then these resources may not be idiosyncratic and imitable. This view is similar to Dierickx and Cool's (1989) assertion that the source of accumulation of resources determines, to a large degree, the extent to which such assets or resources can be imitated.

In information systems, the application of resource-based theory is now gaining ground. It has been used to explain how firms can create competitive value from three IT assets: human, technology and relationship assets (Ross et al., 1996). It has also been used to examine how the use of IT for sustained competitive advantage resides more in the organization's IT managerial knowhow, rather than in the technology itself (Mata et al., 1995). Clemons and Row (1991) examined how differences in structural resources, such as vertical integration, diversification and resource quality, influenced IT innovations.

Grant (1996) also applied the resource-based view, in conjunction with the evolutionary theory of the firm, to develop an information systems capability framework. This examines an organization's capacity to be effective in conceiving of, acquiring, deploying and sustaining the IS requirements needed to support its business objectives. An important element of the IS capability framework is the purposeful action of management in setting the direction for the strategic use of IT. Management plays an active role in building an organization's IS capability by guiding the design, acquisition, deployment and integration of computer-based IS within the organization. Such an emphasis on resources and capabilities is clearly relevant to the study of ICT innovations in organizations. However, the resource-based view has been challenged with the argument that the socio-cultural, political and historical contexts within which decisions are made also influence the nature of such decisions (Oliver, 1997a).

According to this view, decision-making and organizational actions are not just based on the level and type of resources that organizations possess, but also on some taken-for-granted assumptions about how to do things within the organization. Decisions are also based on widely-held beliefs and expectations from the broader environmental context about the appropriate ways of doing things in the organization's environment. These widely-held beliefs originate from the environment of the organization. They find their way into the organization either through political or regulatory demands, or through normative prescriptions of professional associations such as management consultants. This is the argument of what is known as the 'new institutional theory' (DiMaggio and Powell, 1991).

Institutional theory posits that the environment of organizations should not be seen only in economic or strategic terms, but as consisting of socially-prescribed and accepted ways of behaving (Scott and Meyer, 1991). This entails a re-conceptualization of the environment of organizations away from the technical-rational perspective to a focus on the social and cultural features of the environment.[1] Such features concern the systems of belief – socially constructed and widely shared – about the purpose(s) of an organization or an organizational sector, and what constitutes appropriate ways of conducting the business of the sector (Powell and DiMaggio, 1991).

According to the theory, these systems of belief could also involve technical procedures or requirements of how to organize. Nevertheless, the view of institutionalists is that, after a certain level of acceptance, these procedures become 'infused with values beyond the technical requirements of the tasks at hand' (Selznick, 1957)[2]. In other words, they become institutionalized and may persist well after their useful technical contributions are past (Scott and Meyer, 1991). By becoming institutionalized, these procedures become taken-for-granted and unquestioned as the appropriate way of doing things. Ultimately, these procedures take on a rule-like structure, as organizations are expected to adhere to them for survival and to achieve legitimacy[3] (Scott and Meyer, 1991).

DiMaggio and Powell (1991) claim that there are three mechanisms through which institutional pressures are spread:

1. the mimetic influences amongst the different organizations in an organizational sector;
2. the coercive power of government and its agencies; and
3. the normative prescriptions of professional organizations.

Building on this work, Swanson and Ramiller (1997) argued that when IS professionals, management consultants and other agents of change move across organizations, they tend to spread their traditions of practice. These traditions, in turn, may impact on the change efforts of organizations; they may also become taken-for-granted rules and prescriptions which govern the practice of utilizing IT, and to which all organizations must adhere in order to survive.

Mimetic influence stems out of the need to reduce uncertainty. The introduction of a new technology or work procedure is usually accompanied by a measure of uncertainty arising from the lack, or inadequate knowledge, of doing new things or utilizing the new technology. To reduce uncertainty, people and organizations tend to imitate others who have gone through similar processes. According to DiMaggio and Powell (1991: 69)[4]: 'when goals are ambiguous and technologies are not properly understood, or when the environment creates symbolic uncertainty, organizations may model themselves on other organizations'. The argument here is that such modelling would provide solutions that are less costly to the imitating organization because the models would have previously been tried and tested by other organizations. Models can also be diffused directly through employee transfer, or indirectly through knowledge-mediating organizations such as consulting firms (Attewell, 1992).

Coercive influence arises as a result of the use of power. It stems from the political influence an organization may exert over other organizations that depend on it for resources or survival. In such cases, the supplying organization might exert some pressure on the dependent organization, and compel or persuade it to conform to certain demands (DiMaggio and Powell, 1991). For a study of IT and organizational change, this means that the ability of the organization to change depends – to a considerable extent – on environmental prescriptions about the appropriate ways of organizing within the institutional context. As a result, organizations do not just change for efficiency reasons, but primarily to achieve legitimacy through conformity. However, a number of studies employing institutional arguments have come up with results that contradict the institutional arguments of conformity.

For instance, Scheid-Cook (1992) examined the response of mental health organizations to a new policy programme and concluded that their responses were highly variable in relation to a common institutional demand. A study by Orru et al. (1991) that applied institutional arguments to the study of businesses in three East Asian countries concluded that, while firms in each of these countries were highly subjected to local institutional traits, they were also highly successful business enterprises. This led the authors to suggest that institutional and technical-rational pressures can both co-exist in organizations, and that institutional pressures do not necessary imply a neglect of efficiency factors.

There have been relatively fewer studies in IS that apply insights from the institutional theory to IS phenomena. Notable exceptions to this are:

- Silva (1997) examined how the adoption and subsequent institutionalization of IS in organizations is a process concerned with political power.
- Kling and Iacono (1989) employed institutional ideas to argue for legitimacy in the practice of IS development, so that there can be congruence between theory and practice.
- Swanson and Ramiller (1997) introduced the concept of 'an organizing vision' of an IS innovation to explain the process whereby new IS innovation is institutionalized to encourage widespread diffusion.
- King et al. (1994) focused on institutional factors in IT innovation, while stressing the importance of institutions and institutional forces in creating and diffusing widespread IT innovation, with an explicit call for an 'institutional point of view in information systems research' (ibid.: 147). The authors argued for the importance of institutions in understanding social change, as institutional theory willingly embraces the wider

context within which any form of social change is embedded, and because IT innovations are 'inseparably bounded up in the network of institutions both as recipients of institutional forces and as shapers of institutional reality' (ibid: 147).

- Bada (2000) applied concepts and ideas from the institutional theory to study the adoption of computer-based information systems (CBIS) in Nigerian banks.
- Christiaanse and Huigen (1997) applied institutional views to the study of inter-organizational information systems implementation and suggested that cultural bias and structural order are among the factors influencing the implementation process.

7.2.1 Institutional and Resource-based Views: Assumptions and Implications for IT and Organizational Change

The above review indicates a fundamental difference in the motives assigned by institutional and resource-based views to organizational actions (Table 7.1). Where the focus is on resources, organizational actions are viewed as being determined by reasons of rationality and efficiency (Oliver, 1997a), with such actions constrained by economic causes defined as barriers to resource acquisition and imitation (Barney, 1986, 1991; Amit and Schoemaker, 1993). From the institutional perspective, however, decisions and actions within the organization are regarded as being motivated mainly by reasons of social justification (or legitimacy) and obligation to institutional rules (Meyer and Rowan, 1977; DiMaggio and Powell, 1991). These decisions are constrained by socially-constructed forces that are essentially human in nature – like norms, habits, traditions and conventions.

The resource-based and institutional views highlight some examples of contradictions that exist in organizations, such as the rational versus social motive for explaining organizational actions. An institutional perspective on the relations between an organization and its environment gives the picture of a powerful and profoundly influential environment, which compels an organization to conform to its demands. The resource-based view, in contrast, gives primary consideration to the stock of resources and capabilities possessed by organizations, and how these can be rationally selected and employed to influence the environment and respond to environmental imperatives, or indeed to exploit opportunities in the environment. This implies an active engagement with the environment and a strong ability on the part of organizations to control and manipulate their environments.

Table 7.1: Comparison of institutional and resource-based theories

	New Institutional Theory	Resource-based Approach
Theoretical Foundation	Social construction of reality (Berger and Luckmann, 1966); institutional environment of the firm (Meyer and Rowan, 1977; DiMaggio and Powell, 1991).	Resource-based view of firm (Penrose, 1959; Wernerfelt, 1984; Barney, 1986).
Nature of Decision Process	Habitual, symbolic and embedded in norms and traditions.	Systematic, deliberate, value-maximizing and purposeful
Key Concepts	Institutions, institutional context, rationalized myths, ritual activities, taken-for-granted assumptions.	Organization's resources, management capabilities.
Implied Change in IT and the Organization	Organizations responding to environmentally-derived, rationalized concepts of work and IT use through coercive, mimetic and normative influences.	Analysing and strategically deploying an organization's IT and other assets to exploit opportunities and circumvent threats in the environment.
Strengths	Focus on ceremonial aspects of organizational behaviour; theory offers the chance to examine the non-rational and taken-for-granted aspects of organizations' behaviour.	Offers the chance of examining organizational resources and competencies.
Weaknesses	Over-socialized view of organizations; conformity to institutional pressures does not always detract from internal efficiency aspects. Organizational responses to environmental demands are not always conformist; organizations define and create their environments.	No adequate consideration of importance of the social and cultural context of decision-making; too much of an emphasis on an economic view of organizations and organizational behaviour.
Contribution to Studies in this Chapter	Analysis of culture of wider environment; decisions and actions influenced by the institutional organizational context; ceremonial aspects of IT and organizational change practices.	Examination of resources and capabilities of an individual bank; decisions influenced by organization's resources and rational considerations.

For IT and organizational change, the resource-based view implies that the factors which facilitate change are the financial, technological and human assets of the firm, and the managerial ability to co-ordinate and deploy these resources effectively. This perspective also suggests that the ability of the organization to implement IT and manage a successful organizational change program will depend on its ability to exploit resources in innovative ways. Grant (1991) clearly makes this point by stating that the firm's resources and capabilities are the *crown jewels* of the organization, and need to be protected as they 'play a pivotal role' in the firm's competitive strategy. He went on to state: 'the essence of strategy formulation then, is to design a strategy that makes the most effective use of these core resources and capabilities' (ibid.: 129).

However, a study of IT and organizational change from an institutional perspective suggests that the ability of the organization to change depends – to a considerable extent – on environmental prescriptions, which may constrain the ability of the organization to change as it wishes. What this means for a study of organizational change is that a technical-rational perspective alone as a basis for studying organizational change processes is not enough, and that socio-cultural factors are equally important in understanding organizational change initiatives.

7.3 CASE STUDIES OF IMPLEMENTING IT AND ORGANIZATIONAL CHANGE IN NIGERIAN BANKS

This chapter address the issues raised in Section 7.1 by drawing on research undertaken between March 1997 and August 1999 as part of a study of IT use within the Nigerian banking system. The cases focused on here concern two of the three oldest commercial banks within the industry, a category referred to locally as 'old generation' banks'. This term is derived from the fact that they were in operation before the liberalization of the industry in 1989, as part of a general government aim of liberalizing the economy; banks that came into existence after liberalization are commonly referred to as 'new generation banks'.

The change initiatives examined in these studies were the culmination of earlier attempts by the banks to transform themselves from regional, government-owned banks to ones with national outlook, and to become major players within the industry. At the time of data collection, the programmes were well advanced in implementation and a substantial amount of human, physical and financial resources had been committed to the projects. The first sets of interviews were conducted between March and May 1997, primarily to understand the level of computerization within the industry in as much detail as possible, as very little then existed in the relevant literature. This was followed in the summer of 1999 by in-depth studies. One of the banks involved was among the first set of banks to implement a major restructuring programme, soon after it was privatized in 1990, and the model upon which the programme was designed was recognized by industry analysts as worthy of note. The other bank created a major storm in 1997 when it sacked about 4000 employees (representing over half of its entire workforce at the time) as a result of its restructuring programme. It is believed that these two cases are representative of the experiences of the older banks in repositioning to face the challenges of a changing environment.

Primary case study data came from interviews with a variety of sources, such as bank operators, IT and operations directors, senior managers in charge of – and involved with – Business Process Reengineering (BPR) initiatives, branch managers and staff, and management consultants. Secondary data sources included training manuals, company memos, annual reports and newspaper articles about the banks. Valuable information was also obtained from books and reports written by former employees of the banks, as well as from financial and banking industry reports written by independent financial audit companies. Interviews were conducted at the head offices of the banks in Lagos and also in a number of branches within Lagos. In all, over fifty interviews lasting between one to three hours were held with different grades of staff both at head offices and in branches. Key informants, such as BPR managers and branch staff and management, were interviewed up to three times.

7.3.1 Reorganization Through 'Reengineering': The Wema Bank Case

> Reengineering is part of the on-going implementation of Wema bank's strategic plan that has transformed the bank into a major player in the banking industry. It is a bold attempt at creating a sample of future Wema branches (internal document produced by Wema's BPR team in 1994).

The guidelines on which this process of change at Wema was based are given in the strategic plans developed by the bank's management in conjunction with consultants, in order to respond to the changes in the environment within which the bank operates. Perhaps the greatest impetus for change in Wema was the deregulation and liberalization of the banking industry that paved the way for its privatization in 1990. This brought it a new focus as a corporate bank to replace its image as a government-controlled one.

Additionally, the liberalization of the industry also brought in a whole new set of banks with different approaches to providing banking services in Nigeria. This new and improved provision of services became the norm: the standard of service provision that customers of the old banks started to expect. As a result, management perceived that the structure of the industry, as well as the norms of practice, were changing. As a result, the bank had to put some structures in place to respond to these changes in its environment. Clearly influenced by developments within the industry, the CEO at that time stated:

> In 1988, the need to plan for the future became a reality as it became increasingly obvious that planning at the corporate level has become a prerequisite for success as a result of the deregulation and increasing competitiveness of the Nigerian banking industry (Adegbite, 1994: 53).

According to the bank's management, changes within the banking industry demanded that it transformed itself completely, and that this transformation was to encompass all areas of the bank, including its culture, management style, staff profile, service provision and use of information technology:

> If Wema's decision to move from being a primarily government-controlled and regional bank to that with a national outlook and coverage is to be realized, then a fundamental change in management approach and organizational culture needs to be accomplished (Adegbite, 1994: 13).

To achieve this, Wema worked with an international management-consulting firm to create a strategic plan. The consultants carried out major diagnostics of the bank and made a number of suggestions based on their understanding of the challenges facing the bank and the most appropriate responses to the challenges. The first strategic plan was drafted in 1990. It provided a statement of management intent about the direction of the bank for the first two years after privatization, which formed the foundation for restructuring plans.

The cardinal features of the first strategic plan were based on achieving a substantial level of change in three key areas: Geographic Spread; Business Focus; and Image Management. In 1993, the first plan was replaced by another strategic plan, which was the blueprint for much of the restructuring that took place in the bank between 1995 and 1999. The major component of this plan was the Branch Process Reengineering initiative. Its central aim was to achieve better service delivery by 'significantly improving retail banking efficiency'.

A close look at the implementation of the BPR project between 1995 and 1999 revealed some interesting issues and events relating to organizational resources, institutional demands and IT-enabled reengineering. Evidence from the implementation process discloses instances of institutional and resource-based decisions that influenced implementation of the programmes in the two banks. Key examples of such decisions are highlighted below, first for this case study and then for the case discussed in Section 7.3.2.

7.3.1.1 Decision 1: the three-tiered approach to restructuring

The first instance of a context-influenced decision taken by management at Wema was to adopt 'a careful and calculated approach to computerization and reengineering'. This cautious attitude meant the BPR project addressed the needs of the diversity of branches in its network using a pragmatic approach to branch automation and investment in information technology. The bank introduced new computer systems only in selected branches, and the level of restructuring that took place was based on the size of the branch, the volume of transaction, the types of customers and whether it was a rural or urban branch. According to the CEO of the bank:

> Based on the effort, financial commitment and time required to roll-out these (new) procedures, it was decided that the inclusion of some branches in the roll-out plan would amount to a waste of resources, given the existing and likely future transaction volumes and business opportunities in these branches (Wema Bank internal memo, 1996).

This entailed a redefinition of BPR, quite different from that envisaged at the onset of the programme. Consequently, it led to the total exclusion of the bank's 21 rural branches and a three-tiered approach to restructuring the remaining 51 branches:

1. Reengineering: investment in state-of-the-art technology, new banking application software and network interconnectivity in a small number of 'strategic' branches – those with 'high-end' customers and which contribute the most to the bank's earnings.
2. Redesign: restructuring but with only the upgrading of existing software and hardware and without the introduction of any new technology, targeted at the largest number of branches regarded as important to the bank's earnings but not strategic enough to warrant investing in new technology.
3. Streamlining: restructuring operations in the remaining branches, but with no technology input – only a reworking of manual systems and the making of changes to the aesthetics of branches, with data still kept essentially on card files and signatures verified manually with the use of mandate cards.

This decision was influenced by both the resource and institutional contexts of the organization. Institutional influences that were found to be at play included the directive from government that all branches opened under the Rural Banking Scheme (RBS)[5] were to be kept open, despite the abolition of the scheme. This meant that the bank had to keep all of its 21 rural branches in operation, despite the fact that some of them are not economically viable. Apart from the government's insistence on keeping the branches alive, close bank-community relations as well as inter-communal strife were also cited as reasons why the rural branches could not be closed down. Because the bank had been forced to open up branches in rival communities due to the RBS, it became difficult to close or merge branches in these communities, given the rivalry that exists between them. If management decided to close down the branch in a community, the people of that community would resist going to the branch in the rival community. In the worst-case scenario, it could lead to an inter-communal clash, as the community with a branch may perceive this as a sign of superiority – to the wrath of the other community.

In other instances, the bank had enjoyed the hospitality of the people of the local community when starting business and thus forged close bank-community ties that are not easily broken, even when economic considerations suggests otherwise. According to the Corporate Affairs Manager[6]:

> In one of our rural branches, the bank was offered a building free of charge by the community when we were about to open. Initially business was good and the bank enjoyed the good reception of the people. Now things are not so good but we still have to bear it, because when business was good they were good to us. These are the sort of situations that do not really allow you to take decisions as you would like to.

To avoid some of these problems, the bank had to keep the branches open and, therefore, to adopt 'a careful and calculated approach to computerization' and branch reengineering in general. This was realized in its three-tiered approach to the BPR project, which enabled the diverse needs of branches in its network to be met on the basis of the specific characteristics of each branch.

Resource-based factors in this decision were the sheer cost of computerizing the branches, the financial strength of the bank and the productivity of each branch. Given that the new Globus banking software costs between 12 and 15 million naira (1 naira = $110 in 2000) to implement, the bank decided to introduce it only into those branches regarded as 'strategic' in terms of volumes of transactions and contribution to the bank's overall earnings. This three-tiered approach to reengineering was to later become the norm or standard within the industry, as subsequent change initiatives in other banks were modelled around this approach.

7.3.1.2 Decision 2: rotating staff for reengineering

Prior to branch process reengineering, a prevalent issue in Wema branches was the poor quality of service from branch staff. Staff generally did not see any need to foster a close relationship with customers, except for personal gains. The average length of time for transacting business within the branch was between two and three hours even for simple transactions, such as checking an account balance or for cash withdrawal. This led to the practice, known locally as 'man know man', where bank customers solicit for favours from branch staff in order to be able to get through the cumbersome process of banking – in return for some form of financial, material or other gratification. Customers who were unfortunate enough not to know anyone were thus left to spend hours in the bank.

To do away with this 'internal help' practice, the consultants suggested that restructuring a branch, and achieving the level of 'rebirth' needed, would entail a complete overhaul of personnel in each branch. The 'man know man' culture was deemed unnecessary in a restructured branch, as every customer will be served on time and with the quality of service that they deserve. Therefore, a complete set of new staff was selected from other branches within the network to symbolize what branch restructuring stood for, and to drive home the point that restructuring was indeed aimed at breaking away from the old ways of doing things. In the words of the O&M Manager:

> We favour moving people when we want to convert because under the old dispensation nobody cares about service delivery, nobody really cares as to whether customers get served or not and so you discover that that system actually gives room for fraudulent and unprofessional practices on the part of staff. So we feel that if we allow such staff to remain within that branch at the early stage, it will go a long way to derailing the exercise. We want customers to go as they come in – first come; first served.

To achieve this aim, it was recommended that the new set of staff should be mostly graduates, because the existing crop of staff had mainly risen through the ranks after long years of service and were perceived as not qualified to work in the new environment of a restructured branch. However, rather than sack the bulk of its workforce and recruit new graduates, as was the case in other banks, management made an important decision to move staff around instead. This particular decision was influenced by the bank's long-standing tradition of promoting what it called the 'Wema family' of staff. Thus, an institutional pressure of sustaining a long-established tradition within the bank largely brought about a rational decision of keeping the bank's stock of human capital and moving people around branches. Table 7.2 summarizes key factors in the changes at this bank.

Table 7.2: Types of adaptations and influential factors at Wema

Adaptations at the Management Level	Resource and Institutional Influences
Three-tiered approach to reengineering.	Government regulations in the form of the Rural Banking Scheme. Size of branch network. Financial strength of bank and cost of computerization. Wider societal expectations due to close ties with rural communities and inter-communal rivalries.
Rotation of staff during reengineering.	Bank's recruitment policy. Culture of a 'Wema family'.

7.3.2 Reorganization Through 'Practical Restructuring': The UBA Case

> Consistent with the need to evolve a coherent business strategy and respond to environmental changes, UBA Plc embarked on a comprehensive, realistic and practical restructuring exercise in 1995 which involved changes in structure, staffing, systems, skills profile and shared values (UBA, 1998: 3).

The process of change at the United Bank for Africa (UBA) was similar to that at Wema, in that it was influenced largely by both the organization's resource context and the demands of its institutional context. A major driving force for change in UBA, as it was in Wema, a was the deregulation of the Nigerian economy and the consequent liberalization of the banking industry, which led to the privatization of the bank in 1994. Privatization immediately brought about a change in management, especially at the board level – where over 60 directors regarded as government 'cronies' were sacked and replaced by young professionals. It was hoped that this would give the bank the new focus of a corporate bank, thereby removing the tag of being a 'government bank'.

The liberalization of the industry and the attendant increase in the number of operating banks, coupled with the new and emerging focus on customer service and improved technology use, led UBA's new management to embark on strategic planning. The aim of its strategic plan was to combine the strength of UBA – which, being an old bank, were its huge customer base and the availability of cheap and stable deposits – with the flexibility, responsiveness and focus on quality service delivery of a new-generation bank.

The result of adopting the strategic plan was the bank's 'restructuring and repositioning' exercise, which commenced in 1995. Describing some of the challenges that had forced the bank to embark on this exercise, the Chairman of the bank noted that:

> the international and local contexts of banking business have been faced by such emerging challenges as the sustained attack on the market share of the big banks by leaner and younger players; ... [and] the growing sophistication of bank customers in an increasingly competitive environment (*Vanguard*, 1997).

According to management, changes within the banking industry demanded that the bank transformed itself completely and that this transformation was to encompass all areas of the bank. This was made clear by one of the directors:

> The board of UBA was convinced that the prevailing corporate culture, organization structure, sheer size, and degree of efficiency of resources needed to be significantly reviewed if the bank was to enter the 21st Century as a major player in the country.

A change-management team, consisting of key officers experienced in different aspects of the bank's operations, was brought together to work with management consultants. Their brief was to assess the bank in terms of its strengths and weaknesses and to come up with a vision of how it would progress in years to come, especially in the context of changes in the banking environment. The team produced a report that formed the nucleus of the bank's strategic plan on which much of the restructuring and repositioning was founded. The prime features of this plan were based on achieving substantial levels of change in four main areas: computerization; operations process reengineering; branch development; and staff training and development.

Inspired by the recommendations of consultants, management treated the task of restructuring UBA with the utmost urgency, based on their perception of the pace of developments within the industry. As such, it was decided that the projects in the four key areas would be carried out concurrently, so that the bank would not lose ground to changes in its environment. Work commenced immediately on the implementation of the plan, and teams were formed to handle the different projects.

The Strategic Management team was formed to handle branch network development and the Business Process Reengineering team for dealing with process reengineering and staff training. The existing IT unit was upgraded by bringing in new staff to take over the computerization part of the plan. Much of the computerization initiative centred on implementing at all the branches the home-grown applications software named Branch Accounting and Information Systems (BRAINS). However, by the time data was gathered in 1999 on the status of the restructuring exercise, much of the original contents in the strategic plan had been either dropped or modified. The implemented change, at the time the data was collected, showed a number of changes that can be explained by a combination of both institutional and resource-related factors (Table 7.3).

Table 7.3: Types of adaptations and influential factors at UBA

Adaptations at the Management Level	Resource and Institutional Influences
Radical plan, based on an incremental implementation.	Staff strength. (Non) availability of 'capable' staff.
Two-tiered approach to inter-connectivity.	Government regulations an influence on establishing new branches. Size of branch network and cost of computerization.

7.3.2.1 Decision 3: radical plan, incremental implementation

Incremental implementation was a decision reached by management to implement the strategic plan in a piecemeal approach, as opposed to the radical overhaul that was originally envisaged at the start of the project. By the middle of 1997, about 18 months into the strategic plan's implementation, the restructuring exercise took a turn. Management realized that the implementation was not going as smoothly as expected. Due to the changes taking place, there was a series of strikes by staff who were fearful of the impact of the restructuring on their jobs. The bank spent the whole of 1996 in negotiations with the union about the impending rationalization of staff, and in appeasing staff complaints about the pace of change taking place. In addition, the bank realized that it did not have the required skills and staff to carry out the intended plans at the required pace. In an interview, a manager in the Strategic Management unit stated:

> In 1995, we started off with a grand design to change every area of the bank. However, in reality the implementation proved difficult; we realized we could not change everything all at once. We cannot change things overnight because people have a limited ability to absorb change and also because we are short of people to lead the change. Even the ones who are leading the change now have a limited ability to control things; there are only 24 hours in a day and 7 days in a week. People's abilities are limited even where they are 400% committed to the plan.

In effect, this led to management's decision to reconsider its strategy. At the onset of the change programme, management – armed with the recommendations of the consultants and burning with eagerness to wipe the slate clean – had decided the best way forward was to change everything, all at once. However, the reality of the organization's resource context was that there were not adequate resources to carry on as intended, with all projects carried out at the same time. Instead, it was decided that, given the available resources, the scope of the change should be redefined and implemented in phases.

7.3.2.2 Decision 4: the two-tiered approach to inter-connectivity

Similar to Wema, UBA's computerization strategy (especially branch networking) was influenced by both the resource characteristics of the bank – in terms of the diversity of its branch network – and influences from the institutional environment, in the form of the RBS rural banking scheme. Given the variety of types of branches in its network and the level of business activities that takes place in them, management decided that it was not going to be cost effective to connect all the branches. Instead, a two-way strategy was adopted, in which 'strategic branches' were connected using the VSAT[7] technology with all other branches connected via a hub system. In the hub system, a networked regional branch acts as a gateway to other branches within the region. In an interview, the IT Manager explained the major reason for this choice of system:

> Although it is desirable for the bank to have all its branches connected and to be able to access and to determine the financial situation or balance of every branch at a go and at the beginning of every day, but there are constraints. These constraints are in the areas of resources – do you install expensive systems in marginal branches, or do you first concentrate on key branches and then expand the scope for the others?

Two types of resources are referred to here: the financial strength of the bank and the bank's customer reach in terms of its branch network, which is the third largest in the industry with over 200 branches, of which 87 are in rural areas. The cost of installing state-of-the-art technology and wide-area networks into all these branches (especially those regarded as 'unprofitable') led to the adoption of the two-tier hub system to link up branches. As a result, a rational decision to implement state-of-the-art technology into only 'profitable' branches was largely influenced by resource-related factors, such as the financial strength of the bank and its branch network, as well as institutional pressures in the form of the RBS and the government's insistence on keeping all branches opened under this scheme.

7.3.3 Discussion of Cases: Influence of Resource and Institutional Contexts in IT and Organizational Change

Analysis of findings from these two case studies revealed some interesting insights into the role of resources and institutional pressures in implementing

IT-based organizational change initiatives in the two banks. Both the resource and institutional contexts influenced the change process by providing the 'ammunition' for people to draw upon in interpreting and redefining the plan for change, and also by providing 'ready' solutions – where no conscious effort was needed to implement change. Employing concepts and ideas from the resource-based view and the institutional theory, we will discuss both internal and external factors as well as rational and symbolic aspects. This is consistent with Van de Ven and Poole's (1988) and Pettigrew et. al's (1992) guidelines for employing rational and non-rational ideas in explaining change.

In providing ready solutions for change, institutional rules – in the form of the Rural Banking Scheme (RBS) – presented themselves as solutions to the logistical and financial problem of computerizing the large number of branches in both banks. Expectations from the social community also meant that some rural branches would be kept open, even if the RBS permitted their closure. In both banks, the resource base, in terms of the staff profile, also presented solutions which management made use of in their decisions on staff rationalization within the change process. At Wema, the culture of promoting a family of employees had led to a stable bank-employee relationship and a stable and experienced team of professionals, which made management's decision not to lay off staff that much easier.

The situation with UBA was slightly different. Given the highly political environment within which the bank operated before privatization, the new managers that took control after privatization were eager to get rid of staff who they regarded as government stooges. Therefore, the bank's staff profile, the series of staff strikes and the long drawn-out union negotiations were important factors beyond management's technical control. From when the new management took control and the restructuring process began, it was clear that there was going to be some rationalization of staff. However, the actual method was not clear initially, so the series of strikes and union foot-dragging were significant in shaping the pace and direction of change. Expanding the discussion on the role of the institutional context further, from a historical perspective we could also see how the history of the two banks and their origin influenced staff rationalization.

Wema was founded by a group of Nigerian investors with the sole purpose of providing loans and credit facilities, mainly to Nigerian businessmen and women who were discriminated against by the colonial banks operating in the country at that time. Throughout its adolescent years, the bank received support in the form of grants from the government of the western region, where around 80 per cent of its customers are based and around 90 per cent of its branches are located. In addition, as much as 75 per cent of its staff are from the western part of Nigeria, due to its historical ties with this area. Therefore, throughout its history the bank had a close attachment with that region of Nigeria, which may have influenced the decision not to lay off staff. The emotional attachment or 'management of affection' exhibited by the Wema Board reflects deeply in its history and culture, which can be traced back to its founding. This management of affection, therefore, could be seen as an attempt by management to sustain the age-long tradition or norms of practice within the bank.

UBA, on the other hand, was a bank with an international outlook from the beginning; when it was established, the bank was wholly owned by a consortium of foreign banks. In 1977, when the Nigerian government introduced the Indigenization Decree, government bought a controlling 60 per cent of its shares. This was sold off when the bank was privatized in 1994. However, despite the majority share ownership by Nigerian investors after privatization, foreign shareholders held as much as 40 per cent of the shares in the company in 1999 (UBA, 1999: 10) and continue to have an important influence in the running of the bank (*Vanguard*, 1998). Unlike Wema, UBA also has its branches spread more widely across the country. This wide spread is reflected in its staff mix, which is more diverse than Wema. Therefore, the influence of foreign investors, the highly political climate as a result of heavy government involvement before privatization and the wholesale change at the top after privatization meant that there was little or no emotional attachment to staff, which perhaps made the task of laying off staff that much easier. It could also be seen as an attempt by the new Board to sustain the long-term relationship the bank has with the foreign investors and international shareholders who maintain a major stake in the bank.

The resource and institutional contexts of organizations also specify the desirability and feasibility of implementing IT-based change practices in organizations. IT-enabled change programmes may be deemed desirable to adopt but not feasible to implement, perhaps due to a misalignment with the culture of the organization or the established ways of doing things within the organizational context. In such cases, organizations may be unwilling to implement IT and organizational change techniques due to the difficulty of altering life-long habits within the organization, or through the unconscious perpetuation of these age-long habits.

Applying this conceptualization to the case studies, deregulation and liberalization had stimulated banks to start engaging in strategic planning, which was seen as the appropriate response to the changing environment. Influenced by the 'success' stories of BPR in the 'west', bank managers and consultants found BPR and its promise of 'quantum leap improvement' appealing in the context of the liberalization changes. Thus, they proceeded to restructure their branches. The process of restructuring started as a top-down, rational approach of employing consultants to carry out a SWOT analysis of the bank and to design strategic plans that formed the basis of the reorganization initiatives.

However, the situation became rather different at the implementation stage. In contrast to the intentions stated in the strategic plans, management began to pay attention to the realities of the resource and institutional contexts, some of which were at odds with the original plans. Thus, some of the rules and procedures of the change technique were considered not feasible to implement given the demands of these two contexts. At Wema, the suggestion to sack staff and start from a 'clean slate' was not feasible to implement because it contradicts the established ways of doing things within the organization and the bank's traditional link with a particular region of the country. In addition to instances of rituals and symbolism, both banks were also rational and calculating in their implementation of technology and organizational change. Their approach to implementation was influenced by resources available, like the financial strength of the bank and locational assets in terms of strategic branches and customer reach (size of branch network). Due to the high cost of restructuring branches and installing new IT systems, management decided to reengineer and implement new systems in 'strategic' branches first. These branches contribute the most to the banks' earnings, given the worth and the volume of business activities that takes place.

Although the decision to start implementation with strategic branches was motivated by resource-related factors, the history of computerization in both banks also reveals a further insight into the nature of the decision, and adds a different dimension to it. Historically, the introduction of new IT systems in the two banks had always favoured selecting 'important branches' to implement these systems, given the expected return from the branches. When Wema began implementation of its Customer Accounting Package (CAPs) system in 1989 and 1991, it started with some of its 'important' branches. Similarly, when UBA started the implementation of the B1 Accounting Package, the MicroBoss Accounting System and BRAINS in 1985, 1989 and 1993 respectively, it started with some of its 'strategic' branches in Lagos. Thus, a seemingly rational decision to select 'cost-effective' branches is also steeped deeply in established norms of practice within the banks. Therefore, the implementation of technology-based change programmes happened under the influence of both rational considerations and symbolic forces.

7.4 CONCLUSIONS

The important theoretical implication of this chapter's analysis for management decision-making and actions is that symbolic or ritual actions and socio-political factors are not necessarily dysfunctional. Johnson (1990) examined how strategic change can be galvanized through symbolic acts within the organization. Similarly, Kamoche (1995) examined how organizational reality can be socially constructed through a combination of ritual and language. Westphal and Zajac (1998) posited that symbolic corporate actions, in the form of long-term incentive plans (LTIPs) that symbolize congruence between CEO and shareholder interests, can engender significant positive stockholder reactions. In the two bank case studies in this chapter, we have demonstrated how management and other bank staff, acting in the realm of known practices, were able to successfully implement the change programmes to suit their context of operations. An implication of adopting resource-based and institutional perspectives to study IT and organizational change is that, together, they can overcome a key limitation of the technical-rational view of organizational behaviour in general, and more specifically of utilizing IT in organizations: incompleteness of the technical-rational view for the study of IT-enabled organizational change because it cannot consider the 'irrationalities' and 'idiosyncrasies' of the local context.

REFERENCES

Adegbite, S.I. (1994), *Path To Greater Heights: Facts Behind Wema Bank's Turnaround Years (1982–1992)*, Ibadan: Nigeria, Spectrum Books Limited.

Amit, R. and P.J.H. Schoemaker (1993), 'Strategic Assets and Organizational Rent', *Strategic Management Journal*, **14** (1), 33–46.

Astley, W.G. and A.H. Van de Ven (1983), 'Central Perspectives and Debates in Organization Theory', *Administrative Science Quarterly*, **28**, 245–73.

Attewell, P. (1992), 'Technology Diffusion and Organizational Learning: The Case of Business Computing', *Organization Science*, **3** (1), 1–19.

Bada, A.O. (2000), 'Institutional Intervention in the Adoption of Computer-Based Information Systems: The Case of the Nigerian Banking Industry', in C. Avgerou and G. Walsham (eds), *Information Technology in Context: Implementing Systems in the Developing World*, Aldershot, UK: Ashgate Publishers, 168–81

Barney, J. (1986), 'Strategic Factor Markets: Expectations, Luck and Business Strategy', *Management Science*, **32** (10), 1231–41.

Barney, J. (1991), 'Firm Resources and Sustained Competitive Advantage', *Journal of Management*, **17** (1), 99–120.

Berger, P. and Luckman T. (1966), *The Social Construction of Reality: A Treatise in the Sociology of Knowledge,* Garden City, NY: Doubleday.

Christiaanse, E. and J. Huigen (1997), 'Institutional Dimensions in Information Technology Implementation in Complex Network Settings', *European Journal of Information Systems*, **6**, 77–85.

Clemons, E.K. and M.C. Row (1991), 'Sustaining IT advantage: The Role of Structural Differences', *MIS Quarterly* (September), 275–92.

Dacin, M.T. (1997), 'Isomorphism in Context: The Power and Prescriptions of Institutional Norms', *Academy of Management Journal*, **40** (1), 46–81.

DeCock, C. (1996), 'An Investigation into the Introduction of Planned Organizational Change: Theoretical and Empirical Considerations', Ph.D. Thesis, Manchester: Manchester Business School, University of Manchester.

Dierickx, I. and K. Cool (1989), 'Asset Stock Accumulation and the Sustainability of Competitive Advantage', *Management Science*, **35** (12), 1504–11.

DiMaggio, P.J. and W.W. Powell (1991), 'The Iron Cage Revisited: Institutional Isomorphism and Collective Rationality in Organizational Fields', in W.W. Powell and P.J. DiMaggio (1991) (eds), *The New Institutionalism in Organizational Analysis*, Chicago: University of Chicago Press, 63–82.

Goodman, P. (1982), *Change in Organizations: New Perspectives on Theory, Research, and Practice*, San Francisco, Jossey-Bass Publishers.

Grant, G.G. (1996), 'The Strategic Dimensions of Information Systems Capability: Case Studies in a Developing Country Context', Ph.D. Thesis, London: London School of Economics.

Grant, R.M. (1991), 'The Resource-Based Theory of Competitive Advantage: Implications for Strategy Formulation', *California Management Review* (Spring), 114–35.

Hrebiniak, L.G. and W.F. Joyce (1985), 'Organizational Adaptation: Strategic Choice and Environmental Determinism', *Administrative Science Quarterly*, **30**, 336–49.

Hung, S. and R. Whittington (1997), 'Strategies and Institutions: A Pluralistic Account of Strategies in the Taiwanese Computer Industry', *Organization Studies*, **18** (4), 551–75.

Johnson, G. (1990), 'Managing Strategic Change: The Role of Symbolic Action', *British Journal of Management*, **1**, 183–200.

Kamoche, K. (1995), 'Rhetoric, Ritualism, and Totemism in Human Resource Management', *Human Relations*, **48** (4), 367–85.

King, J.L., V. Gurbaxani, K.L. Kraemer, F.W. McFarlan, K.S. Raman and C.S. Yap (1994), 'Institutional Factors in Information Technology Innovation', *Information Systems Research*, **5** (2), 139–69.

Kling, R. and S. Iacono (1989), 'The Institutional Character of Computerized Information Systems', *Office Technology and People*, **5** (1), 7–28.

Kling, R., K.L. Kraemer, J. Allen, Y. Bakos, V. Gurbaxani and J. King (1992), 'Information Systems in Manufacturing Coordination: Economic and Social Perspectives', presented at the Thirteenth International Conference on Information Systems, Dallas, TX: ACM Publications.

Lippman, S. and R. Rumelt (1982), 'Uncertain Imitability: An Analysis of Interfirm Differences in Efficiency Under Competition', *Bell Journal of Economics*, **13**, 418–38.

March, J.G. and J.P. Olsen (1976), *Ambiguity and Choice in Organizations*, Bergen: Universitetsforlaget.

Mata, F.J., W.L. Fuerst and J.B. Barney (1995), 'Information Technology and Sustained Competitive Advantage: A Resource-based Analysis', *MIS Quarterly*, **19** (4), 487–505.

Mehra, A. (1996), 'Resource and Market Based Determinants of Performance in the U.S. Banking Industry', *Strategic Management Journal*, **17**, 307–22.

Meyer, J.W. and B. Rowan (1977), 'Institutionalized Organizations: Formal Structure as Myth and Ceremony', *American Journal of Sociology*, **83** (2), 340–63.

Oliver, C. (1991), 'Strategic Responses to Institutional Processes', *Academy of Management Review*, **16** (1), 145–79.

Oliver, C. (1997a), 'Sustainable Competitive Advantage: Combining Institutional and Resource-Based View', *Strategic Management Journal*, **18** (9), 697–713.

Oliver, C. (1997b), 'The Influence of Institutional and Task Environment Relationships on Organizational Performance: The Canadian Construction Industry', *Journal of Management Studies*, **34** (1), 99–124.

Orru, M., N.W. Biggart, and G. Hamilton (1991), 'Organizational Isomorphism in East Asia', in W.W. Powell and P.J. DiMaggio (1991) (eds), *The New Institutionalism in Organizational Analysis*, Chicago: University of Chicago Press, 361–89.

Penrose, E. (1959), *The Growth of the Firm*, Oxford: Basil Blackwell.

Peteraf, M.A. (1993), 'The Cornerstones of Competitive Advantage: A Resource-Based View', *Strategic Management Journal*, **14** (3), 179–91.

Pettigrew, A., E. Ferlie and L. McKee (1992), *Shaping Strategic Change*, London: Sage Publications.

Powell, W.W. and P.J. DiMaggio (1991) (eds), *The New Institutionalism in Organizational Analysis*, Chicago: University of Chicago Press.

Prahalad, C.K. and G. Hamel (1990), 'The Core Competence of the Corporation', *Harvard Business Review*, **90** (May–June), 79–91.

Ross, J.W., C.M. Beath, and D.L. Goodhue (1996), 'Developing Long-Term Competitiveness Through IT Assets', *Sloan Management Review*, **38** (1), 31–42.

Rumelt, R.P. (1984), 'Toward a Strategic Theory of the Firm', in R. Lamb (ed), *Competitive Strategic Management*, Prentice-Hall, Englewood Cliffs, NJ, 1984.

Scheid-Cook, T.L. (1992), 'Organizational Enactments and Conformity to Environmental Prescriptions', *Human Relations*, **45** (6), 537–55.

Scott, R. and J. Meyer (1991), 'The Organization of Societal Sectors: Propositions and Early Evidence', in Powell, W.W. and P.J. DiMaggio (1991) (eds), *The New Institutionalism in Organizational Analysis*, Chicago: University of Chicago Press, 108–40.

Selznick, P. (1957), Leadership in Administration, Evanston, Ill: Row Peterson

Silva, L. (1997), 'Power and Politics in the Adoption of Information Systems in Organizations: The Case of a Research Center in Latin America', Ph.D. Thesis, London: London School of Economics and Political Science.

Swanson, E.B. and N.C. Ramiller (1997), 'The Organizing Vision in Information Systems Innovation', *Organizational Science*, **8** (5), 458–73.

UBA (1998), *Annual Report, 1998*, Lagos: United Bank for Africa (UBA).

UBA (1999), *Annual Report, 1999*, Lagos: United Bank for Africa (UBA).

Van de Ven, A. and M.S. Poole (1988), 'Paradoxical Requirements for a Theory of Organizational Change. Paradox and Transformation: Toward a Theory of Change', in R. Quinn, and K. Cameron, (eds), *Organization and Management*, Cambridge, MA, Ballinger.

Vanguard (1997), 'UBA's Bello-Osagie Lists Challenges of Banking', 13 November.

Vanguard (1998), 'International Investors Take Five Seats on UBA Board', 12 December.

Wernerfelt, B. (1984), 'A Resource-based View of the Firm', *Strategic Management Journal*, **5** (2), 171–80.

Westphal, J.D. and E.J. Zajac (1998), 'The Symbolic Management of Stockholders: Corporate Governance Reforms and Shareholder Reactions', *Administrative Science Quarterly*, **43**, 127–53.

NOTES

1. It is worth noting that institutionalists argue that environments, in this respect, do not just involve the immediate environment of organizations, but that organizations are also involved in non-local and vertically-structured relationships (Scott and Meyer, 1991).
2. Quoted in DiMaggio and Powell (1991).
3. Legitimacy is explained as an evaluation method that places emphasis on meeting societal expectations, and which may be at odds with the internal efficiency needs of the organization (DiMaggio and Powell, 1991).
4. Quoting March and Olsen (1976).
5. The Federal Government introduced the Rural Banking Scheme in 1977. Through it, government compelled all banks to increase their presence in rural areas by allocating to each bank a minimum number of branches they had to establish within a specified length of time. The aim was to encourage rural banking habits, and also to mop up excess liquidity. However, the Scheme was abandoned after the industry was liberalized in 1989, as it was argued that such a policy of establishing branches in 'unprofitable' areas conflicts with the tenets of profitability and efficiency which the government was trying to encourage with the introduction of the Structural Adjustment Programme.
6. Many of the quotations from bank managers and staff in this chapter come from interviews for the study on which the chapter is based and don't have a published source. Confidentiality agreements mean names cannot be revealed.
7. VSAT is the generic term used to describe Very Small Aperture Terminal earth stations. These earth stations are high-capacity digital satellite communication technology, capable of accommodating a host of interactive communications applications, LAN–LAN connectivity, digital audio broadcasting and business television.

PART THREE

Innovation in the organizational setting of ICT use

8. New Socio-technical Perspectives of IS Innovation in Organizations

Chrisanthi Avgerou

8.1 INTRODUCTION

In this chapter, I present and discuss the understanding of 'innovation' associated with ICTs at the organizational level that has been formed in the stream of IS research which draws on social theory. I take IS innovation to mean both the process leading to a new technology-mediated organizational practice and the results of such a process, that is, a novel way of technology-mediated practice.

The term innovation is not actually widely used in the IS literature. As a field with the mission to elaborate on the process of accommodating ICT artefacts in the practices of an organization, IS has been preoccupied with the nature and comparative merits of specific activities through which artefacts are produced and organizational practices change, such as 'development', 'implementation' and 'design'. Also, IS research endeavoured to understand the nature of innovation as the outcome of a process of IS development, implementation or design. Thus, from an early stage, a great deal of debate has been directed at shaping the understanding of the result of IS development processes as new socio-technical arrangements for handling information in an organizational context, rather than as a new technology system. Although no accurate definition of the concept of 'information system' has ever been agreed, there is a discernible tacit agreement in the IS field that it refers to information content and social context, as well as technologies.

This perspective raises several issues regarding the process of ICT innovation in organizations. A major question is about the nature of the inter-relationship between the two constitutive parts of IS innovation: the change of organizational practices and the acquisition or construction of technology artefacts. Can we expect the development or acquisition of new ICT systems to drive, and necessitate the working out of, specific new organizational practices and structures, such as customer-oriented practices or network structures? Is it the other way round, that is, effective take up of ICTs require specific structural characteristics and established modes of work practice? Or is there a different way of understanding the relationship between ICT and organizations that does not assume one is determined by the other? Another related question concerns the kind of effort involved in IS innovation. Is it a matter of methodical and skilful technical tasks, of managerial competencies, of political manoeuvring? Can the process of IS innovation be controlled by engineering, management and policy – or should it be seen as an inherently uncertain process of social change?

It is also worth asking how innovation in the local context of an organization is associated with the advent of new technologies and the prevalence of particular organizational practices and structures in the broader context of IT and management-consultancy industries, competitor firms or any other influential organizations. Are organizations in a position to work out new technology-mediated practices or are they, perhaps with the exception of a few 'leaders', merely imitating what has proven to be successful ICT-based practice elsewhere?

I argue in this chapter that the process of IS innovation is not determined by the material properties of the technology or by the structural properties of the social context implicated in the innovation. Nor is it under the control of a team of management and technology professionals. Instead, the construction or configuration of new technology artefacts and the working out of organizational arrangements unfold by a mix of technical/rational tasks, institutionalized enactments and improvisational action, as people make sense of the potential of ICTs in their work context and seek to appropriate it. IS innovation is inevitably situated in the organization concerned, although most technology components are acquired as standard 'solutions' from the IT industry and many IS implementation efforts are aimed at introducing what are seen as established 'best practice' elsewhere.

The next section explores this further by tracing the changing setting of IS innovation, from the days when all computer-based information systems were constructed 'in-house' to meet an organization's specific predetermined 'requirements' to the situation in the early 21st Century where most information systems are constructed from generic packaged software – often with the mandate to change radically an organization's structures and practices. The subsequent sections outline and discuss the main types of IS innovation in contemporary organizations and the main theoretical aspects of the current understanding of the socio-technical process of IS innovation. Finally, I discuss the contribution this perspective makes and explain why the socio-theoretical stream of IS studies is crucial for the development of critical professional judgement for interventions at both the organizational and societal levels, although it is neither instrumental by itself nor feeds directly into normative professional practice.

8.2 THE CHANGING SETTINGS OF IS INNOVATION

8.2.1 Life-cycle Computer Applications Development

From its emergence around the late 1970s as a distinct academic field that studies IT in organizations, IS has had a particular conception of IT innovation centred on the notion of the 'life cycle'. With its roots in engineering, the life cycle played a multifaceted role in the development of the field. Most obviously, it provided a model to structure professional practice for the construction of IS applications in organizations. Beyond this prescriptive role, the life cycle shaped the general discourse on innovation in IS as a series of purposeful actions. These were based heavily on an analysis of both the information-processing requirements an IT application under construction should fulfil and the design of technical components of the application, mainly the data structures and data processing built into software. Consequently, this discourse gave rise to a specific research agenda that crystallized the set of intellectual and practical questions with which the IS community became preoccupied. Prominent among these have been:

- the methodological merits and philosophical basis of alternative analysis and design techniques (Lyytinen, 1987; Avison and Fitzgerald, 1996);
- the relationship between technical professionals (analysts and designers) and 'users' (Kyng and Mathiassen, 1982; Land and Hirschheim, 1983; Suchman, 1994); and
- the relationship of 'before' and 'after' events and actions implied by the cut-off point of implementation in the life cycle of an IT-based system (Land, 1982; Swanson and Beath, 1989).

According to this conception, IS innovation in organizations resides in the construction of the technical artefacts that are seen to be required by the business circumstances of the organization concerned. The prevailing view has been that a firm's competitive needs justify the investment in new technology, and its operational particularities determine the information processing functionality of the chosen new technology. The outcome of such an innovation depends on various organizational change processes and technical tasks, involving cooperation and negotiation among management, technical experts and users.

Advances in ICT and changes in the innovation expectations of organizations have lessened the relevance of the life cycle as a model of practice, as a determinant of the discourse of innovation and as a source of research questions for the IS community. IT changed both in terms of what it does (the functionality of the technology) and how it is made available to organizations (the market of products and services). With layers of 'user friendly' systems and application software, and with an abundance of software products and services in the market, a great deal of IT enters organizations in the form of directly usable artefacts. This current state of IT contrasts sharply with that of the time almost all IT applications were developed 'in house', when a software construction process had to be set up to make usable artefacts from the then-available raw materials: compilers and computers (with a rudimentary interface).

In effect, the advent of packaged software and user-friendly computer interfaces has broken the life-cycle model of systems development into two parts, each of which may be seen as comprising its own cyclical pattern of activities. The first is located in software production firms and is concerned with the construction of generic products that address a range of alternative 'requirements', according to standard processes found in modern organizations. The second is located in 'user' organizations and is concerned with the configuration of a purchased generic product for their specific structures and processes. The size and technical sophistication of each of the two parts varies for different types of software applications. In general, the overall process of innovation is more complex than life-cycle-based systems construction, as it is mediated by a plethora of consultancy support services and in-house initiatives and improvisations carried out by technical experts and users.

8.2.2 Implementation of IS Infrastructure

The innovation expectations of organizations became both uncertain in terms of target organizational features and mimetic of fast changing fads. According to the IS literature, although the benefits of productivity and efficiency remained strongly associated with IT innovation, expectations shifted to 'enabling' restructuring in search of patterns of practice suitable for the emerging 'new economy'. IT innovation in organizations is seen as being intertwined with efforts for moving towards new forms and norms of organizing. It should be noted that, in the broad context of contemporary business, various weakly-institutionalized organizational forms coexist and compete for legitimacy, such as the matrix structure, the network organization and the platform organization (Avgerou, 2000). This implies a fundamental change for the process of IT innovation, in so far as new technology artefacts in organizations are not derived as requirements for supporting the information processes of an existing organizational setting; instead, the artefacts are enablers of imaginary new organizational states. For example, packaged enterprise resource planning (ERP) systems are often acquired with the expectation of transferring 'best practice' for integrating a range of typically fragmented functions, such as orders, sales, payments, inventory control and procurement. Such a process of change involves a substantial, often massive, intervention for the redesign of work processes in parallel with the customization of the ERP software.

With such changes, the IS field has been faced with new challenges, both in terms of informing professional practice and of explaining the role of new technology in organizations (for example, see Currie and Galliers, 1999). It became clearer that IS innovation is not confined to the actions concerned with taking up (designing or transferring) new technologies, but is also concerned with issues of information, knowledge and changes of organizational structure and practice, such as changes in the content and structure of work tasks. In the intertwined technical and social processes of IS innovation, therefore, the social context is a constitutive part of innovation itself – not merely the container of technical artefacts and processes (Lea et al., 1999).

In the next section, I trace the main IS innovation practices that have emerged since the early 1990s, and discuss the way they are associated with organizational change. A change of terminology is indicative of a shift of focus in the activities comprising IS innovation. For instance, it has become most likely that an IS project will be called 'implementation' rather than 'development', signifying the importance of the effort involved in fitting a generically-designed software product into an organization.

8.3 KEY TYPES OF IS INNOVATION IN ORGANIZATIONS

Three types of technologies have been most prevalent in the IS literature since the early 1990s: computer supported collaborative work (CSCW), ERP and intranets[1] or Internet-based network systems. There is a great deal of literature on a variety of other, often more specific, information systems, such as business-to-business (B2B) and business-to-customer (B2C) e-commerce infrastructures. However, in terms of their construction efforts, these comprise – or are combinations of – the three categories of ERP, CSCW and network-based information systems. Each of these requires a different course of effort for its implementation.

8.3.1 Computer Supported Collaborative Work

CSCW systems are technology infrastructures intended to support cooperative work arrangements (Bannon, 1998). Most of them use generic packaged software application products, which require relatively minor technical work to install in order to begin operations. The most demanding part of the CSCW innovation process in an organization is the taking up of the technical system in an organization's practices, through the shaping of new processes of work in teams of co-workers.

Orlikowski (1996) analyses the way a CSCW application comes to bear on an organization's task as a process of emergent organizational change. A number of aspects of her analysis are important to highlight. The implementation of a CSCW technology, such as Lotus Notes, does not imply a particular work practice. Whether it leads to changes of practice, and whether the benefits generally associated with these technologies are achieved, depend on whether an organization's actors are interested in changing the way they work by exploiting CSCW's technical features and the capacity they have to take initiatives to transform their work. Capacity for such action varies in different organizational contexts. For example, organizations with a collaborative culture are more likely to accommodate CSCW technology keenly, making it a platform for reorganizing communication for the sharing of knowledge and the provision of mutual support to co-workers. In Orlikowski's research sample, employees in organizations with an individualistic and adversarial culture showed little interest in exploiting the possibilities for new ways of sharing and collaboration that such technical tools provide (Orlikowski, 2000).

Nevertheless, studies elaborating on the shaping of information systems through practice may be misleading with regard to the extent to which the flexibility of the technology can be taken for granted, and consequently the extent to which the initial design and configuration of the software system matters. Other studies show that the technical features of CSCW systems have constraining effects. Although they are intended to be flexible, it is not always possible to shape the systems to support the preferred practices of a team. Initial assumptions about desirable team performance may lead to technical properties that restrict team practice. For example, Sach's (1995) study of a computerized dispatching system intended to increase the efficiency of a team of co-workers showed that the way the system was configured to improve the efficiency of individual tasks created problems for the overall and long-term performance of the team. Such problems could not be overcome by adjusting work arrangements; it required the redesign of the technical components of the system.

8.3.2 Enterprise Resource Planning

The question of the possibilities opened up for shaping technology and technology-mediated practice according to the particularities of an organization is more pressing in cases of technologies that are not built to be flexible. One of the most rigid of more recent IT applications is ERP. As described in the literature, the processes of implementing such systems and changing organizational practice to accommodate them differ significantly from those that involve CSCW systems.

ERP is understood as 'an integrated IT-based system that supports the management of all enterprise resources including information, people, money products and services, materials and equipment' (Howcroft and Truex, 2001: 14). Such systems almost always make use of packaged software; they are not purpose-built for a specific organization. ERP software packages are complex, generic, typically modular products that require a substantial technical effort to configure for the circumstances of a particular organization. Three contentious issues about such systems are of interest to our analysis in this chapter.

First, to the extent that they require a major technical effort for 'customizing' the software product to the specifics of an organization's practice, ERP systems involve many of the technology-construction problems highlighted in the life-cycle-centred discourse of information systems development. The configuration of ERP packages bears many of the features of planned and methodical systems development familiar in purpose-designed information systems (Bancroft et al., 1998; Markus et al., 2000; Markus and Tanis, 2000; Kawalek and Wood-Harper, 2002). For example, according to Bancroft et al. (1998), the implementation of an ERP system involves four phases[2]:

1. 'as is' covers a detailed analysis of current business processes, the installation of the package, mapping of the business processes on to the ERP functions and training of the project team;
2. 'to be' concerns the design of the new system, including interactive prototyping to reach approval for the detailed features of the new system and the new business processes;
3. 'construction and testing' deals with the development of a comprehensive configuration for the system and testing with real data; and
4. 'actual implementation' involves tasks similar to those of the implementation stage in the life-cycle model: putting in place the network infrastructure, installing the necessary technology components, training users and 'going live'.

This kind of approach seeks to determine information processing requirements accurately, once and for all at the very beginning of the innovation process. That confronts analysts with difficulties in trying to resolve the clashes of meaning and interest among technical professionals, managers and 'users', as well as the restrictions that rigid information systems infrastructures impose on organization practice for years to come.

A second contentious ERP issue is that this innovation is further complicated by the linking of the configuration and implementation of the selected technology with the design and enactment of desirable organizational changes (Besson and Rowe, 2001). Thus, an ERP implementation tends to combine two design activities: the redesign of organizational structure and practice, and the design for the configuration of technology infrastructure to support the intended new structure and practice. There are practical issues here regarding the linking of the two processes and the containment of the entailed risks.

ERP implementation has been closely associated with business process reengineering (BPR), a management practice expected to lead to the radical re-shaping of the way an organization conducts its business and aimed at major gains of efficiency and effectiveness in achieving an organization's output. Despite the criticism that BPR-type interventions attracted throughout the 1990s (Jones, 1994; Galliers and Swan, 1999), such organizational reengineering is often included in ERP projects – either before, or in parallel with, the software configuration. In some cases, the reengineering of the organization is intended to fit the organizational processes to those inscribed in the ERP software package, either as a way of transferring 'best practice' or because it is considered much more complex and risky to change the software package to fit the particular way a company organizes its processes (Kawalek and Wood-Harper, 2002). In other cases, reengineering is seen as necessary to work out improvements in the processes of the organization before these are fixed through an inflexible technical infrastructure (Besson and Rowe, 2001).

The third significant issue concerns the extent to which ERP implementation allows for the search for novel technology-mediated organizational structures and practices. The question is whether the designed-in functionality of the technology leaves scope for working out new socio-technical arrangements, or takes organizations towards standard routes of arranging and performing work processes. Indeed, in many cases, this is the reason organizations embark on ERP projects: they expect to be driven to emulate ways of organizing and acting that are generally considered efficient, effective and 'modern'. This shift of attention to ERP implementation in the 1990s actually marked a turning in the IS literature from the discourse that emphasized innovative thinking for purposes of competitive advantage – the 'strategic IS' literature – to a discourse that sought the tidying up of core business processes for purposes of efficiency gains, albeit with a radical rhetoric such as BPR.

Thus, the hallmarks of ERP innovation are the adjustment of organizational structures and processes to prevalent norms, and the following of prevailing standards of organizing business firms by making use of technologies that are proven robust market leaders in a worldwide software market. Moreover, ERP technology infrastructure is understood to be rigid once it is put into organizational practice. It binds and controls organizational actors to comply with its functionality. There may be some leeway of manoeuvring and manipulation by the users to accommodate their own meanings and tasks within the complex software system. Overall, however, the controlling, restrictive, binding character of this kind of system is highlighted by both the message from the vendors and consultants through which ERP systems are diffused and the empirical evidence from research studies.

8.3.3 Intranets and Internet-Based Systems

The way intranets and Internet-based information systems are implemented and associated with organizational change has attracted relatively little attention. The few accounts of the activities involved in setting up and using these technologies suggest an unstructured and largely improvisational process of prototyping (Beynon-Davies et al., 2000; Damsgaard and Scheepers, 2000). No normative frameworks have been proposed for the methodical steering towards specific structures and practices, despite the general association of such technologies with radically new organizational forms, such as the 'virtual' organization. The deployment of network infrastructures can be contrasted to the rigid implementation of ERP systems in terms of the scope provided for diversity and local creativity.

This contrast is shown in Ciborra's (1996a; 2000) studies of the efforts pursued in a large pharmaceutical company, Hoffmann–La Roche, to develop an information infrastructure for its 'Strategic Marketing' function. This started with the development of MedNet, a corporate network with a portfolio of common applications to support the consulting of literature and access to data on clinical trials, as well as to enable office automation. MedNet was a centralized effort intended to integrate, standardize and unify the marketing activities of the various national affiliates of the company, which enjoyed a great deal of autonomy due to the nature of the nationally regulated pharmaceutical industry. The implementation of MedNet was discontinued, according to Ciborra's (1996a) analysis, partly because its aim of overcoming the autonomous national feuds through global networking met with resistance, and partly because of its high cost and technical competence requirements.

The second phase of Hoffmann–La Roche's efforts to create an IS infrastructure in Strategic Marketing abandoned MedNet's objective of unifying and standardizing, and allowed the formation of a networking infrastructure through decentralization, autonomy and loose coupling. Ciborra (2000) describes the emergence in this phase of a multiplicity of Web sites for internal and external communication in the company's headquarters and affiliates. Multiple initiatives with little coordination created network systems with different technical features, content and functionality. Interestingly, despite the significance of confidentiality in the pharmaceutical industry, the picture presented in Ciborra's analysis is one of highly improvisational innovation in a very decentralized, loosely-coupled knowledge community that spans organizational boundaries and involves outside stakeholders, such as the scientific community, the public, national health services and medical doctors.

Ciborra's studies suggest that the implementation of intranets and Internet-based information systems shifts attention away from data processing to issues of networking and information content. The matter of central concern becomes neither the design of technology per se nor the design of organizational practice, but the fostering and harnessing of the communication potential and the information content. Key issues include the design of information content, the policy of access to external and internal information sources, the mechanisms of safeguarding the integrity of information and transactions, and the management of the dynamics of networking and information communication.

8.3.4 Inter-organizational Systems

Inter-organizational information systems, such as industrial networks and B2B and B2C e-commerce systems, combine and extend the functionality of the three types of systems outlined above. The implementation and operation of such systems are often overseen by a dominant company (Sydow, 1992). The new IS may be an extension of the dominant company's ERP, in which case the implementation of the technical system is methodically organized, aiming at establishing a long-lasting basis for standardized inter-organizational series of activities – and thus often accompanied by the redesign of cross-organizational processes of business activities (Kumar and Christiaanse, 1999).

Sometimes, the development of inter-organizational information systems involves more radical organizational interventions, such as the development of intermediary organizations charged with the tasks of operating and managing the new technical infrastructure as a common, collaborative resource for the competing firms of an industry (Knights et al., 1997a). Inter-organizational information systems, therefore, also involve combinations of technology configurations and organizational interventions, which may be organized either in strict formal technical mode, or as open-ended processes of the formation of new patterns of interactions.

8.4 THE NEW SOCIO-TECHNICAL DISCOURSE ON IS INNOVATION

The concerns of IS innovation seen as designing systems aimed at fitting technology to an organizational context continue to be relevant in the types of innovation discussed in the previous section, particularly in ERP projects. However, these more recent types of IS innovation established a new discourse that became prevalent in the IS field. In this new discourse, IS innovation is explicitly linked with the organizational search for characteristics suitable for the changing broad socio-economic context and the harnessing of networking capabilities for the creation and exploitation of information content.

As already mentioned, the association of the development of technology-based information systems with organizational change is not new. The accounts of even the earliest computer applications in organizations suggest that technology innovation was understood to bring about business benefits by enabling new organizational processes, rather than by automating existing ones (Land, 1999). Enid Mumford's efforts to associate technical design with the redesign of work arrangements (Mumford and Weir, 1979) was central in the socio-technical design tradition of IS development of the 1970s and early 1980s. Similarly, issues of information content and communication were always part of the pragmatic and theoretical concerns of the IS field (Ackoff, 1967; Stamper, 1973). However, on the whole, IS research and practice paid lip service to organizational questions, and it was only in the 1990s that IS innovation became directly linked with the search for new organizational forms that preoccupied business and management practitioners and scholars (Drucker, 1988; Applegate, 1994; Ciborra, 1996b; DeSanctis and Fulk, 1999).

During the 1990s, IS research continued to address itself to vocational considerations of business management and the IS consultancy industry, directing a great deal of effort towards predicting trends and suggesting appropriate courses of technical and managerial activities (Davenport and Short, 1990; Scott Morton, 1991; Hammer and Champy, 1993; Galliers and Baets, 1998). But, in that period a stream of publications marked the emergence of theoretical perspectives that examine the IS and organizational change relationship through conceptual lenses drawn from the social sciences (Baskerville et al., 1994; Orlikowski et al., 1996; Bloomfield et al., 1997a; DeSanctis and Fulk, 1999). In effect, IS research became engaged in the broader theoretical debate about the relationship of technology and society, the character of ICT-mediated socio-economic forms and the role of IS innovation in contemporary globalization trends.

8.4.1 Structuration and Social Constructionist Theories

Two major theoretical influences have dominated debates on the IS and organizational change relationship: structuration theory (Giddens, 1984) and the social constructionist theories of the sociology of technology (Law, 1991; Bijker and Law, 1992; Grint and Woolgar, 1997)[3]. There are ongoing debates on the merits of the analytical perspectives each of these affords to IS research and the particular theoretical arguments derived from each theory (Walsham, 1997; Jones, 1999; Monteiro, 2000; Orlikowski, 2000). Nevertheless, structurational and social-constructionist analyses have together contributed to the elaboration of an understanding of IS innovation as a socio-technical process that implicates three constitutive elements (Barley, 1986; Orlikowski, 1992; Walsham, 1993; Orlikowski, 1996; Orlikowski, 2000):

1. organizational structure and culture (i.e., the institutionalized ways of going about the tasks organizational actors perform);
2. organizational actors' initiatives to appropriate the technical capabilities within the enactment of their jobs (i.e., the agency of the organizational participants); and
3. structural/material properties of the technologies used in the innovation process (i.e., the technical features that enable certain organizational conditions while constraining others).

Thus, new IS innovation theory attaches significance to the material properties of ICTs, for example in debates on the differences of communication afforded by alternative media, such as conversation in co-presence, conversation via telephone, or e-mail (Lee, 1994; Markus, 1994). But it avoids forming cause-and-effect relationships between technology properties and organizational outcomes. Instead, the development and use of ICT artefacts are understood to be embedded in particular social contexts. ICT-based information systems are formed by the cultural setting of a social environment, while at the same time they contribute to its change by means of their technical properties (Mitev, 1996; Monteiro and Hanseth, 1996; Walsham, 1997; Monteiro, 2000). Consequently, research oriented to exploring this dynamic simultaneous shaping of technologies and re-shaping of social context suggests the following picture of the innovation process.

IS innovation results from the mobilization of networks of actors, either in formal design activities or in informal adjustments of existing artefacts. Furthermore, it involves the appropriation of artefacts in enactments of work practices, that is, in routine organizational roles and in the capacities of understanding and acting when confronted by unexpected events. Action for the shaping of technology artefacts and the transformation of work practices encompasses much more than the technical/rational activities of formal IS projects. In fact, the central effort of the IS field to develop methods for steering the innovation process towards predetermined goals was intensely critiqued by several authors, who pointed out the situated and emergent nature of action in organizations in general, and more specifically of action comprising innovation (Suchman, 1987; Orlikowski, 1996; Ciborra, 1999; Ciborra and Associates, 2000).

8.4.2 The Significance of Improvisation

Ciborra (1999) uses the notion of improvisation to highlight those decisions and actions that are not formally/rationally pre-planned, but that are taken spontaneously – on the spur of the moment – just as an actor experiences the situation confronting the course of an innovation. In this sense, improvisation is not 'irrational', but relies on an actor's past experience and ability to comprehend the situation and deploy spontaneously relevant competent behaviour. From such a phenomenological perspective, Ciborra argues that the general models for rationally-calculated action and methodical organization of systems development rarely works. Instead, IS innovation involves a great deal of spontaneous action and idiosyncratic decisions. Rather than resulting from preconceived views of successful outcomes, managerial control activities and methodical tasks of supervision, such innovation is inherently a process that addresses the unknown and requires the ability to respond to unforeseen circumstances. It also needs empathy and caring for the technologies that are put together to form new information systems.

Moreover, action in organizations has political dimensions. For example, Knights et al. (1997b) discuss IT strategy in organizations as a political process. They see the 'discourse on strategy' – the ideas and methodical ways according to which IS innovation is an activity that should be pre-planned and systematically performed – as a mechanism for managers to secure discipline and compliance to their own authority. In their words: 'IT-strategy is involved in the constitution of what is meaningful, becomes part of the internal self-discipline of subjects, provides a sense of security and confidence, and demonstrates managerial competence internally and externally' (Knights et al., 1997b: 29). This view reverses the common logic: that the formulation of an IT strategy is the rational way to find out what is needed, and to plan for executing what needs to be done to meet that requirement. It suggests IT strategy does not just capture and model what is required for an unambiguously understood area of business but, in contributing to a particular way of understanding what an information systems should be, the strategy contributes to 'the constitution of what is meaningful'. Political behaviour is not an incidental dysfunctional behaviour, but a fundamental mechanism for holding the organization together as a social entity. In particular, it is a mechanism through which managers secure the legitimacy of their authority inside and outside the organization.

8.4.3 Actor Network Theory

Several authors have used actor network theory (ANT) to discuss IS innovation as a process involving the mobilization of actors with diverse interests towards a particular powerful actor's view of what the problem is, and what solution should be pursued (see, for example, Mitev, 1996; Bloomfield et al., 1997b; Hanseth and Monteiro, 1998). Whether a process of innovation actually gets launched, the extent to which it is pursued and whether it produces the outcomes intended by the actors who conceived it, depends on the power relations of this network of actors and on the influence of other networks that might erode or support it. A particular aspect of ANT is that technologies themselves are seen as powerful actors that may be mobilized to enforce a network.

An example suffices to demonstrate the difference of such thinking from the traditional technical rationality. ANT's socio-technical perspective sees a systems development methodology, or a set of automated tools to support systems development activities, as an actor that is mobilized by the analysts in a systems development project to strengthen their role and assist in leading the project towards what the analysts consider is important: typically, a reliable and efficient technology-based information system. This view does not take for granted either the value of the goal of the innovation process or the role of the technologies involved. Both are contestable. No assumption is made about the de facto desirability of a reliable and efficient system. And rather than being neutral instruments, technical artefacts – such as the automated tools used by systems analysts – take part in the innovation process as allies in networks of interests and power; they are constructed to carry inscriptions of organizational practice that privilege certain actors and constrain others.

The new socio-technical perspective sheds a different light on the issue of innovation diffusion too. As discussed by Madon in Chapter 4, IS innovation is always shaped within specific, historically-formed social circumstances. Technology artefacts and practice extracted from the particular organizational setting within which they were designed or emerged may take the form of products or 'best practice' guidelines and methods, thus being transferable – or diffusible – to other settings. Yet, such 'immutable mobiles'[4] are not just adopted and then fitted into the information systems of another social context. They trigger a situated process for the construction of locally-meaningful technical tools and practices, thus involving the negotiation of their meaning and role by local participants. Such a situated process re-shapes the transferred artefacts and methods and de-scribes (reconstructs) their original social inscriptions, thus forming new socio-technical networks – which is the essence of IS innovation. In other words, IS innovation is the perpetual re-making of ICT artefacts and organizational practice in specific social settings.

8.5 CONCLUSIONS

The theoretical perspectives of IS innovation outlined in this chapter do not result in knowledge that informs action in a direct and instrumental way, but they do identify the ingredients of successful IS innovation. Indeed, they reveal the significance of actions other than technical/rational in the course of innovation, such as sense-making of a situation in hand, improvisation, power alliances, mimetic behaviour, or unquestioned performance of taken-for-granted tasks rather than strategic analyses, market-oriented decision processes and engineering activities.

For example, while structurational analysis points out the significance of agency in exploiting the potential afforded by particular technologies, it deliberately avoids a functionalistic orientation towards reaching conclusions as to what action might contribute to desirable innovation (Orlikowski, 1996). No a priori assumption of a universally desirable innovation process is made. Innovation results from the enactment of roles that are meaningful and possible within the historically-shaped circumstances of an organizational context. This does not deny the utility of technical/rational activities, such as the processes of strategy making, or the use of techniques for carrying out engineering tasks – but it associates an organization's capacity to enact such activities with the social conditions of its existence. Similarly, ANT's view of innovation as a process of 'translation' of a particular actor's interests and perceptions into a durable heterogeneous network of humans and technology artefacts does not tell us what kind of new socio-technical networks are desirable, or what action brings about such networks successfully.

Current research in the socio-technical perspective of IS innovation tends to combine interpretivist and critical approaches. Both recognize that the instrumental orientation which has historically dominated IS research has severe limitations. In many situations, it is not clear what the problems or the necessary 'improvements' are, and possible solutions and improvements are not a matter to be decided and executed on the basis of technical expertise alone. According to the interpretivist approach, what the problem is, what might be an improvement of a situation and how an improvement may be worked out are subject to the interpretation of various participants and observers. Typically, analysts and managers should expect to find multiple interpretations of a situation, and they should be aware that their views are also interpretations according to their professional knowledge and personal life experience. Thus, at best, they can act as facilitators for organizational change and processes of IS innovation, but cannot control the decisions and actions involved. A good example of this perspective is the role Checkland's (1981) 'soft systems' approach assigns to professional analysts.

Critical approaches, on the other hand, challenge the alleged facilitator's role of experts. Technology experts and management professionals, involved in an inherently political organizational context, have their own interests (Bloomfield and Danieli, 1995: 23-46; Avgerou, 2002). Negative as this may sound, such theoretical perspectives are very important – not only because they contribute to avoiding mistakes by over-reliance on the ability of professionals to be in control of innovations, but also because they build the analytical ability to see more fundamentally what IS innovation in organizations means within modern society.

Direct consequences for professional practice arise from the shifting of the theoretical perspective of innovation from analysing the relative merits of methodical technical/rational activities for the construction of artefacts and the design of organizational practice to studying the situated action through which technical artefacts and organizational practice are shaped. This shift positions conscious design activities in a broader context, where technological capabilities are interpreted and appropriated by actors in the organization enacting their roles.

From such a broader perspective, attention to improve planned and methodical action (either in carrying out the IS innovation process itself, or in creating effective organizations through it) does not necessarily have positive effects. Method-driven innovation may frustrate actors' sense-making, improvisational and creative capabilities; planned courses of action towards predetermined technology-mediated practice are often intolerant to slow and uncertain processes of cultivating the capacity to accommodate the newcomer technologies in the social fabric of the organization; and information systems that seek to control the performance of an organization may deprive it of its vital capacity to cope with the messy and complex circumstances of contemporary organizing.

Seen in relation to the general socio-economic theories of technology innovation, the research literature I draw on for this chapter re-enforces the understanding that IS innovation is not just diffused from the setting within which ICT artefacts first emerged to other settings by means of the competent execution of technical activities, such as the making of 'correct' estimates of the competitiveness of a business firm, the acquiring of software with advanced functionality and the redesigning of business processes. The literature puts forward a view of IS innovation as a process of purposive action situated within organizations, or alliances of organizations, the outcomes of which depend on the negotiations of values, meanings and competencies of actors in the organizational setting concerned.

This has implications for development policy. In much of the economic development literature, ICT is seen instrumentally as a factor for improving economic performance and major national and international institutions have been engaged in promoting 'technology transfer', dedicating resources to the diffusion of computers, the Internet, etc. The socio-theoretical perspective put forward here does not deny that these technologies are rightly considered as potential enablers of developmental benefits. But the actual economic value achieved (or not) from their acquisition, results from socio-technical processes of innovation situated in the organizations of the countries importing the technologies and/or the new management ideas. Certain capabilities for such an innovation process may be created by appropriate policy interventions. Nevertheless, the socio-technical analysis suggests that the innovation process depends on the situated actors' capacity to make sense of the value of the new artefacts and organizing techniques, and to accommodate them in their historically-formed enactments. The risk – all too visible in the widespread 'failures' of IS projects in developing countries – is that technology-diffusion policies which push specific technologies as 'drivers' to desirable 'impacts' or business 'best practice' distort local economic activities and frustrate, rather than enable, improved performance.

REFERENCES

Ackoff, R.L. (1967), 'Management Misinformation Systems', *Management Science*, **14** (4), 147–56.

Applegate, L.M. (1994), 'Managing in an Information Age: Transforming the Organization for the 1990s', in R. Baskerville, S. Smithson, O. Ngwenyama and J.I. DeGross (eds), *Transforming Organizations with Information Technology*, Amsterdam: North-Holland, 15–94.

Avgerou, C. (2000), 'IT and Organizational Change: An Institutionalist Perspective', *Information Technology and People*, **13** (4), 234–62.

Avgerou, C. (2002), *Information Systems and Global Diversity*, Oxford: Oxford University Press.

Avison, D.E. and G. Fitzgerald (1996), *Information Systems Development: Methodologies, Techniques and Tools*, Oxford: Blackwell.

Bancroft, N., H. Seip and A. Sprengel (1998), *Implementing SAP R/3*, Greenwich, UK: Manning Publications.

Bannon, L.J. (1998), 'Computer Supported Collaborative Working: Challenging Perspectives on Work and Technology', in R.D. Galliers and W.R.J. Baets (eds), *Information Technology and Organizational Transformation: Innovation for the 21st Century Organization*, Chichester, UK: Wiley, 37–63.

Barley, S.R. (1986), 'Technology as an Occasion for Structuring: Evidence from Observations of CT Scanners and the Social Order of Radiology Departments', *Administrative Science Quarterly*, **31** (1), 78–108.

Baskerville, R., S. Smithson, O. Ngwenyama and J.I. DeGross (1994) (eds), *Transforming Organizations with Information Technology*, Amsterdam: North-Holland.

Besson, P. and F. Rowe (2001), 'ERP Project Dynamics and Enacted Dialogue: Perceived Understanding, Perceived Leeway, and the Nature of Task-related Conflicts', *The Data Base for Advances in Information Systems*, **32** (4), 47–66.

Beynon-Davies, P., H. Mackay and D. Tudhope (2000), '"It's Lots of Bits of Paper and Ticks and Post-it Notes and Things...": A Case Study of a Rapid Application Development Project', *Information Systems Journal*, **10** (3), 195–216.

Bijker, W.E. and J. Law, (1992) (eds), *Shaping Technology/Building Society*, Cambridge, MA: MIT Press.

Bloomfield, B.P. and A. Danieli (1995), 'The Role of Management Consultants in the Development of Information Technology: The Indissoluble Nature of Socio-political and Technical Skills', *Journal of Management Studies*, **32** (1), 23–46.

Bloomfield, B.P., R. Coombs, D. Knights and D. Littler (1997a) (eds), *Information Technology and Organizations: Strategies, Networks, and Integration*, Oxford: Oxford University Press.

Bloomfield, B.P., R. Coombs, J. Owen and P. Taylor (1997b), 'Doctors as Managers: Constructing Systems and Users in the National Health Service', in B.P. Bloomfield, R. Coombs, D. Knights and D. Littler (eds), *Information Technology and Organizations: Strategies, Networks, and Integration*, Oxford: Oxford University Press, 112–34.

Checkland, P. (1981), *Systems Thinking Systems Practice*, Chichester, UK: Wiley.

Ciborra, C.U. (1996a), 'Mission Critical: The Use of Groupware in a Pharmaceutical Company', in C.U. Ciborra (ed.), *Groupware and Teamwork: Invisible Aid or Technical Hindrance?*, Chichester, UK: Wiley.

Ciborra, C. (1996b), 'The Platform Organization: Recombining Strategies, Structures, and Surprises', *Organization Science*, **7** (2), 103–18.

Ciborra, C.U. (1999), 'A Theory of Information Systems Based on Improvisation', in W.L. Currie and B. Galliers (eds), *Rethinking Management Information Systems*, Oxford: Oxford University Press, 136–55.

Ciborra, C.U. (2000), 'From Alignment to Loose Coupling: From MedNet to www.roche.com', in C.U. Ciborra and Associates (eds), *From Control to Drift*, Oxford: Oxford University Press, 193–211.

Ciborra, C.U. and Associates (2000) (eds), *From Control to Drift*, Oxford: Oxford University Press.

Currie, W.L. and B. Galliers (1999) (eds), *Rethinking Management Information Systems: An Interdisciplinary Perspective*, Oxford: Oxford University Press.

Damsgaard, J. and R. Scheepers (2000), 'Managing the Crises in Intranet Implementation: A Stage Model', *Information Systems Journal*, **10** (2), 131–49.

Davenport, T.H. and J.E. Short (1990), 'The New Industrial Engineering: Information Technology and Business Process Redesign', *Sloan Management Review*, **31** (Summer), 11–27.

De Sanctis, G. and J. Fulk (1999) (eds), *Shaping Organization Form,* Thousand Oaks, CA: Sage.

Drucker, P. (1988), 'The Coming of the New Organization', *Harvard Business Review*, **66** (January–February), 45–53.

Galliers, R.D. and W.R.J. Baets (1998), *Information Technology and Organizational Transformation: Innovation for the 21st Century Organization*, Chichester, UK: Wiley.

Galliers, B. and J. Swan (1999), 'Information Systems and Strategic Change: A Critical Review of Business Process Re-engineering', in W.L. Currie and B. Galliers (eds), *Rethinking Management Information Systems,* Oxford: Oxford University Press, 361–87.

Giddens, A. (1984), *The Constitution of Society: Outline of the Theory of Structuration*, Cambridge: Polity Press.

Grint, K. and S. Woolgar (1997), *The Machine at Work: Technology, Work and Organization*, Cambridge: Polity Press.

Hammer, M. and J. Champy (1993), *Reengineering the Corporation, A Manifesto for Business Revolution*, London: Nicholas Brealey.

Hanseth, O. and E. Monteiro (1998), 'Changing Irreversible Networks', in *Proceedings of the 6th European Conference on Information Systems (ECIS)*, Aix en Provence.

Howcroft, D. and D. Truex (2001), 'Editorial, Special Issue on Critical Analysis of ERP Systems: The Macro Level', *The Data Base for Advances in Information Systems*, **32** (4), 14–8.

Introna, L.D. (1997), *Management, Information and Power: A Narrative of the Involved Manager*, Basingstoke, UK: Macmillan.

Jones, M. (1994), 'Don't Emancipate, Exaggerate: Rhetoric, Reality and Reengineering', in R. Baskerville, S. Smithson, O. Ngwenyama and J.I. DeGross (eds), *Transforming Organizations with Information Technology*, Amsterdam: North-Holland, 357–78.

Jones, M. (1999), 'Structuration Theory', in W.L. Currie and B. Galliers (eds), *Rethinking Management Information Systems*, Oxford: Oxford University Press, 103–35.

Kallinikos, J. (1996), *Technology and Society: Interdisciplinary Studies in Formal Organizations*, Munich: Accedo.

Kawalek, P. and A.T. Wood-Harper (2002), 'The Finding of Thorns: User Participation in Enterprise System Implementation', *The Data Base for Advances in Information Systems*, **33** (1), 13–22.

Knights, D., F. Murray and H. Willmott (1997a), 'Networking as Knowledge Work: A Study of Strategic Inter-organizational Development in the Financial Services Industry', in B.P. Bloomfield, R. Coombs, D. Knights and D. Littler (eds), *Information Technology and Organizations*, Oxford: Oxford University Press, 138–59.

Knights, D., F. Noble and H. Willmott (1997b), '"We Should be Total Slaves to the Business": Aligning Information Technology Strategy – Issues and Evidence', in

B.P. Bloomfield, R. Coombs, D. Knights and D. Littler (eds), *Information Technology and Organizations*, Oxford: Oxford University Press, 13–35.

Kumar, K. and E. Christiaanse (1999), 'From Static Supply Chains to Dynamic Supply Webs: Principles for Radical Redesign in the Age of Information', *Proceedings of the 18th International Conference on Information Systems (ICIS)*, Atlanta, GA: Association for Information Systems (AIS).

Kyng, M. and L. Mathiassen (1982), 'Systems Development and Trade Union Activities', in Bjørn-Andersen N. (ed.), *Information Society, for Richer, for Poorer,* Amsterdam: North-Holland, 247–60.

Land, F.F. (1982), 'Adapting to Changing User Requirements', *Information and Management*, **5**, 59–75.

Land, F. (1999), 'A Historical Analysis of Implementing IS at J. Lyons', in W.L. Currie and B. Galliers (eds), *Rethinking Management Information Systems,* Oxford: Oxford University Press, 310–25.

Land, F.F. and R.A. Hirschheim (1983), 'Participative Systems Design: Rationale, Tools and Techniques', *Journal of Applied Systems Analysis*, **10**, 91–107.

Latour, B. (1987), *Science in Action*, Cambridge, MA: Harvard University Press.

Law, J. (1991) (ed.), *A Sociology of Monsters: Essays on Power, Technology and Domination*, London: Routledge.

Lea, M., T. O'Shea, and P. Fung (1999), 'Constructing the Networked Organization: Content and Context in the Development of Electronic Communications', in G. DeSanctis and J. Fulk (eds), *Shaping Organization Form: Communication, Connection, and Community*, Thousand Oaks, CA: Sage, 295–325.

Lee, A.S. (1994), 'Electronic Mail as a Medium for Rich Communication: An Empirical Investigation Using Hermeneutic Interpretation', *MIS Quarterly*, **18** (2), 143–57.

Lyytinen, K. (1987), 'A Taxonomic Perspective of Information Systems Development: Theoretical Constructs and Recommendations', in R.J. Boland, Jr. and R.A. Hirschheim (eds), *Critical Issues in Information Systems Research*, Chichester, UK: Wiley, 3–42.

Markus, M.L. (1994), 'Electronic Mail as a Medium of Managerial Choice', *Organization Science*, **5** (4), 502–27.

Markus, M.L. and C. Tanis (2000), 'The Enterprise Systems Experience – from Adoption to Success', in R.W. Zmud (ed.), *Framing the Domains of IT Research: Glimpsing the Future Through the Past,* Cincinnati, OH: Pinnaflex Educational Resources, 173–207.

Markus, M.L., S. Axline, D. Petrie, and C. Tanis (2000), 'Learning from Adopters' Experiences with ERP: Problems Encountered and Success Achieved', *Journal of Information Technology*, **15** (4), 245–65.

Mitev, N. (1996), 'Social, Organisational and Political Aspects of Information Systems Failure: the Computerised Reservation System at French Railways', in *Proceedings of 4th European Conference on Information Systems (ECIS)*, Lisbon.

Monteiro, E. (2000), 'Actor-Network Theory and Information Infrastructure', in C. Ciborra and Associates (eds), *From Control to Drift*, Oxford: Oxford University Press, 71–83.

Monteiro, E. and O. Hanseth (1996), 'Social Shaping of Information Infrastructure: On Being Specific About the Technology', in W. Orlikowski, G. Walsham, M.R. Jones and J.I. DeGross (eds), *Information Technology and Changes in Organizational Work*, London: Chapman & Hall, 325–43.

Mumford, E. and M. Weir (1979), *Computer Systems in Work Design: The ETHICS Method*, London: Associated Business Press.

Orlikowski, W.J. (1992), 'The Duality of Technology: Rethinking the Concept of Technology in Organizations', *Organization Science*, **3** (3), 398–427.

Orlikowski, W.J. (1996), 'Improvising Organizational Transformation Over Time: A Situated Change Perspective', *Information Systems Research*, **7** (1), 63–92.

Orlikowski, W.J. (2000), 'Using Technology and Constituting Structures: A Practice Lens for Studying Technology in Organizations', *Organization Science*, **11** (4), 404–28.

Orlikowski, W.J., G. Walsham, M.R. Jones and J.I. DeGross (1996) (eds), *Information Technology and Changes in Organizational Work*, London: Chapman & Hall.

Sachs, P. (1995), 'Transforming Work: Collaboration, Learning and Design', *Communications of the ACM*, **38** (9), 36–44.

Scott Morton, M.S. (1991), *The Corporation of the 1990's, Information Technology and Organizational Transformation*, Oxford: Oxford University Press.

Stamper, R.K. (1973), *Information in Business and Administrative Systems*, London: Batsford.

Suchman, L. (1987), *Plans and Situated Action*, Cambridge: Cambridge University Press.

Suchman, L. (1994), 'Working Relations of Technology Production and Use', *Computer Supported Cooperative Work*, **2**, 21–39.

Swanson, E.B. and C.M. Beath (1989), *Maintaining Information Systems in Organizations*, Chichester, UK: Wiley.

Sydow, J. (1992), 'On the Management of Strategic Networks', in H. Ernste and V. Meier. (eds), *Regional Development and Contemporary Industrial Response: Extending Flexible Specialization*, London: Belhaven Press,

Walsham, G. (1993), *Interpreting Information Systems in Organizations*, Chichester, UK: John Wiley.

Walsham, G. (1997), 'Actor-Network Theory and IS Research: Current Status and Future Prospects', in A.S. Lee, J. Liebenau and J. DeGross (eds), *Information Systems and Qualitative Research*, London: Chapman & Hall, 466–80.

Zuboff, S. (1988), *In the Age of the Smart Machine*, New York: Basic Books.

NOTES

1. Intranets are systems that use Internet technologies for internal communication and coordination in organizations. Typically, intranets are developed in large organizations with multiple sites and functional departments. By using Internet technologies (communications protocols and standards), intranets allow communication across 'proprietary' systems of the various departments of the organization, in the same way that the Internet at large allows communication across a variety of computer systems.
2. Other authors describe different phases, but indicate similar tasks. For example, Markus and Tanis (2000) describe three phases: building a case for an enterprise system (chartering); getting the system up and running in one or more organizational units (project); and the period from 'going live' until 'normal operations' are achieved (shakedown).
3. For other efforts in theorizing the relationship between IS and organizational change, see Zuboff (1988), Kallinikos (1996) and Introna (1997).
4. Immutable mobile is a term suggested by Latour (1987) to make the point that technology artefacts inscribe particular social relations and practices, thus constituting actors in their own right who subsequently circulate and take part in further efforts that shape socio-technical networks.

9. Information Systems and New Technologies: Taking Shape in Use

Tony Cornford

9.1 INTRODUCTION

The origins of the information systems field can be seen as arising from a fundamental concern with how new and unknown, or unproven, technologies are to be understood, evaluated, taken up and employed in productive activity within business and administrative organizations. The newness or novelty of such technologies, and their untested and ambiguous potential, has always been, implicitly, a central issue for people who work in the field. Discovering or imagining the character and significance of new technologies has been acknowledged as a part of IS work from the very earliest days as shown, for example, by Leavitt and Whistler's (1958) classic article 'Management in the 1980s'.

Despite this general acknowledgement and enthusiasm for new technologies, and for finding them a place within business processes and organizational structures, this newness – with its implications of some mystery, hidden rationales or uncertain outcomes, as well as of new opportunities and new solutions – has not been placed at the centre of concerns or fruitfully pursued within IS. Essentially, the means to deal with the new has been understood through a particular and limiting concept of design, a trimming of the new to fit the established in terms of business activities, organizational structures and human needs. From the most aggressive business process re-engineering to the most intimate and reflective socio-technical project, such design has been identified and promoted as the means to make new technologies useful, predictable, acceptable and sustainable.

In this chapter, however, we seek to look beyond design, certainly as conceived of in the traditional accounts of information systems development and embodied in established information systems practices and methodologies. Instead, we look to the domain of the use of technology in the world of users. It is perhaps ironic that despite a long tradition of concern for users, understood as a homogeneous group of difficult people who need to be brought into IS development work, there is far less of a tradition of study or concern for the uses they find for ICT. These users, or their representatives, are certainly understood as needing to be found a place in design – hence the traditional concern for, and recommendation of, participation (Land and Hirschheim, 1983). Nevertheless, this interest has not extended into any sustained concern with the uses that people and organizations find for technologies, and the way they understand and appropriate technology's potential (its 'affordances') as they interact with technologies over time. This aspect of the uses made of technologies within information systems in the context of operational life is explored in this chapter as an expression, and a working through, of the newness (and at times strangeness, opaqueness, rigidity and malleability) of technology.

9.2 A ROLE FOR THE NEW

9.2.1 Fleeing Forward Towards Technological Novelty

Boland (1999) characterizes the IS field in terms of its unwillingness to stand and reflect upon practice, and its casual exploitation of the new (or newer still) as an easy get out: 'When faced with a problem, we find ourselves instead "fleeing forward" in hopes that a new round of technology advances in processors, storage, transmission or display devices will eliminate the difficulty' (Boland, 1999: 239). He makes these comments in relation to the information systems research tradition, and in contrast to the stability he sees as offered for Accounting researchers by the long established and essentially unmoving representations of accounting practice around which research and debate in that field has developed, such as the balance sheet or income statement.

For Boland, the continual arrival of new and newer-still technologies has diverted the IS field from retaining a focus on, or even identifying, the equivalent timeless essentials. He sees the newness of new ICTs as essentially an ephemeral distraction from the primary significance of information systems as creating representations (boundary objects) that serve some organizational ends, or represent interventions with consequences. In this respect, Boland is arguing along a somewhat similar line to that taken in this chapter, and we can agree with him that information systems research has indeed 'a well established concern with the process of developing systems, but little evidence of reflecting upon the various kinds of representations our systems are employed to create' (ibid.: 239), though we would not say 'employed to create', reflecting as it does the traditional concept of prior design, but rather 'implicated in the creation of'.

However, Boland's account of the distracting attention paid to the newness of new technologies does need to be challenged, and here we wish to reshape his account of the essential unimportance of the new and newer yet. We argue that, in order to understand information systems, we must acknowledge that the new things that are on their way, to which we 'flee forward', are of real and substantial significance and should indeed be at the heart of information systems research and practice. The argument made here is that the IS field has not paid too much attention to the new, but too little. To make this assertion stand, we need to understand where this 'newness' is to be found. For Boland, it is in a new round of technology advances: 'a new processor, a new storage and retrieval system, or a new development methodology' (ibid.: 234) – seeing the new as the product of laboratories, research departments and a limited number of legitimated interest groups.

We could directly question this account of such advances in technology as amounting to no more than a distraction, and do so later in this chapter, on the grounds that new technologies – such as networks, client-server computing or packaged software from the market place – have indeed changed things in significant ways. But the main argument pursued here is that we need to shift forward our understanding of where the new is to be found, offering an account through the experience of people as they interact with such technologies, imbue them with their own new meanings and accommodate them in their working lives. The new is not then (just) defined or found in technology with different characteristics or performance figures, or in refined development (design) methodologies, but is found and manifested in the perception and working through of the mystery, hidden rationales or uncertain outcomes which come with a new technology. That is, the newness is in the experience of technology, not the thing itself. Boland's critique may then be well taken if we understand it as reflecting the paying of too much attention to fitting the new into the established and to trying to understand the new as solutions to extant problems, while paying too little attention to understanding the open and uncharted aspects that come into play when we start to use any new technology.

9.2.2 The Importance of Design to IS Professionals

During most of the period of computer use up to the present day, practitioners' concerns have indeed focused primarily on making a more or less given technology work to good effect in given situations of information handling, mediated through design. At any moment in time, these situations are understood as given in terms of available technologies and understandings of technologies, as well as of organizational needs. This 'given-ness' that constrains the understanding of the new can be characterized in a number of ways, for example as what Swanson and Ramiller (1997) from the macro and institutional perspective call organizing visions or Ciborra and Lanzarra (1994), from the contextual, introduce as formative contexts.

A far less sophisticated account was prevalent for perhaps the first 20 years of widespread IS development activity, through the 1960s and 1970s, and remains at the core of the field. This view was driven quite explicitly by an understanding that established ways of handling information and data, based on pre-computer procedures, were to be translated into a new technological manifestation of essentially the same processes, though often with a strong Tayloristic bias when envisioning the functional structure into which new information systems based on the technology would fit (Friedman and Cornford, 1989). Such a bias draws on a fundamental understanding of technology (or, as expressed later in this chapter, an interpretation of technology or a shared technological frame) as a machine for data processing with specific attributes of rule-following and accuracy, matched by economies of control, expertise and scale. The newness of technology is understood here essentially in terms of potential for efficiency, a very particular and focused technological determinism based on viewing computers as an exogenous factor within a supply-side production function. An example of such a concern today is seen in the continuing debate over the productivity paradox (Brynjolfsson, 1993), classically expressed in the comment attributed to the economist Robert Solow that 'computers are seen everywhere except in the productivity statistics' (Landauer 1996: xi).

The understanding outlined above is the heritage of the IS field. It brings with it the strong allegiance to design as a prior and necessary activity, and as the prime responsibility of suitably qualified professionals. Design is seen as necessary in order to marshal the potential (the newness) of new technology within a focused development effort, to shape it to organizational and social ends, and to provide the entrée for the skilled cadre of professionals with the knowledge and, more importantly, the legitimacy to act to shape technology to serve within an information system. Of course, how well this design work is done, what aspects of the organization and its environment it recognizes and reflects, and how 'professional' the practice really is, is a subject for debate, though not one we pursue here. The significance for this chapter is that such an area of design activity has been carved out and colonized as a means of controlling the new.

9.2.3 Use in the Context of the IS Life-cycle Model

The primary role for design in the IS field has been underpinned by the information systems life cycle, an engineering-based and linear account of how systems are developed and put to use (Friedman and Cornford, 1989; Avgerou and Cornford, 1998; Avgerou, Chapter 8). Key ideas that support this are the linked concepts of requirements extracted from the organizational milieu, of model building through (graphical) abstractions of boxes and arrows, and of phased transitions from analysis to design to a frozen realization in shaped technology and work practices, all within the broad model of unfreeze, change and refreeze introduced by Lewin (1951). A vast literature in academic and professional spheres has pursued this account, and it has formed the basis for not only practice but also for most of the research, education and training in the field. This is particularly true if we understand the concern with information systems strategy that emerged in the 1980s as essentially a similar account of planned change (design) in response to new technologies, predicated on prior analysis and design.

Although, as Avgerou argues in Chapter 8, packaged software and user-friendly systems have challenged the life-cycle model, it is still dominant in much IS practice. Within the life cycle, an information system *in use* is posed as a fairly unproblematic and uninteresting concept – unproblematic, that is, if the prior activity is done well and properly: by drawing on appropriate expertise, models and tools and being expressed and delivered essentially in technical forms. Setting a system into use (conventionally referred to as 'implementation') is certainly acknowledged as a risky time, and hence as requiring yet more careful analysis and planning. In the mainstream literature, this is most often addressed through a model of diffusion, implicitly based on a 'black boxed' system that is to be 'adopted' by a user community (Kwon and Zmud, 1987). The one persistent irritant which is acknowledge is in the notion of 'resistance' (Keen, 1981; Markus, 1983) and 'resistors' (or counter implementers). This has been influential in reinforcing the notion of implementation as a political process (Walsham, 1993), a battle between those in the know, with the power and in the right, and the ignorant and malicious others who at best just do not understand. But even so, once this potential ambush is avoided, or the resistors are co-opted or defeated, a new system is expected to function more or less as it was designed.

The traditional approach does acknowledge two activities that help to sustain a new system in use: evaluation and maintenance. Even so, evaluation is usually described in terms of its omission in practice and maintenance is the least regarded professional task within information systems practice. It is certainly understood that systems should be evaluated, but they are not, and perhaps for good reasons (Powell, 1992; Farbey et al., 1999). However, even if they are, evaluation tends to become an accounting for the effort and resources consumed in systems development, for the processes used and for the ability of a new system to meet the original design parameters. Seldom is evaluation linked directly to the ongoing activity of a system in use, the situation of its users or its productive and organizational potential (Avgerou, 1995). More cynically, we might say that evaluation is undertaken, if it is undertaken, for the apportionment of blame; in the popular aphorism of the final stages of project management: 'for the punishment of the innocent and the exoneration of the guilty'.

Maintenance is rather more interesting to consider, even if it is treated with hardly veiled contempt within IS practice. Organizations with existing information systems need to keep them working. In general, this is a non-trivial task and is acknowledged to absorb a high percentage of the total operating costs (Swanson and Beath, 1989). Maintenance may be required for essentially three reasons: because the delivered (implemented) system is judged wrong in terms of meeting actual requirements; because the delivered system lacks integrity internally; or because requirements have changed since the system was delivered. Thus, maintenance is often categorized in terms of corrective, perfective and adaptive dimensions (Swanson and Beath, 1989). But, as noted above, maintenance is usually seen as a just-about necessary evil, and certainly not the central concern of those who work as part of a system (users), information systems managers, information systems professionals or, even, researchers (Swanson and Dans, 2000). A system is expected to be essentially and coherently formed in design, based on the requirements identified, including perhaps some projection of future needs (Fitzgerald, 1990). Swanson and Dans (2000) suggest that the effort to maintain systems in organizations may be more positively appreciated if it is not understood as aimed at extending the useful life of a given system (given at the time of design), but rather that useful lives give cause to extend the effort in maintenance. This observation helps us to redirect our attention to ask what it is that constitutes a 'useful life' for a system, and to see maintenance as less an implicit judgement of the quality of the preceding design and more as a working through of an understanding of the significance of technologies, as they are used or consumed.

9.2.4 New Perspectives on the Relationship between Technology and Organization

The account based on the life cycle given above is, of course, backward looking as it seeks to find some enduring aspects of half-a-century's experience in dealing with the newness presented by rapidly-changing technologies. The fundamental character, as sketched above, has been one of dealing with the new by ignoring or restraining absolute novelty, challenge or potential and by taming, truncating or domesticating technologies through design and through development structures that seek to pre-form technologies to organizational needs. However, a significant change in understanding can be perceived more recently. We might say the new technology of the 1970s and 1980s (new then) was accommodated 'politely' within organizations in functional roles, by legitimated professionals and through their chosen medium of design. Since then, the shift to a process perspective, the pervasiveness of technology and the potential for interconnections have led to some revisions in understanding. Evidence for such a shift can be found, for example, in the explosion of interest in the 1980s in IS strategy, interpreted as a response to the appreciation that IT was here for good, had long-term and transformative consequences and could not be 'kept in its box' – see, for example, Earl's (1989) account of the 'DP era' vs the 'IT era' or the work of the Massachusetts Institute of Technology's *Management in the 1990s* programme (Scott Morton, 1991).

Thus, in the contemporary era we have seen the inward-looking, design-oriented model sketched above being overrun and distorted in many ways. Here, we note four key ideas that have contributed to this challenge, shifting the understanding of the relationship between technology and organization and reinforcing the need for changed perspectives on both development and use, and the approach we take to dealing with the new.

The first idea is the nature of the core technology itself. This was transformed in the ten-year period of the 1980s from being essentially centralized, separated and monolithic to becoming distributed, integrative and fragmentary – a paradoxical set of adjectives. This move was paralleled in the shift from the use of the abbreviation IT (information technology) to that of ICT (information and communication technology), where 'communication' emphasizing the passing of messages, rather than their processing.

This leads to the second key idea, of this technology as a (communications) infrastructure – exemplified by the Internet – with a role as an open channel for information flows, within and beyond the organization and into markets and communities. New conceptions such as 'e-commerce', 'e-government' or 'virtual organizations' then offer a very distinct and different account of the purpose of technology and where it leads, and how it acts as a mechanism of the market – equally relevant to the demand side as to the supply side – that also has significant consequences for processes of technology development and deployment. Open standards, network externalities (of manifest networks), lock-in and temporal and spatial relocation of activity become a main concern. In addition, as technology serves the social it becomes implicated in consumption as much as in production (Silverstone and Haddon, 1996; Dahlbom, 2000; Hanseth, 2000).

The third motivating idea we expose here, as seen from within the IS discipline, is the concept of knowledge, knowledge work and knowledge workers (Scarbrough, 1999). In IS, this move can be linked back to Zuboff's (1988) distinction made in the late 1980s: between uses of technology that *automate* as opposed to those that *informate*. Of course, knowledge work (as with managerial work) is at least as old as Taylorism, and probably a lot older. However, such ideas have provided a very specific set of challenges within the IS field. They imply a new set of relations around data: with a break in the simple formulation of information as processed data and a confusing expansion of the notion of a 'high end' user from a generic 'manager' with decisions to make to becoming knowledge workers with their own quirky needs, their own ideas and their own networks to align – and all this seen as being quite context-specific. This has produced, almost out of a conjurer's hat, a new set of people we know little about, but who need (we suppose) systems to support their work (or systems to take back control of their work?). Technologically, we can see this as being addressed (in both senses) through computer supported cooperative work, through intranets, and through a whole new array of (perhaps dubious) knowledge-management technologies (Ciborra, 1996; Alavi and Leidner, 2001; Avgerou, Chapter 8).

The final motivating idea introduced here is the establishment of a market in software services and packages that has transformed both the organizational and professional's experience of technology. The development of an information system was once predicated on a local (usually in-house) team activity to establish details and to program. Now, in many, perhaps most, cases the expectation is to buy in the market – to buy expertise, to buy consultancy, to buy services, to buy software and, in all this, to buy 'best practice' (Madon, Chapter 4; Avgerou, Chapter 8). The economic analysis of such build-or-buy decisions through transaction-cost economics has offered one of the most sustained theoretical strands to the information systems discipline (Ciborra, 1993). More fundamentally, this shift has recast the development activity, which is no longer about making something specific for some specific place and time and community. Rather, we now seek to accommodate something that is inherently general and has, at the outset at least, weak links to the local context of its use.

9.3 LIMITS OF DESIGN: A SYSTEM IN USE

9.3.1 Challenging the Primacy of Design

The discussion above indicates the challenge that has been made to the primacy of design in IS as a means of dealing with the new, and from there leads us to a concern over the lack of interest in, or sophistication of analysis of, technologies within information systems in use. In terms of the overall intent of this volume, this is a rather significant omission. When economists and other social scientists come to be interested in information technology and information systems because of their consequences within economic or social structures – such as organizations, administration and national economies – then they want to know what happens as technologies start to be used. However, as shown above, traditional models of information systems have a weak conception of the system in use, other than in some binary notion of 'success' and 'failure'. In this sense, the information systems field has provided only a prologue to technology in its construction-oriented account of a process of requirements determination, analysis, design and implementation – what has been described as a planned change approach (Orlikowski, 1996a). Any system, once developed and installed, is conceptualized in use essentially as a more-or-less efficient mechanism to achieve pre-established information handling activities.

Nevertheless, as information and communication technologies become ever more pervasive aspects of organizational domains, and expectations of the consequences of systems become more varied and complex, alternative models developed within the field have attempted to characterize and understand use. These models focus on the dynamics created around a technology finding a place within information handling activities, and the various consequences for organizations and individuals (and technologies too) as they participate in (and shape) information activities. A growing number of contemporary accounts of ICT acknowledge this character, though they do so in a variety of ways. The result is a new and fuzzy vocabulary of the ecology of information systems, including concepts of structuration, emergence and opportunism, improvisation, drifting, hospitality, appropriation and enactment (Orlikowski, 1996b; Orlikowski and Hofman, 1997; Ciborra, 1999; Ciborra and Associates, 2000).

9.3.2 The Social Shaping of Technology

The new(er) IS approaches often draw explicitly, or otherwise, on the social shaping of technology movement (SST) and various applications or derivatives of structuration theory. SST is concerned, in general, with the way organizational, political, economic and cultural factors influence the process of technological innovation and change. Such views include the systems approach (Hughes, 1986; Hughes, 1987), actor network theory (ANT) (Callon, 1986; Latour, 1987) and the social construction of technology (SCOT) (Bijker et al., 1987; Bijker and Law, 1992). Each approach provides us with interesting and challenging alternatives to any narrow technological determinism, by proposing that changes around technologies, and to technologies, are shaped by the conditions of their creation and use. Thus, there are always a number of possible outcomes in the way technologies are conceived, designed, used and understood (MacKenzie and Wajcman, 1985; Edge, 1995). By drawing on these ideas, IS researchers have found it possible to expose, in a variety of areas, the different processes of 'shaping' taking place, the different histories being told and drawn upon, and the different set of stakeholders paraded and prioritized. In this concept of shaping, and depending on the flavour of SST, we can find an account of how the new is created, perceived or made available within organizational and social contexts.

To achieve this, SCOT studies have introduced the concept of 'interpretive flexibility': the idea that technological artefacts are both culturally constructed and interpreted, with flexibility manifested in how people think of, or interpret, artefacts that surround them – as well as in how they design them (Pinch and Bijker, 1987). More controversially, SCOT approaches discuss how a technological artefact may become 'closed' or 'stabilized', where the problems relating to their introduction are resolved or appear, to the relevant social groups, to be solved. Stabilization can thus be seen as a process of creating the new artefact and making it available for wider diffusion, and the newness is constrained and directed to worked-out ends in this stability, if it is achieved.

Bijker (1995) explains that when the relevant social groups have invested so much in the artefact that its meaning becomes quite fixed, the artefact forms a part of a hardened network of practices, theories and social institutions. Actors with a low inclusion level in the technological frame – in the interactions around attribution of the meanings to a technical artefact or its constitution – then have little ability to change the artefact, so have to 'take it or leave it'. The degree of inclusion of an actor in a technological frame indicates to what extent the actor's interactions (thinking and behaviour) are structured through that frame. This process of stabilization depends on many factors, including economic and political interests as well as the ability of inventors or innovators to engage other parties in the production and promotion and the enrolment of relevant social groups.

Actor network theory develops some of the same ideas, but does so in a distinctive and, to some, provocative manner. In place of the stabilizing technological frame, the shared and pre-constraining understanding of what is new, ANT uses the notion of 'translation' to express how different actors may be coopted (enrolled) to support a particular innovation or project as part of a heterogeneous network. A network can also express technology in various forms and manifestations as an actor in a situation of use. In ANT terms, innovations (and an information system is seen here as an innovation) are developed and adopted (or not) through the building of networks of alliances between such human and non-human actors (Monteiro, 2000). The translation process includes any means of persuasion to get actors to believe that the goals of a particular project correspond to their own goals, or that they at least might serve them in some way.

What distinguishes ANT from other approaches is its outright rejection of any analytical distinction between technology and society. Rather, it proposes that both should be studied in the same way, through the same (or interchangeable) language, metaphors, etc. In order to be persuaded to play their parts in a network, actors (human or non-human) must be transformed. This means their attributes must be changed to fit other components of the network (Callon, 1986), with such transformations – individually and collectively – creating the new within, or as a manifestation of, the network. For the network to succeed or be sustained, such a transformation must become stronger. However, and in some contrast to ideas of stabilization as closure, this stability remains difficult to sustain because actors in the network have a tendency to revert to the old status, or to move on or defect to participate in new networks. Thus, it is fundamental to the ANT perspective that yet another account of the new, as a new or reshaped set of alliances, is always understood as possible.

Both ANT and social constructivism are criticized on a number of points, in particular for their relativism (Russell, 1986; Button, 1992; Winner, 1993). In this instance, relativism implies lack of an evaluative stance or any moral or political principles that might guide people in their judgement regarding the possibilities of new technologies – perhaps a key issue if information systems activity is seen as driven by some judgement or evaluation of the new. For example, SCOT does not indicate who decides (and how) which social groups are relevant or the way some groups with an interest in technology who are not powerful/visible enough to influence it may be excluded. In addition, SCOT's concept of stabilization of an artefact is disputed by those who point out that technologies are highly malleable, not only at the stage of conceptualizing and designing them but also during use (Cooper and Woolgar, 1993; Woolgar, 1996).

Drawing in part on such constructivist ideas and attempting to apply structuration theory (Giddens, 1984) to technological development and use, Orlikowski (1992) proposes a slightly different account in her notion of the duality of technology. She suggests that 'technology is created and changed by human action, yet it is also used by humans to accomplish some action' (ibid.: 405). In this way, she proposes that technology embodies some of the *rules and resources* constituting the structure of an organization; arguably, a neo-technological deterministic position. However, in a recent paper (Orlikowski, 2000), and in some contrast to her earlier writings, she suggests that it is misleading to accept the notion of technology itself embodying fixed characteristics, and thus leading to the perception of technology as an embodiment of structure.

The first reason she gives for this new view is the problematic nature of the presumption that technologies embody specific stable structures; as discussed above, technologies are not static and are continuously modified by their users and by other actors in their surrounding context. Second, she insists only technologies-in-use, when this use is *routinized and habitual*, can be seen as rules and resources (constituting structures), not the technology itself. That is, in order to understand the consequence of technology in specific or more general contexts, or to pursue any such consequence, it is necessary to consider the issues of habitual use. Developing such a line of argument, we then see that technologies are not to be understood as being predetermined in design, either as technologies or as organizationally-driven development projects, but rather as being enacted over time in the local and situated frame within which they are used. This position leads to a shift in the focus from the design and shaping of technology to its habitual and routinized use within specific contexts.

Finally, in contrast to Orlikowski's structurationally-influenced approach, with its concern for use with a routine and habitual character (which we might see as a resolution of the issues of the new), Ciborra (1999) provides an account of the arrival of technology within organizational life that is quite explicit in recognizing new technology as enigmatic and ambiguous, and likely to remain so. This sees the relationship between technology and the social being expressed through the cultural institution of hospitality. As Ciborra proposes it, hospitality is an institutional device to 'cut down on the time needed to merge cultures, and to integrate alien mindsets and costumes' (ibid.:161). While Ciborra makes explicit links to ANT and the work of Latour and Callon, and implicitly the symmetry of the human and the non-human, the notion of hospitality provides a distinct account of heterogeneous networks, with organization as the host and technology a guest. The essential metaphor pursued is of a careful and ritualized engagement between the two, and one that is based on both an obligation and an underlying reserve or mistrust. The relationship between host and guest is fragile and can breakdown, and always bears the risk of misunderstandings. Of course, the stranger is to be treated well, but the stranger's ambiguity is acknowledged and drives efforts to 'make the Other human as well ... to make a paramount symmetry between humans and non-humans' (ibid.: 168).

Our systems development methodologies and approaches, as discussed earlier in this chapter, can then be seen as the established rituals imposed by humans on the technology visitor. However, as Ciborra suggests in discussing a case of groupware in which senior managers revealed the degree of their surveillance, these rituals can breakdown and have powerful consequences when, he notes: 'despite the careful planning and design and the extensive training, new technology appears suddenly to the user as an ambivalent, threatening "stranger"' (ibid.: 166). Finally, and pursuing the idea to its conclusion, we must ask: Who is the host and who is the guest? Is hospitality a human cultural practice to serve the new technology, or is technology equally a host, and does its culture and rituals provide the framework within which the human is hosted, and 'systems development becomes the intriguing business for humans to find ways of being hosted by the technology' (ibid.: 169)?

9.4 CONCLUSIONS

The views and positions discussed above provide an enticing account of the new, and are gaining wider acceptance in the IS field as information systems are seen as more pervasive, autonomous, complex and interactive, with an orientation that shifts to encompass organizational and social realizations of life with, and through, technology. Work in the information systems discipline increasingly highlights not only the local and the situated meanings that ICT acquires during the design and implementation processes, but equally meanings gained through use and emergent features of deployed information systems, the improvisational acts that surround them and their planned and unexpected consequences.

The message conveyed in such work is that there is no single or simple model of the place for information technology within crafted and stabilized information systems through the route of design, and that outcomes are dependent on complex and interrelating socio-technical factors. These factors are drawn all the way from the micro context to the macro and socially construct technologies themselves, the systems or networks they are part of and, critically, the account of their significance and consequence that we circulate. In all this, different stakeholders may perceive and appropriate the newness of new technology in many different ways, seek different things from it, make local decisions as to what it is to become for them – and thus judge its essential affordances accordingly.

For those who study the field, and who try to make some linkage between IS and other social science disciplines, the implications of such work are significant, and perhaps profound. The first implication we draw here is that systems development, an organizational endeavour fundamentally concerned about dealing with and channelling the new, is uncontrollable; certainly, the illusion of control that the standard approaches offer is just that: an illusion. This suggests that to study information systems through the IS professionals and what they do – through design – is at best to miss the main story. These professionals, with their repertoires of techniques and competencies, are no more than the prelude. Indeed, they are being more and more pushed aside, with both their functional role and organizational legitimacy weakened. The story of information systems and the potential of new technologies, their newness, is far more in the hands of the community into which they are introduced and which will create its own meaning and role for technology. It is to them, and to technology itself once it enters the world of use, that we need to look to find the authentic account of the new. And along the way, as researcher or practitioner, we must work at cultivating an alertness and responsiveness to where, how and through whom the new is manifested.

REFERENCES

Alavi, M. and D.E. Leidner (2001), 'Review: Knowledge Management and Knowledge Management Systems: Conceptual Foundations and Research Issues', *MIS Quarterly*, **25** (1), 107–36.

Avgerou, C. (1995), 'Evaluating Information Systems by Consultation and Negotiation', *International Journal of Information Management*, **15** (6), 427–36.

Avgerou, C. and T. Cornford (1998), *Developing Information Systems: Concepts, Issues and Practice*, Basingstoke, UK: Macmillan.

Bijker, W.E. (1995), *Of Bicycles, Bakelites, and Bulbs: Towards a Theory of Sociotechnical Change*, Cambridge, MA: MIT Press.

Bijker, W.E., T.P. Hughes and T. Pinch (1987) (eds), *The Social Construction of Technological Systems: New Directions in the Sociology and History of Technology*, Cambridge, MA: MIT Press.

Bijker, W.E. and J. Law, (1992) (eds), *Shaping Technology/Building Society*, Cambridge, MA: The MIT Press.

Boland, R. (1999), 'Accounting as a Representational Craft: Lessons for Research in Information Systems', in W.L. Currie and B. Galliers (eds), *Rethinking Management Information Systems*, Oxford: Oxford University Press, 229–44.

Brynjolfsson, E. (1993), 'The Productivity Paradox of Information Technology', *Communications of the ACM*, **35** (December), 66–77.

Button, G. (1992), 'The Curious Case of the Vanishing Technology', in G. Button, *Technology in Working Order: Studies of Work, Interaction, and Technology*, London: Routledge.

Callon, M. (1986), 'Some Elements of a Sociology of Translation: Domestication of the Scallops and the Fishermen of St Brieuc Bay', in J. Law (ed.), *Power, Action and Belief*, London: Routledge & Kegan Paul, 196–233.

Ciborra, C.U. (1993), *Teams, Markets and Systems: Business Innovation and Information Technology*, Cambridge: Cambridge University Press.

Ciborra, C.U. (1996), *Groupware and Teamwork: Invisible Aid or Technical Hindrance?*, London: Wiley.

Ciborra, C. (1999), 'Hospitality and IT', in F. Ljungberg (ed.), *Informatics in the Next Millennium*, Lund, Sweden: Studentlitteratur, 161–76.

Ciborra, C.U. and Associates (2000) (eds), *From Control to Drift*, Oxford: Oxford University Press.

Ciborra, C.U. and G.F. Lanzarra (1994), 'Formative Contexts and Information Systems: Understanding the Dynamics of Innovation in Organizations', *Accounting, Management and Information Technology*, **2** (4), 61–86.

Cooper, G. and S. Woolgar (1993), *Software is Society made Malleable: The Importance of Conceptions of Audience in Software and Research Practice*, PICT Policy Research Paper No. 25, Swindon, UK: Economic and Social Research Council.

Dahlbom, B. (2000), 'Postface: From Infrastructure to Networking', in C.U. Ciborra and Associates, *From Control to Drift*, Oxford: Oxford University Press, 212–26.

Earl, M. (1989), *Management Strategies for Information Technology*, New York: Prentice Hall.

Edge, D. (1995), 'The Social Shaping of Technology', in N. Heap, R. Thomas, G. Einon, R. Manson and H. Mackay, *Information Technology and Society: A Reader*, London: Sage Publications.

Farbey, B., F. Land and D. Targett (1999), 'The Moving Staircase: Problems of Appraisal and Evaluation in a Turbulent Environment', *Information Technology & People*, **12** (3), 238–52.

Fitzgerald, G. (1990), 'Achieving Flexible Information Systems: The Case for Improved Analysis', *Journal of Information Technology*, **5** (1), 5–11.

Friedman, A.L. and D.C. Cornford (1989), *Computer Systems Development: History, Organization and Implementation*, Chichester, UK: Wiley.

Giddens, A. (1984), *The Constitution of Society: Outline of the Theory of Structuration*, Cambridge: Polity Press.

Hanseth, O. (2000), 'The Economics of Standards', in C.U. Ciborra and Associates, *From Control to Drift*, Oxford: Oxford University Press, 56–70.

Hughes, T.P. (1986), 'The Seamless Web: Technology, Science, etcetera, etcetera', *Social Studies of Science*, **16**, 281–92.

Hughes, T.P. (1987), 'The Evolution of Large Technological Systems', in W.E. Bijker, T.P. Hughes and T. Pinch (eds), *The Social Construction of Technological Systems: New Directions in the Sociology and History of Technology*, Cambridge, MA: MIT Press.

Keen, P. (1981), 'Information Systems and Organizational Change', *Communications of the ACM*, **24** (1), 24–33.

Kwon, T.H. and R.W. Zmud (1987), 'Unifying the Fragmented Models of Information Systems Implementation', in R.J. Boland and R.A. Hirschheim (eds), *Critical Issues in Information Systems Research*, Chichester, UK: Wiley, 227–52.

Land, F. and R. Hirschheim (1983), 'Participative Systems Design: Rationale, Tools and Techniques', *Journal of Applied Systems Analysis*, **10**, 91–107.

Landauer, T.K. (1996), *The Trouble with Computers*, Cambridge, MA: MIT Press.

Latour, B. (1987), *Science in Action*, Cambridge, MA: Harvard University Press.

Leavitt, H.J. and T.L. Whistler (1958), 'Management in the 1980s', *Harvard Business Review*, **36,** 41–8.

Lewin, K. (1951), *Field Theory in Social Science*, New York: Harper Row.

MacKenzie, D. and J. Wajcman (1985) (eds), *The Social Shaping of Technology: How the Refrigerator got its Hum*, Milton Keynes, UK: Open University Press.

Markus, M.L. (1983), 'Power, Politics and MIS Implementation', *Communications of the ACM*, **26** (6), 430–44.

Monteiro, E. (2000), 'Actor–Network Theory and Information Infrastructure', in C. Ciborra and Associates (eds), *From Control to Drift*, Oxford: Oxford University Press, 71–83.

Orlikowski, W.J. (1992), 'The Duality of Technology: Rethinking the Concept of Technology in Organizations', *Organization Science*, **3** (3), 398–427.

Orlikowski, W.J. (1996a), 'Improvising Organizational Transformation Over Time: A Situated Change Perspective', *Information Systems Research*, **7** (1), 63–92.

Orlikowski, W.J. (1996b), 'Evolving with Notes: Organizational Change around Groupware Technology', in C.U. Ciborra (ed.), *Groupware & Teamwork: Invisible Aid or Technical Hindrance*, Chichester, UK: Wiley, 23–60.

Orlikowski, W.J. (2000), 'Using Technology and Constituting Structures: A Practice Lens for Studying Technology in Organizations', *Organization Science*, **11** (4), 404–28.

Orlikowski, W.J. and J.D. Hofman (1997), 'An Improvisational Model for Change Management: The Case of Groupware Technologies', *Sloan Management Review*, **38** (2), 11–21.

Pinch, T.J. and W.E. Bijker (1987), 'The Social Construction of Facts and Artefacts: or How the Sociology of Science and the Sociology of Technology Might Benefit Each Other', in W.E. Bijker, T.P. Hughes and T.J. Pinch (eds), *The Social Construction of Technological Systems: New Directions in the Sociology and History of Technology*, Cambridge, MA: MIT Press.

Powell, P. (1992), 'Information Technology Evaluation: Is It Different?' *Journal of the OR Society*, **42** (1), 29–42.

Russell, S. (1986), 'The Social Construction of Artefacts: A Response to Pinch and Bijker', *Social Studies of Science*, **16**, 331–46.

Scarbrough, H. (1999), 'The Management of Knowledge Workers', in W.L. Currie and B. Galliers (eds), *Rethinking Management Information Systems*, Oxford: Oxford University Press, 474–98.

Scott Morton, M.S. (1991) (ed.), *Management in the 1990s: Information Technology and Organizational Transformation*, Oxford: Oxford University Press.

Silverstone, R. and L. Haddon (1996), 'Design and the Domestication of Information and Communication Technologies: Technical Change and Everyday Life', in R. Mansell and R. Silverstone, *Communications by Design*, Oxford: Oxford University Press, 44–74.

Swanson, E.B. and C.M. Beath (1989), *Maintaining Information Systems in Organizations*, Chichester, UK: Wiley.

Swanson, E.B. and E. Dans (2000), 'System Life Expectancy and the Maintenance Effort: Exploring their Equilibrium,' *MIS Quarterly*, **24** (2), 277–97.

Swanson, E.B. and N. Ramiller (1997), 'The Organizing Vision in Information Systems Innovation', *Organization Science*, **8** (5), 458–74.

Walsham, G. (1993), 'Implementation', in G. Walsham, *Interpreting Information Systems in Organisations*, Chichester, UK: Wiley, 210–31.

Winner, L. (1993), 'Upon Opening the Black Box of Technology and Finding it Empty: Social Constructivism and the Philosophy of Technology', *Science, Technology and Human Values*, **18** (3), 362–78.

Woolgar, S. (1996), 'Technologies as Cultural Artefacts', in W.H. Dutton (ed.), *Information and Communication Technologies: Visions and Realities,* Oxford: Oxford University Press.

Zuboff, S. (1988), *In the Age of the Smart Machine*, New York: Basic Books.

10. Perspectives on ICT Innovation and Organizational Context

Rodrigo Magalhães

10.1 INTRODUCTION

This chapter starts by showing how the three topics of interest to this book – business economics, ICT innovation and information systems governance – converge towards the issue of organizational context as a common denominator. It approaches these topics from the point of view of the information systems discipline, treating the expressions information systems and information technology (IS/IT) as being equivalent to the expressions information and communication technology (ICT). It then puts forward a fresh view on the formation process of organizational contexts, climates or cultures, as an aid to a better understanding of ICT innovation phenomena. This incursion into the fields of organization and organizational behaviour is useful because of the centrality of the concept of organizational context for the successful diffusion, absorption and integration of the capabilities afforded to organizations by all types by information and communication technologies.

The intention, however, is not to provide prescriptions or recipes on how to build a 'better' or more 'appropriate' organizational context to be applied to ICT innovation. Instead, the aim is to put forward a model that will help in understanding what it is we are talking about when using concepts such as the 'learning organization', 'organizational maturity', 'learning', 'knowledge' or 'culture'. Following Checkland and Holwell's (1998) advice, the chapter explains why the building up of a more solid stock of knowledge on organizations and organizational issues among the IS/IT community is an important step in achieving improved levels of ICT-related innovation.

10.2 ICT INNOVATION FROM THREE VANTAGE POINTS

The perspectives from which ICT innovation might be approached are manifold. For example, it might be seen from the point of view of the economic impact of applying ICT to firms. In turn, economic impact could be tackled from the perspective of effectiveness, as measured through savings in production, through improvements in the quality of products or services or through an enlargement in market share which reflects success in competitive positioning. All such measures of effectiveness can be approached from a macro or micro perspective. The macro viewpoint (for example, country-wide ICT-related savings) is not particularly useful if one's interest is in how to manage ICT innovation inside an organization. A far more useful point of view from which to address that interest is the micro economic perspective, which is the one explored in this chapter.

Approaching ICT innovation from a micro or business economics perspective also depends on the particular school of thought being followed within the discipline that is adopted. Business economics has various such schools, including the neo-classical, Bain-type industrial economics or Williamson's transaction cost theory (see Conner, 1991 for a historical review of five such schools). A recent theoretical approach to surface in business economics is known as 'resource based'. This emphasizes variables within the organizational context as being the key for analysing competitive behaviour among firms (Hansen and Wernerfelt, 1989; Nordhaug and Gronhaug, 1994; Spender, 1996). The resource-based approach has also had a strong impact in strategic management over the last decade (Prahalad and Hamel, 1990; Hamel and Prahalad, 1994). Hence, if ICT innovation is approached from the point of view of business economics, there is a likelihood that the approach taken will also emphasize organizational-context variables.

Interestingly, the same is also likely to happen when approaching ICT innovation from the process point of view. Questions that might be asked in this area of enquiry are, for example: 'What are the stages of the innovation process?', 'What is the content of innovation process stages?' or 'What is the relationship between ICT innovation and the organization's level of maturity?'. Answering these questions requires turning partly to the literature on technical innovation and partly to the information systems literature, which are the key fields of the study of ICT innovation as a process. The trend in these areas seems to entail a move from object-oriented to action-oriented approaches, where organizational context variables also prevail (Eveland, 1987; Roberts, 1987; Slappendel, 1996).

Finally, turning to the literature on IS/IT management containing the most useful advice for managing ICT-related innovation, one observes a similar turning towards organizational issues. Earl (1996) supports this point of view, when arguing that in the realm of IS/IT management the strategic dimension was prevalent in the 1980s, but this had changed to the organizational dimension in the 1990s. As a reflection of this change, Earl has suggested, for example, the introduction of the expression 'IS governance' to replace 'IS management'. Figure 10.1 represents the intellectual developments and turns we have just outlined.

Figure 10.1: Three perspectives for analysing ICT innovation

10.2.1 The Organizational Learning Turn in Business Economics

Theories of the firm have been advanced by economists since the writings of Coase (1937) in order to explain why firms exist, as well as the role of firms in the economy. Several theories have been put forward over the years, but the one which has had the greatest impact on the management literature recently has been the resource-based theory (Conner, 1991). This proposition changes the focus of attention from the external environment to the internal environment of the firm and the internal capacity of organizations to accumulate knowledge and skills. The resource-based approach has been developed primarily by researchers affiliated to the field of strategic management (Wernerfelt, 1984) rather than by those from industrial economics, as was the case with the earlier theories of competitive advantage (Porter, 1980; 1985). Due to the new emphasis on resources as the locus of advantage over the competition, the resource-based theory marks a significant turn in business economics towards organizational and behavioural issues.

The resource-based approach is not new. It can be traced back to Penrose ([1959] 1995) and to the notion that a firm grows because of the accumulated experience and knowledge from within the company – not the price mechanism from the market. However, the approach suggested by Penrose's writings in the late 1950s lay dormant until the 1980s, probably due to the period of fast economic growth that followed in the 1960s and part of the 1970s. The work on evolutionary economics by Nelson and Winter (1982) has provided a renewed foundation from which to develop the resource-based view. Nelson and Winter's views are centred on knowledge and competence as assets. In addition to endeavouring to find which knowledge states are amenable to description and quantification, they seek to identify which control variables can be used to alter these knowledge states. Finding such variables, however, has not been an easy task, as Winter (1987: 164) recognizes:

> The tradition of viewing the firm as a unitary actor with well-defined preferences has long been challenged by organization theorists and social scientists outside of economics, and by a few economists of heretical bent ... There are indeed some key issues in the strategic management of knowledge assets that relate to whether the firm can hold together in the face of conflict among the diverse interests of the participants (Winter, 1987: 164).

Resources can be considered by a widely-used technique for assessing the competitive potential of firms, the 'SWOT' analysis. This covers anything that might be considered as a strength (S) or a weakness (W) – the internal part of the analysis – as opposed to opportunities (O) and threats (T), which are the foci of the external part of the method. Resources are the tangible and intangible assets tied semi-permanently to the firm. They can be classified under three categories: physical capital resources, human capital resources and organizational capital resources (Barney, 1991). Physical capital resources include the physical technology, a firm's plant and equipment, its geographic location and its access to raw materials. Human capital resources include the knowledge of individual workers: their skills, experience and contacts. Organizational capital resources include the formal and informal organizational structures, as well as the relationships among individuals and groups within and outside the firm. Examples of resources include brand names, trade contacts, machinery, capital and in-house knowledge of technology.

The organizational issues that are behind the management of such resources have also surfaced as priority areas. Hamel and Prahalad (1994), who have developed the concept of 'core competencies', define a competence as 'a bundle of skills rather than a single discrete skill or technology' (ibid.: 202). They define core competencies as 'the sum of learning across individual skill sets and individual organizational units [which] is very unlikely to reside in its entirety in a single individual or small team' (ibid.: 203). Teece (quoted in Conner and Prahalad, 1996: 494) reinforces this view by saying that 'it is not only the bundle of resources that matter, but the mechanisms by which firms learn and accumulate new skills and capabilities, and the forces that limit the rate and direction of this process'.

Mahoney (1995) puts forward a 'resource-learning theory', as a synthesis of resource-based theory and of learning theories focusing on the development of human resources and of organizational capabilities in general. Mahoney explains that, on its own, resource-based analysis is not sufficient – as it is unable to articulate the management practices that enable firms to earn rents[1]. On the other hand, process-oriented models inspired by theories of organizational behaviour are also incomplete because they cannot make the distinction between what is strategically relevant from what is strategically irrelevant. The solution rests on the development of a theory emphasizing the managerial skills that, jointly with other resources, produce rents for the firm.

Managerial skills are part of a larger whole, known as 'organizational skills'. These skills are the sum total of the organization's ability to apply collectively the competencies held individually by organizational members. Competencies are sets of skills, which enable individuals to carry out their work. Individual skills, in turn, are the outcome not only of personal knowledge and experience, but also of values, attitudes and exhibited personal characteristics. The transformation of individual into organizational skills goes through a process known as 'competence interplay' (von Krogh and Roos, 1996). This is a crucial concept for an understanding of how collective competence or task-specific organizational knowledge is formed. Competence interplay can be thought of as the outcome of each discrete group-level event, which contributes towards the formation of group-level competence.

Competence interplay is also restricted by various other factors, namely 'hard' structural factors and 'soft' cultural aspects. The hard factors include the formal organizational structure – which makes the 'identification, formation and implementation of groups possible' (ibid.: 108) – and 'organizational slack'. Organizational slack refers to the pressures in the organization, either in terms of time or financial resources, which also have an effect on the level of achieved effectiveness in competence application. Among the cultural factors are the leadership style and the organizational climates, which are crucial factors in the formation of a collective 'mind-set' regarding, for example, activities involving cooperation and collaboration in the organization, such as information sharing.

This view is shared by various authors who defend the idea that the organization's cultural factors are also part of the resources that create competitive differentiation (Barney, 1986; Fiol, 1991; Bartlett and Ghoshal, 1993; 1994). Cultural factors are an important part of the organization's context, through the strong influence they exert on the level of effectiveness in applying competence at the organizational level. Cultural factors limit or enhance the overall capacity for the organization to apply effectively its overall stock of competencies.

The resource-based approach has been applied to IS/IT strategy and management by Mata et al. (1995). They have analysed four types of IS/IT attributes in relation to their potential for creating competitive advantage: capital requirements, proprietary technology, technical IT skills and managerial IS/IT skills. From this research, it has been concluded that capital requirements, proprietary technology and technical IT skills are not the kinds of resources which might bring any form of advantage to firms. However, the building up of IS/IT-related managerial skills has been found to be crucial for an improvement of the effectiveness of IS/IT implementation and, therefore, for an improvement of the effectiveness of ICT innovation. This leads us into our next topic: the issue of ICT innovation viewed as an organizational process.

10.2.2 ICT Innovation Viewed as a Process of Organizational Maturity and Learning

The view of ICT innovation as a process of organizational maturity utilizes the analogy of the organization as a living organism. Thus, innovation is seen as a process of learning and growth within the organization, which is partly influenced by external (ICT-related) factors and partly subjected to the history of ICT management in that particular organization. In this section, we will look at two approaches to ICT innovation as a process. The first is a stream of research on IS/IT implementation inspired by technical innovation and diffusion theory, as developed by Kwon and Zmud (1987), Cooper and Zmud (1990) and Saga and Zmud (1994). The second approach is a well-known attempt to establish the 'maturity stages' which the introduction of ICTs is presumed to go through in organizations, pioneered by the work of Nolan (1979). Although both approaches conceptualize ICT innovation as a process based on stages of development, they are substantially different as regards both the rationale and the contents of the development stages.

The research developed by Zmud and colleagues is important because it suggests that many of the conclusions that can be drawn about the process of technical innovation can be applied to the process of ICT innovation. The key contribution is the suggestion that a process of innovation can, and should, be split up into stages. The six stages that form the main body of Cooper and Zmud's (1990) model are derived from the phases of a technical innovation and diffusion process. They are:

1. Initiation;
2. Adoption;

3. Adaptation;
4. Acceptance;
5. Routinization; and
6. Infusion.

In discussing the dynamics of implementing innovations, Eveland explains why technical innovation is a process which goes through stages:

> Putting technology into place in an organization is not a matter of a single decision, but rather of a series of linked decisions and nondecisions. People make these choices and choices condition future choices ... Researchers have developed the idea of innovation stages as a way of categorizing decisions and defining how this leverage operates, that is, seeing how some decisions of necessity precede and shape later ones (Eveland, 1987: 313).

However, the research stream led by Zmud has often been criticized on the grounds that the implementation stages represent a linear and object-oriented view of the innovation process, divorced from the organizational context. An object-oriented view of innovation is one where the stages are described in terms of the content of the decisions, rather than in terms of the actions taken at each stage of the process. According to Eveland (1987: 313), technical innovation must be seen as an action-oriented or change process of 'gradual shaping of a general idea, which can mean many different things to different people, into a specific idea that most people understand to mean more or less the same thing'. Roberts (1987) expresses a similar view, emphasizing also the action component of technical innovation. He observes: 'technical innovation is a multistage process, with significant variations in the primary task as well as in the managerial issues and effective management practice occurring among these stages' (ibid.: 4).

The view of innovation as a linear process where the technology is first identified, then implemented and then presented to the users goes directly against the ICT development models inspired by socio-technical thinking. Innovation is a process of change, and according to Pettigrew and Whipp (1991: 27) organizational change 'does not move forward in a direct, linear way nor through easily identifiable sequential phases. Quite the reverse, the pattern is much more appropriately seen as continuous, iterative and uncertain'. In the innovation literature, there also seems to be some consensus regarding the incremental and learning nature of technical innovation processes (Cohen and Levinthal, 1990). Nelson and Winter (1982) propose that innovations are not just incremental, but that they are also the result of the combination of old organizational routines.

Slappendel (1996) reviews the trends in the innovation literature and concludes that the 'interactive process' perspective is likely to become the most prevalent. Such a trend assumes that innovations are the outcomes of an interactive process between individuals, the organization and the structural factors of the technology. Moreover, Slappendel argues that the aim of the process view of innovation is to explain organizational change in terms of 'probabilistic rearrangements of discrete events over time rather than to establish efficient causes through the study of variance' (ibid.: 118). Going back to the resource-based approach to business economics, we note that this view of the technical innovation process is remarkably close to an orientation in strategic management which emphasizes the relevance of purposeful managerial action in the development of organizational contexts disposed towards innovation, collaboration and learning (Bartlett and Ghoshal, 1993; 1994).

The other attempt to conceptualize ICT innovation as a process of organizational learning and growth was carried out under the label of 'organizational maturity stages'. The best known stages model has been proposed by Nolan (reviewed in King and Kraemer, 1984). It comprises the following six stages:

1. Initiation;
2. Contagion;
3. Control;
4. Integration;
5. Data Administration; and
6. Maturity.

Nolan's objective was to formulate a predictive model of IS/IT evolution which might be generalizable to organizations of all types. He has postulated that IS evolution in organizations follows two S-shaped learning curves. The first starts with very low levels of learning at the initiation stage, followed by rapid growth through contagion, levelling off at the control and integration stages. The second curve starts at the levelling off of the previous curve, has slow growth at first and then more rapid growth through the data administration stage, levelling off again at the maturity stage.

Although Nolan's stages are essentially object-oriented in nature, this work has left two important theoretical contributions. Firstly, it drew attention to the fact that the growth of computing is due to the influence of forces both inside (i.e., organizational learning) and outside the organization (i.e., market pressures). Secondly, it introduced the notion that managements go through periods of 'slack' and 'control' throughout the evolution of IS/IT in organizations. Huff et al. (1988) have reached similar conclusions, but have renamed the key dependent variables as 'expansion' and 'control'. Expansion means that the introduction of a new type of technology triggers the need for the organization to learn and to expand, either in terms of knowledge or of computing resources. But after such periods of expansion, there is usually a need on the part of management to contain the expenditure; a period of tighter control of the development of computing then follows.

Choo and Clement (1994) express an alternative view of the evolution of ICT in organizations. They suggest that IS/IT maturity is a function of the degree of control and influence over computing resources exercised by users, versus the control and influence over computing resources on the part of IS/IT staff. They suggest, further, that such control and influence could be ascertained over a number of criteria (e.g., hardware and software acquisition, information centre policies, IS training, etc), and that these criteria can be used to establish whether an organization is more user-driven or more IS/IT-driven. Although this may sound too simplistic an idea, it does draw attention to what is a key element in IS organizational maturity or learning: the political and sometimes conflictual nature of the relationship between users and IS/IT specialists.

Such a conflicting relationship is part of a crucial issue in IS/IT management, involving the balance established between the centralized versus decentralized control of IS/IT resources. This debate between the demands and expectations of the technology platform versus the demands and expectations of the business platform is a 'push-pull' dilemma (Zmud, 1988). In order to facilitate technological innovation in the business platform, 'need pull' and 'technology push' are required; and in order to facilitate technological innovation in the technology platform, 'technology pull' and 'need push' are required. There is a delicate balance to be sought between the push from the technology platform, backed by the forces from the ICT market, and the organizational absorption capacity of the business platform. The attainment of such a balance of forces in the organization is crucial because it means potential success for ICT-related innovation. And, like any other management dilemma, the prime requisite is for the creation of an organizational context supportive of cooperation and partnership-building between users and IS/IT staff.

Brown and Ross (1996) reinforce the 'push-pull' dynamics by pointing out that organizations strive constantly towards the maintenance of a balance between the development of an IT infrastructure and the building of partnerships between IS/IT staff and IS/IT users. A centralized corporate IT infrastructure brings benefits such as a more cost-effective utilization of computing resources, the synergistic effects of having these resources under a common management structure and all the operational benefits of using standard technology platforms (Von Simson, 1990). Strong IS/IT staff-users partnerships create other benefits, such as an IS management style which is more responsive to local business needs, a shared understanding of IT capabilities and business unit needs, and information systems that are targeted directly at customer needs (Henderson, 1990).

In viewing ICT innovation as a process of organizational maturity and growth, four types of learning can be singled out with regard to:

1. ICT-related expansion: learning about technological choices; procurement procedures; infrastructure building; and outsourcing decisions;
2. ICT-related managerial control: learning about IS/IT planning and evaluation of costs versus benefits;
3. the culture gap between users and specialists: learning about partnership building; and
4. the ICT innovation process itself: learning about ICT-related managerial action and leadership.

The last point leads directly into our next topic.

10.2.3 Information Systems Management with a Changing Emphasis on Governance and Learning

As outlined in the previous section, 'push-pull' dynamics are also one of the central issues in IS/IT management. Overall, IS/IT management comprises the following four major operational areas (Sprague and McNurlin, 1998):

1. computer operations: running and maintaining computers and networks;
2. systems development: developing, maintaining and updating systems;
3. architecture development: providing a framework of policies and standards for information technologies and information contents; and
4. business information requirements: helping users to articulate their needs in terms of the systems architecture.

These traditional functions of IS/IT departments are undergoing major changes, due to a variety of factors. These can be grouped into two major categories. Firstly, changes from within the organization, where a combination of more user-friendly technologies and users more knowledgeable about IT can, in some ways, replace the work of traditional IS/IT specialists. Secondly, changes from outside the organization, where all kinds of new computer services are being offered that make it more cost-effective for many companies to outsource, rather than insource, various types of IT services. All such changes are creating a need for new types of relationships in the organization, which forge a new 'ethos' comprising the new technologies and accompanying new modus operandi.

This new ethos is adequately described by a transition from information systems management to 'information systems governance', an expression introduced by Michael Earl (1996) but left largely undefined. In using the term, Earl intended to highlight the involvement of a variety of stakeholders in the process of formulating IS/IT strategy. However, we believe that IS governance could become a very useful concept – if given a wider coverage and made to encompass not only strategy formulation but also strategic and operational implementation, as well as the daily management of IS/IT-related routines.

Monks and Minow (1995: 1) define corporate governance as 'the relationship among various participants in determining the direction and performance of corporations'. The primary participants in corporate governance are the shareholders, the management (led by the chief executive officer) and the board of directors, in addition to a second line of participants made up of employees, customers, suppliers and the wider community. The key objectives of corporate governance are all concerned with coordination and alignment, such as 'alignment of information, incentives and capacity to act and alignment of responsibilities and authorities of all the various constituencies to achieve the optimal conditions for growth and renewal' (Monks and Minow, 1995: 257).

Hence, the notion of IS/IT corporate governance must be based, in the first instance, on the roles and relationships of all the players involved in the process. The top level of players or stakeholders are the:

1. top management, represented by the member of the board in charge of the information systems/technology function (in the USA sometimes known as the Chief Information Officer);
2. information systems/technology manager; and
3. senior line managers, who increasingly have functional responsibilities in the area of information systems/technology.

These stakeholders form a high-level triangle which dominates all IS-related decision making in organizations. But there are also other players whose roles are equally important when considering the impact of such decision making on the rest of the organization, as well as the new opportunities coming from the external market and the constraints felt from within the organization in order to take up such opportunities. The other important players are (following on the above number sequence):

4. middle managers, who establish the link between senior managers and the end-users, and who constitute the first line of contact with IS/IT-related constraints;

5. non-managerial end-users, whose local IS/IT-related learning should be a key element in IS/IT management, both as a constraint and an opportunity; and
6. suppliers of IS/IT products and services, who provide the interface between the organization and the external market.

IS governance can thus be seen as a system of interlocking roles (i.e., the stakeholders) and their relationships. But neither roles nor relationships are static. In Earl's (1996) words, they are the 'keystone' of the implementation of information systems strategy because they evolve and change continuously, forming the 'constitution process'. He defines this as follows:

> [The constitution process] can influence the setting of the organization's strategy, for example, when tensions or fault-lines in design of the host organization become manifest as information management issues. It can affect the capability and effectiveness of IS strategy-making, for example, in encouraging teamwork and partnership. It can influence the quality of IT strategic decisions, and the subsequent buy-in to them, by education, development and propaganda programmes (ibid.: 498).

Thus described, the constitution process is one of learning or, better said as we have suggested above, an ensemble of learning processes – but this time the emphasis is on the stakeholders involved. Figure 10.2 represents an expanded vision of IS/IT corporate governance. In it, three interacting learning processes (or loops) are depicted. The first, labelled (a), is the top-level loop, where top managers, information systems managers and senior line managers jointly learn about IS/IT strategy formulation while working on IS/IT managerial decisions, such as outsourcing, selection of major software packages or restructuring of the IS/IT function at corporate level.

The second learning loop, (b), involves the users, their direct supervisors (the middle managers) and the senior line managers whose roles encompass two different levels of learning. It is within this second loop that most of the learning directly concerned with IS/IT-related innovation actually occurs, because non-managerial end users are, in most organizations, not only the largest group but also the group with the closest contact with clients. It is through the contact with clients that much IS/IT-related innovation comes about, both through the detection of information-related needs and through the innovative use of the tools made available by the organization's technology platform. The middle managers form a crucial link between the outcome of IS/IT-related managerial decision-making processes, conveyed by the senior line managers, and the activity of non-managerial end users.

The third learning loop, (c), involves both external and internal stakeholders. They include suppliers of IS/IT-related products and services as

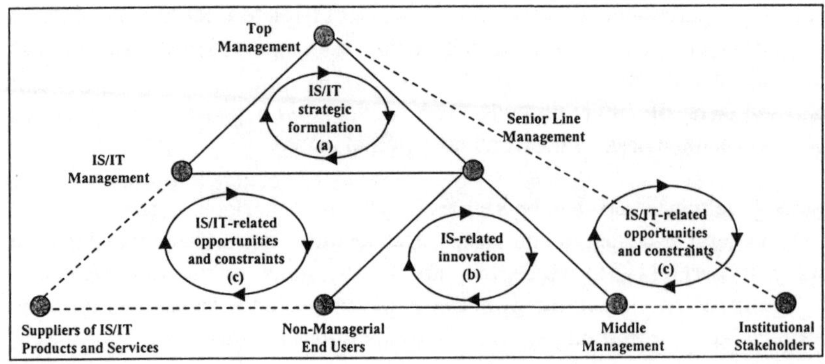

Notes
(a) The area where IS /IT-related managerial learning occurs; it influences the overall conditions for the effective implementation of IS-related innovation.
(b) The area where IS-related innovation actually occurs through experiential learning involving the matching of top-down implementation of managerial choice and of bottom-up detection of business/ innovation needs. The increasing relevance of line management's role must be noted, thus moving the focus of IS-related innovation from the IT platform to the business platform.
(c) Areas of influence from external market players and institutional stakeholders on internal actors in the organization, and of mutual learning about IS/IT-related opportunities and constraints.

Figure 10.2: Interlocking roles and learning loops for IS governance

the marketing power of the players in the IS/IT marketplace is overwhelming and affects each and every individual stakeholder in the organization. Such influence can be very harmful if the organization does not have appropriate IS/IT governance structures, but can also be extremely beneficial if all the players involved have a good grasp of both the opportunities and constraints of new technological offerings. Increasingly, suppliers of IS/IT-related products and services are considered as partners and not just as vendors, thus assuming a participative role in the governance of ICTs in organizations. If such a role is accepted as legitimate by the internal stakeholders, the conditions are set for suppliers to become part of the organization's communities of practice, and for organizational learning to ensue.

The third learning loop also encompasses other external stakeholders, which we have called 'institutional stakeholders'. These are the individuals or organizations which, in one way or another, exert an influence in the internal governance of IS/IT. Often, such influence is of a political nature and applies mostly to large publicly-funded organizations. Political influence, however, can play a major role both as a facilitator or as an inhibitor of new IS/IT-related initiatives, especially when they involve large capital investments.

IS/IT managers or directors, therefore, have to learn how to play the micro-political games which are imposed on the organization via the institutional stakeholders. But this is not a one-way process. Institutional stakeholders can also derive gains from learning about the inner workings of large IS/IT-related initiatives, for example through personal or institutional prestige or reputation. Hence, a learning loop about IS/IT-related opportunities and constraints is also established at this level.

Corporate governance of information systems is an important supporting concept for a comprehensive and holistic approach to IS/IT development and implementation procedures and processes. This brings together strategic formulation, technological development and organizational implementation aspects of IS/IT. It is a middle-of-the-road approach with a strong emphasis on communication and coordination, which has been discussed in the IS/IT strategic development literature under various names: 'eclectic approach' (Sullivan, 1985); 'multiple strategies' (Earl, 1989) or 'mixed development strategies' (de Jong, 1994). In the broader management field, it is intellectually affiliated to the thinking of mainstream strategic management authors such as Nonaka and Takeuchi (1995) and Bartlett and Ghoshal (Bartlett and Ghoshal, 1993, 1994; Ghoshal and Bartlett, 1998), who place leadership or managerial action at the centre of the problem of any kind of implementation.

Both the notion of IS corporate governance and the so-called 'eclectic approach' to IS/IT development place new needs on the organizational context through the stakeholders, including their skills and capabilities for coordination, motivation and leadership. In order to follow an eclectic approach, the level of organizational maturity related to IS/IT must be high. Going back to the stages-of-growth models discussed above, an eclectic approach is possible only at the most advanced stages, where contexts of cooperation, interaction and coordination are the required ingredients (see, for example, Galliers and Sutherland's model quoted in Galliers, 1991).

Hence, let us now turn to the issues of what organizational contexts are, and how they come to be.

10.3 THE PROCESS OF CONSTITUTION OR FORMATION OF ORGANIZATIONAL CONTEXTS

The notion of 'constitution' is not new in management literature. It has been used by different authors under different labels to signify the generative mechanism behind the formation of organizational contexts. For instance, Normann (1985: 235) talks about the organizational constitution as an equivalent to culture or a 'long-term strategic action capability which determines what can and cannot be done'; for Barnard ([1938] 1968), constitution is the same as the organization's 'cooperative system'; Burns and Stalker (1961) have identified organizational 'codes of conduct' as the bases of organizational constitution; and Ghoshal and Bartlett (1998) discuss the 'feel of the place' as the organization's overall climate or context. Constitution is used in the management literature to signify a process of formation of organizational climates (equivalent to contexts) by means of 'structuration' (Giddens, 1984) or 'sensemaking' (Weick, 1995).

The notions of organizational climate and organizational context overlap to a great extent. Authors from industrial economics or strategic management tend to talk of 'context' instead of 'climate', but the content of the two notions tends to be exactly the same. Hansen and Wernerfelt (1989) have identified the need to establish an 'organizational model' of the firm, which would enable them to develop comparisons with an 'economic model' and draw conclusions about company performance. These authors complain that such an organizational model (as opposed to the economic model) is difficult to arrive at because there are so many alternative theories trying to explain organizational performance and effectiveness. However, while agreeing that the construct 'organizational climate' is useful for establishing the basis of an organizational model, they use the expressions 'climate' and 'context' interchangeably. Bartlett and Ghoshal (1993; 1994) and Ghoshal and Bartlett (1998) also use the expressions 'context' and 'climate' with interchangeable meanings.

Given the difficulty in finding definitive descriptions for these concepts, we too will not make any distinctions among the expressions 'organizational contexts', 'organizational climates' and 'organizational cultures', which we will use interchangeably.

Ashforth (1985), Falcione et al. (1987) and Schneider (1990) have all suggested definitions of organizational climate along theoretical lines that might be summed up as defining organizational climate or context as: an inter-subjective phenomenon that is continuously being structured and restructured by organizational members in an effort to make sense of their organization, its values and their roles in it. This definition highlights the fact that the constitution process of the organizational context is tied not only to action in the form of organizational roles and relationships, but also to action in the form of organizational values.

This reasoning is supported by autopoiesis theory (Maturana and Varela, 1980; 1987). Autopoiesis supports a 'constitutive' ontology (as opposed to a 'transcendental' ontology) for the construction of a reality where values and facts are inseparable in the formation of knowledge. As Varela (1992: 260) reminds us: 'to the extent that we move from an abstract to a fully embodied view of knowledge, facts and values become inseparable', i.e., 'to know is to evaluate through our living, in a creative circularity'.

Autopoiesis is a theory initially conceived to explain the development of living organisms in the biological sciences, but which has been imported by the field of socio-cybernetics since the 1980s. In emphasizing the self-organizing, self-reproducing and self-steering qualities of individuals and groups, this theory provides underpinnings for the conviction that society cannot be steered 'from above', i.e., from a transcendental force, but is a bottom-up process in essence. This was especially relevant in the first post-war decades when institutions and agencies such as the Rand Corporation or the American CIA felt attracted to cybernetics as a means for steering societal development in a desired direction. The scientific community of the 1960s generation objected and protested – and such intentions were, fortunately, never pursued (Geyer and van der Zouwen, 2001).

Thus, social systems and organizations, as part of the reality around us, are also 'constituted' through the action of their members. Such action, in its most basic element, takes the form of language or conversations. According to Maturana (1988):

> Each social system is constituted as a network of co-ordinates of actions or behaviours that its components realize through their interactions in mutual acceptance ... (ibid.: 67) ... as a particular social system is realized and conserved through the participation of its members in the network of conversations that constitute it, [such a network] specifies the characteristics and properties that its members must have (ibid.: 69).

However, we are primarily affected by emotions even before we engage in the use of language and in conversation – 'our mood or *emotioning* is an ever-present background to our use of language. It conditions our stance or attitude (are we happy or sad, caring or self-concerned, deferential or confident, angry or upset?) and thereby the course of our conversation' (Mingers, 1995: 79, added emphasis).

The managerial world tends to think of logic and rationality as something which can be separated from emotions. However, as autopoiesis shows, emotions form the background of the embodiment of all our knowledge and cannot be separated from logic. To understand the role of emotions or emotioning is also crucial for an understanding of the nature of social (and organizational) systems. Maturana (1988) argues that emotions are the key ingredient that makes social phenomena possible, through mutual acceptance ('love', in his terminology). Without mutual acceptance, cooperation and social action are not possible. He notes:

> A social system is a closed system that includes as its members all those organisms that operate under the emotion of mutual acceptance in the realization of the

network of co-ordinations of actions that realize it. Due to this, the boundaries of social systems are emotional ones (Maturana, 1988: 69).

Nevertheless, some management authors argue that organizational values are also crucial elements in the formation of organizational contexts. Such is the case of Bartlett and Ghoshal. They start by defining organizations as social structures, stating: 'even though actions of and within organizations may be motivated by a variety of economic and other objectives, they emerge through processes of social interactions that are shaped by the social structure' (Bartlett and Ghoshal, 1993: 43). In adopting this interpretivist view, unusual in mainstream strategic management circles, they bring to the fore the constructs of values, roles and relationships as the principal shapers of organizational context. These authors are concerned with characterizing the 'context' of the organization, both for external purposes (i.e., the role of firms in the economy) and internal aspects (i.e., the role of workers and of management in the firm). In doing this, Ghoshal and Bartlett (1994: 110) propose four key organizational value dimensions, about which they comment: 'Concepts like Stretch, Discipline, Trust and Support have little relevance in existing theory. Yet, we believe they are of central importance for the analysis of organizational effectiveness.'

The concept of organizational role is also well established in the management literature. For example, in his influential effort to set the agenda for a 'science' of administration and to identify the organization as the prime locus for such an undertaking, Simon ([1945] 1997: 19) notes that, 'we are concerned with a role system known as organization'. Katz and Kahn (1966: 186), in one of the earliest authoritative texts on organizational behaviour, define human organizations as role systems, giving 'the role concept a central place in the theory of organizations'. Roles in organizations usually have a formal aspect (i.e., functional roles) in terms of a job description; but they also have an informal aspect, which is strongly influenced by the system of values prevalent in the organization. According to Selznick (1957: 80), organizational roles are 'formal and informal patterns of behaviour associated with a position in the social system to which individuals are expected to conform'.

This is consistent with Fiol's (1991) notion of 'identity' or contextual frames. Fiol has suggested that, because it is difficult to establish a one-to-one link between values and behaviour, we need to find mediators between the organizational values that form organizational contexts and the more overt forms of behaviour. Fiol has collectively labelled such mediators as the identity, referring to the organizational roles that make up the contextual frames which link organizational values and inter-personal behaviours.

The above discussion introduces the ideas that form the descriptive model of the organizational context formation process illustrated in Figure 10.3. At both levels of analysis in the model – behavioural and conceptual – the cycle starts with the impact of values: the behavioural are individual values and conceptual are organizational. At the individual level, values can be defined as the ideas, beliefs or principles behind the way individuals think or feel about certain facts, events or other people (Schein 1992). Values, in turn, affect attitudes and what are viewed as appropriate behaviours in a given situation (Bowditch and Buono, 1997). Attitudes include a cognitive (i.e., languaging) and an affective (i.e., emotioning) component. These can be thought of as individual predispositions to respond to a stimulus, which can be a fact, an event or other people.

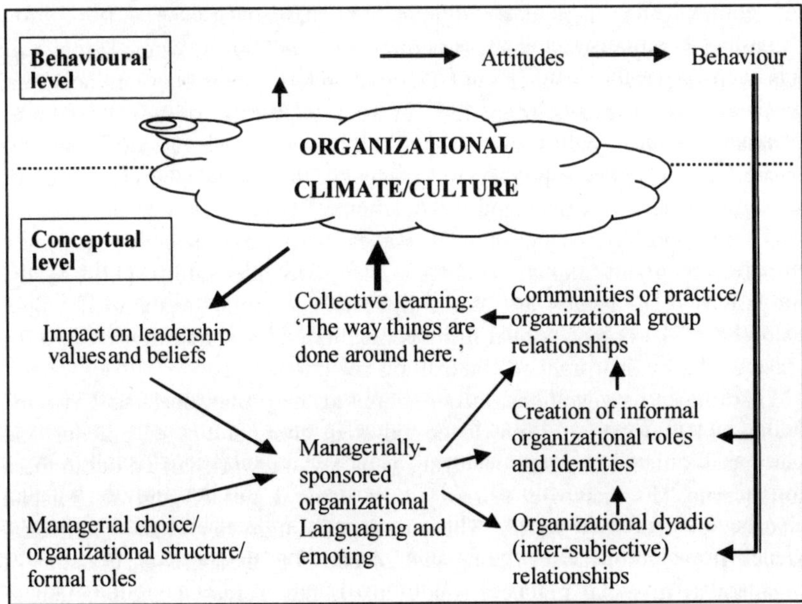

Figure 10.3: The process of organizational context formation

The cognitive component of behavioural attitudes refers to the knowledge derived from a factual evaluation of the stimulus, while the affective component refers to the emotional part of such evaluation. In other words, when talking about attitudes, it is difficult (or impossible) to unscramble facts from emotions (Damasio, 1994). Attitudes also have a behavioural component, which is the inclination that individuals have to behave in certain ways (Bowditch and Buono, 1997). Individual behaviour, in turn, has a direct impact on the relationships between organizational members when they interact, either as dyads or as groups.

Moving now to the conceptual level, the constitutive process also starts with values, which can appropriately be called organizational values. Although they are values of a social group, ultimately values pertain to individuals; so, organizational values might also be termed socialized individual values. Hence, organizational values can be understood as ideas, beliefs or principles that have been socialized by organizational members, and which are behind the way individuals in the organization think or feel about a given situation and about the way 'things should be done' in that organization (Bowditch and Buono, 1997). Managers play a vital role in the process of socialization of individual values, given their responsibility as leaders. Individual organizational members naturally adopt many of the values conveyed to them in the attitudes and behaviour of their leaders.

Formal organizational roles, structural rules and norms which result from acts of managerial choice are imposed on the relationships between individual organizational members when they interact, primarily, on a dyadic basis. However, both dyadic and group relationships are affected by the organizational values espoused and made visible through the actions of its managers. The way values and the outcome of managerial decision making affect relationships is through messages and meta-messages, or cues, perceived by organizational members in their daily interactions. These dyadic and group relationships are also influenced by the organizational values espoused by all organizational members, as individuals, and infused into the organization by their implicit and explicit behaviour.

Learning in organizations occurs mainly at the group level. As Lave and Wenger (1991) explain, knowledge exists in communities of practice and learning is situated in action occurring as part of the work carried out in these communities. Furthermore, learning is an integral part of generative social practice in the real world. This occurs through 'legitimate peripheral participation', a construct offering an explanation of the incremental nature of engagement in social practice, which entails the increased participation of newcomers from the periphery in the centre of the activity in question. Such participation, in turn, is intimately linked to the identity or role formation process discussed above: the process behind informal role formation is actually the same process behind learning in communities of practice.

To complete the cycle of context formation, we have the collective beliefs about 'the way things are done around here' arising from the learning which occurs at the level of the various groups or communities of practice in the organization. While the collective learning associated with participation through informal roles is highly situational and emergent in nature, the notion of organizational context/climate/culture is very stable in its characteristics.

Such stability comes from the autonomous, closed and self-referential nature of autopoietic social systems (von Krogh and Roos, 1995). This means that because individuals set up their own interpretative schemes and become self-referential, the relationships between individuals also become closed, self-referential systems. By the same token, organizations which are made up of relationships between individuals and groups of individuals also become self-referential systems that are quite resistant to change. And when we speak of 'the organization', we speak of the values-roles-relationships loop – itself a closed and self-referential loop – acting as the key constitutive force of the organizational context.

10.4 CONCLUSIONS: THE RELATIONSHIP BETWEEN ICT INNOVATION AND ORGANIZATIONAL CONTEXT

The above analysis indicates there are three broad categorizations of the relationship between issues of ICT innovation and organizational context:

1. resource-based;
2. a process view; and
3. as an issue of IS corporate governance.

10.4.1 The Resource-based Approach to ICT Innovation

The resource-based approach provides much of the intellectual justification for an organizationally-oriented approach to ICT innovation, at least in the areas of management and economics. In any discussion about business or competitive differentiation related to ICT innovation, the issue of organizational effectiveness will undoubtedly come up if the resource-based approach is underpinning the discussion. Variables such as individual and organizational competencies become paramount in research involving, for example, inter-firm comparisons. However, the variables used to identify and define organizational contexts are not amenable to research designs involving large samples and large numbers of observations, as is customary in the quantitative methods favoured by the economics community.

10.4.2 The Process View of ICT Innovation

With regard to the view of ICT innovation as a process of organizational maturity that progresses through identifiable stages of growth, the same constraint applies to the design of research samples. In other words, cross-sectional studies with academic respectability are difficult to implement in view of the differences among organizations within a survey sample. What characterizes a stage of growth in one company may be very different from the characteristics of the same stage of growth in another firm. However, longitudinal studies can be of great interest in the stages-of-growth approach. If a small sample of organizations can be followed up over a period of a few years, the results can be very valuable in terms of the evolution of specific items of ICT innovation across several stages of growth, in each organization. Qualitative comparisons can also be carried out among the organizations in the sample in a longitudinal study.

Moreover, the organizational maturity approach to ICT innovation may be of use to practitioners if attention is turned to the types of learning needed to overcome the various stages of ICT-related growth. As outlined in Section 10.2.2, such learning can be usefully categorized under four interconnected headings: ICT-related expansion; ICT-related control; the bridging of the ICT-related cultural gap; and the required managerial action to lead and manage the ICT-related innovation process. Under each heading, there are a number of practical areas worthy of managerial attention, such as: how to expand the organization's ICT infrastructure; how to control the balance between ICT outsourcing and ICT insourcing; and how to structure the IS/IT department so as help in the gradual dissolution of the cultural divide.

10.4.3 ICT Innovation as an Issue of IS Corporate Governance

As demonstrated in Section 10.3, further dissection and investigation at a more micro level can be applied to both the approach to ICT innovation from the vantage point of the accumulation of internal resources of the firm and the view of ICT innovation as a process of organizational maturity and learning defined through stages of growth. For example, the issue of role or identity formation as regards new ICT-related roles in the organization probably has a high impact on the managerial effort to bridge the cultural gap between ICT specialists and ICT users. This is one reason why we believe it is important to have not only an organizational perspective of ICT innovation, but also to supplement it with sub- and supra-organizational perspectives. Conceptually, the move to sub- and supra-organizational levels of analysis is achieved through the third perspective discussed in this chapter: ICT innovation as an issue of IS corporate governance.

Governance is defined as sets of relationships among stakeholders fulfilling roles and enacting values *in determining the direction and performance of corporations*. If ICT management practitioners subscribe to this view, it quickly becomes obvious that the management of ICT-related innovation processes is, above all, a leadership issue. The model of organizational context formation presented in Figure 10.2 suggests how roles, values and relationships shape, and are shaped by, the attitudes and behaviours of leaders. Hence, if the process of innovation while progressing through its various stages can be equated to a process of IS/IT governance, then the issues of leadership, roles, values and relationships also apply to ICT-related innovation. From the point of view of research into ICT innovation, the variables relating to governance roles, values and relationships can be used to be matched with, for example, the perceived effectiveness of ICT innovation.

10.4.4 Understanding the Nature of ICT Development Projects

Issues such as organization and organizational behaviour are still foreign to many ICT researchers and practitioners. However, concepts such as the constitution process applied to IS/IT governance can be of great value in bridging such a knowledge gap. Similarly valuable is the IS/IT governance model discussed above, where it shows how the ICT-related innovation process can be split into different kinds or levels of learning: a strategic formulation level; an operational/implementation level with an increasingly crucial role for line managers; and a level of exploitation of new ICT-related opportunities/constraints. Each of these levels makes up one or more 'community of practice'. Given that these communities are the loci of organizational learning, a great deal of attention should be devoted to them, with differentiated learning strategies for each level.

Finally, the notion of corporate governance draws attention to ICT-related development strategies and practices. The expression 'eclectic' defines well the development style recommended for ICT applications, as it means all issues in implementing ICT applications must be dealt with in parallel, not sequentially. For example, operational implementation does not necessarily happen before all strategic formulation is complete, or technical implementation does not necessarily have to follow the full surveying of information needs from users. The balancing acts both within and across the technology and business platforms are so complex that it is virtually impossible to follow streamlined methodologies for the implementation of all ICT applications in the organization. That may be possible for some small, well-localized applications. But well-sequenced methodologies do not work for the majority of large-scale projects involving several sub-projects and the streamlining of many interfaces with legacy systems and manual systems. Thus, we hope that this chapter has also contributed to an understanding of the eclectic nature of ICT development projects.

REFERENCES

Ashforth, B.E. (1985), 'Climate Formation: Issues and Extensions', *Academy of Management Review*, **10** (4), 837–47.

Barnard, C.I. ([1938] 1968), *The Functions of the Executive,* Cambridge, MA: Harvard University Press.

Barney, J.B. (1986), 'Organizational Culture: Can it be a Source of Sustained Competitive Advantage?' *Academy of Management Review*, **11**, 656–65.

Barney, J.B. (1991), 'Firm Resources and Sustained Competitive Advantage', *Journal of Management*, **17**, 99–120.

Bartlett, C.A. and S. Ghoshal, (1993), 'Beyond the M–Form: Towards a Managerial Theory of the Firm', *Strategic Management Journal*, **14**, 23–46.

Bartlett, C.A. and S. Ghoshal, (1994), 'Changing the Role of Top Management: Beyond Strategy to Purpose', *Harvard Business Review* (November–December), 79–88.

Bowditch, J.L. and A.F. Buono (1997), *A Primer on Organizational Behaviour*, New York: Wiley.

Brown, C.V. and J.W. Ross (1996), 'The Information Systems Balancing Act: Building Partnership and Infrastructure', *Information Technology and People*, **9** (1), 49–62.

Burns, T. and G.M. Stalker (1961), *The Management of Innovation*, London: Tavistock Publications.

Checkland, P. and S. Holwell (1998), *Information, Systems and Information Systems: Making Sense of the Field*, Chichester, UK: Wiley

Choo, C.W. and A. Clement (1994), 'Beyond The Stage Models for EUC Management', *Information Technology and People*, **6** (4), 197–214.

Coase, R.H. (1937), 'The Nature of the Firm', *Econometrica* (4), 386–405.

Cohen, W.M. and D.A. Levinthal (1990), 'Absorptive Capacity: A New Perspective on Learning and Innovation', *Administrative Science Quarterly*, **35**, 128–152.

Conner, K. (1991), 'A Historical Comparison of Resource-based Theory and Five Schools of Thought Within Industrial Organization Economics', *Journal of Management*, **17**, 121–154.

Conner, K.R. and C.K. Prahalad (1996), 'A Resource-Based Theory of the Firm: Knowledge versus Opportunism', *Organization Science*, **7** (5), 477–501.

Cooper, R. and R.W. Zmud (1990), 'Information Technology Implementation Research: A Technology Diffusion Approach', *Management Science*, **34** (2), 123–39.

Damasio, A.R. (1994), *Descartes' Error*, New York: Putnam.

de Jong, W.M. (1994), *The Management of Informatization: A Theoretical and Empirical Analysis of IT implementation Strategies*, Groningen, Holland: Wolters-Noordhoff.

Earl, M. (1989), *Management Strategies For Information Technology*, Hemel Hempstead, UK: Prentice-Hall.

Earl, M.J. (1996), 'Integrating IS and the Organization: A Framework of Organizational Fit', in M.J. Earl (ed.), *Information Management: The Organizational Dimension*, Oxford: Oxford University Press.

Eveland, J.D. (1987), 'Diffusion, Technology Transfer and Implementation', *Knowledge: Creation, Diffusion, Utilization*, **8** (2), 303–22.

Falcione, R.L., L. Sussman and R.P. Herden (1987), 'Communication Climate in organizations', in F.M. Jablin, L.L. Putnam, K.H. Roberts and L.W. Porter (ed),

Handbook of Organizational Communication, Newbury Park, CA: Sage.

Fiol, C.M. (1991), 'Managing Culture as a Competitive Resource: An Identity-based View of Sustainable Competitive Advantage', *Journal of Management*, **17** (1), 191–211.

Galliers, R. (1991), 'Strategic Information Systems: Myths, Realities and Guidelines for Successful Implementation', *European Journal of Information Systems*, **1** (1), 55–64.

Geyer, F. and J. van der Zouwen (2001), 'Introduction to the Main Themes in Sociocybernetics', in F. Geyer and J. van der Zouwen (ed.), *Sociocybernetics: Complexity, Autopoiesis and Observation of Social Systems*, Westport, CT: Greenwood Press, 1–14.

Ghoshal, S. and C.A. Bartlett, (1994), 'Linking Organizational Context and Managerial Action: The Dimensions of Quality Management', *Strategic Management Journal*, **15,** 91–112.

Ghoshal, S. and C.A. Bartlett (1998), *The Individualized Corporation: A Fundamentally New Approach to Management*, London: Heinemann.

Giddens, A. (1984), *The Constitution of Society: Outline of the Theory of Structuration,* Cambridge, UK: Polity Press.

Grant, R.M. (1991), 'The Resource-Based Theory of Competitive Advantage: Implications for Strategy Formulation', *California Management Review*, **33** (Spring), 114–35.

Hamel, G. and C.K. Prahalad (1989), 'Strategic Intent', *Harvard Business Review*, **67** (3), 63–76.

Hamel, G. and C.K. Prahalad (1994), *Competing for the Future*, Boston, MA: Harvard Business School Press.

Hansen, G.S. and B. Wernerfelt (1989), 'Determinants of Firm Performance: The Relative Importance of Economic and Organizational Factors', *Strategic Management Journal*, **10,** 399–411.

Henderson, J.C. (1990), 'Plugging into Strategic Partnerships: The Critical IS Connection', *Sloan Management Review*, (Spring), 7–18.

Huff, S.L., M.L. Munro and B.H. Martin (1988), 'Growth Stages of End-user Computing', *Communications of the ACM*, **31** (5), 61–74.

Katz, D. and R.L. Kahn (1966), *The Social Psychology of Organizations*, New York: Wiley.

King, J.L. and K.L. Kraemer (1984), 'Evolution of Organizational Information Systems: An Assessment of Nolan's Stages Model', *Communications of the ACM*, **27** (5 May), 466–75.

Kwon, T.H. and R.W. Zmud (1987), 'Unifying the Fragmented Models of Information Systems Implementation', in R.J. Boland and R.A. Hirscheim (eds.), *Critical Issues in Information Systems Research*, Chichester, UK: Wiley.

Lave, J. and E. Wenger (1991), *Situated Learning: Legitimate Peripheral Participation*, Cambridge, UK: Cambridge University Press.

Mahoney, J.T. (1995), 'The Management of Resources and the Resource of Management', *Journal of Business Research*, **33,** 91–101.

Mata, F.J.F., Fuerst W.L. and J.B. Barney, (1995), 'Information Technology and Sustained Competitive Advantage: A Resource-based Analysis', *MIS Quarterly*, **19** (4), 487–505.

Maturana, H. (1988), 'Reality: The Search for Objectivity or the Quest for a Compelling Argument', *Irish Journal of Psychology*, **9** (1), 25–82.

Maturana, H.R. and F.J. Varela (1980), *Autopoiesis and Cognition: The Realization of the Living*, Dordrecht, Holland: D. Reidel Publishing.

Maturana, H.R. and F.J. Varela, (1987), *The Tree of Knowledge*, Boston, Shambhala.
Mingers, J. (1995), *Self-producing Systems: Implications and Applications of Autopoiesis*, New York: Plenum Press.
Monks, R.A.G. and N. Minow (1995), *Corporate Governance*, Oxford: Blackwell.
Nelson, R.R. and S. Winter (1982), *An Evolutionary Theory of Economic Change*, Cambridge, MA: Harvard University Press.
Nolan, R. (1979), 'Managing the Crisis in Data Processing', *Harvard Business Review*, **57** (2), 115–26.
Nonaka, I. and H. Takeuchi (1995), *The Knowledge Creating Company: How Japanese Companies Create the Dynamics of Innovation*, New York: Oxford University Press.
Nordhaug, O. and K. Gronhaug (1994), 'Competence as Resources in Firms', *International Journal of Human Resources Management*, **5** (1), 89–106.
Normann, R. (1985), 'Developing Capabilities of Organizational Learning', in J.M. Pennings (ed.), *Organizational Strategy and Change*, San Francisco: Jossey-Bass.
Penrose, E. ([1959] 1995), *The Theory of the Growth of the Firm*, Oxford: Oxford University Press.
Pettigrew, A. and R. Whipp (1991), *Managing Change for Competitive Success*, Oxford: Blackwell.
Porter, M. (1980), *Competitive Strategy*, New York: The Free Press.
Porter, M. (1985), *Competitive Advantage*, New York: The Free Press.
Prahalad, C.K. and G. Hamel (1990), 'The Core Competence of the Corporation', *Harvard Business Review*, **90** (May–June), 79–91.
Roberts, E.B. (1987), 'Managing Technological Innovations: A Search for Generalizations', in E.B. Roberts (ed.), *Generating Technological Innovation*, New York: Oxford University Press.
Saga, V.L. and R.W. Zmud (1994), 'The Nature and Determinants of IT Acceptance, Routinization and Infusion', in L. Levine (ed.), *Diffusion, Transfer and Implementation of Information Systems*, Amsterdam: North Holland.
Schneider, B. (1990), 'The Climate for Service: An Application of the Climate Construct', in B. Schneider (ed.), *Organizational Climate and Culture*, San Francisco: Jossey-Bass.
Schein, E. (1992), *Organizational Culture and Leadership*, San Francisco: Jossey-Bass.
Selznick, P. (1957), *Leadership in Administration*, New York: Harper & Row.
Simon, H. ([1945] 1997), *Administrative Behavior*, New York: The Free Press.
Slappendel, C. (1996), 'Perspectives on Innovation in Organizations', *Organization Studies*, **17** (1), 107–29.
Spender, J.-C. (1996), 'Making Knowledge the Basis of a Dynamic Theory of the Firm', *Strategic Management Journal*, **17** (Winter), 45–62.
Sprague, R.H. and B.C. McNurlin (1998), *Information Systems Management in Practice*, Upper Saddle River, USA: Prentice-Hall.
Sullivan, C.H. (1985), 'Systems Planning in the Information Age', *Sloan Management Review* (Winter), 3–11
Varela, F.J. (1992), 'Whence Perceptual Meaning? A Cartography of Current Ideas', in F.J. Varela and J-P Dupuy (eds), *Understanding Origins*, Dordrecht, Holland: Kluwer Academic Publishers.
von Krogh, G. and J. Roos (1995), *Organizational Epistemology,* Basingstoke, UK: Macmillan.
von Krogh, G. and J. Roos (1996), 'Arguments on Knowledge and Competence', in G. von Krogh and J. Roos, *Managing Knowledge: Perspectives on Cooperation*

and Competition, London: Sage.
Von Simson, E.M. (1990), 'The Centrally Decentralized IS Organization', *Harvard Business Review* (July–August), 158-62.
Wernerfelt, B. (1984), 'A Resource-based View of the Firm', *Strategic Management Journal*, **5**, 171–80.
Weick, K.E. (1995), *Sensemaking in Organizations*, Beverly Hills, CA: Sage.
Winter, S.G. (1987), 'Knowledge and Competence as Strategic Assets', in D.J. Teece, *The Competitive Challenge: Strategies for Industrial Innovation and Renewal*, Cambridge, MA: Ballinger Publishing Co.
Zmud, R.W. (1988), 'Building Relationships Throughout the Corporate Entity', in J. Elam (ed.), *Transforming the IS Organization*, Washington, DC: ICIT Press.

NOTES

1. In view of the ambiguity associated with definitions of profit, the academic literature increasingly utilizes the expression 'rent' to refer to 'economic profit'. Rent is the surplus of revenue over the real or 'opportunity' cost of the resources used in generating that revenue. The opportunity cost of a resource is the revenue it can generate when put to an alternative use in the firm, or the price that the resource can be sold for. Such an interpretation of 'rent' is also known as 'Ricardian rent'. When applied to the resource-based view of strategy, a Ricardian rent means the returns to a given resource (e.g., managerial skills) that confer competitive advantage to the firm over and above the real costs of such a resource (Grant, 1991).

Conclusions

Chrisanthi Avgerou and Renata Lèbre La Rovere

In this concluding section to the book, we draw on the various perspectives presented in the preceding chapters to highlight key aspects of ICT innovation. To begin with, we revisit the ICT diffusion model of five translations by Gillespie et al. (1995) that we referred to in the Introduction. Subsequently, we make some general observations about the commonalities and differences of perspective found in the analyses contributed by the authors of this volume.

Diffusion models oversimplify a much more complex group of multi-dimensional processes, as do most linear models. Of course, simple intuitively-sound models have a clear utility as sense-making devices and frameworks for structuring activities. Moreover, they are valuable for analytical purposes, in so far as they articulate concepts and relationships that invite further empirical and theoretical elaboration. Two elements of the Gillespie et al. ICT diffusion model have this quality of being a useful structure for communication and practice, despite triggering analysis that reveals a more complex set of socio-economic processes: the innovation/adoption relationship and the macro/micro distinction as contexts of action.

C.1 LIMITATIONS OF THE INNOVATION/ADOPTION DISTINCTION

In its simplest form, the diffusion perspective seeks to explain under what conditions, and through what facilitatory mechanisms, a novel technology or organizational practice – a software application, new management method or combination of the two, such as an enterprise resource planning system – is introduced in organizations (adopted) and impacts on the conduct of their business performance. Thus, for new ICT artefacts and ICT-based practices, e.g. electronic data interchange (EDI) or e-commerce, the main concerns relate to how their use is spread once they become available in the laboratory and market place, and the nature of related economic impacts. This focus has drawn the attention of scholars from diverse currents of Economic theory, as shown in this book by Tigre and La Rovere (Chapter 6).

Following this logic, a plethora of new ICT artefacts, as well as business practice prescriptions, originate in specialized industries and research programmes (e.g. the software industry, management consultancy corporations, business schools, computer science academic departments and R&D initiatives, such as the succession of EU R&D 'Framework' programmes[1]) and are then introduced as distinct products or services in 'user' or 'client' organizations. It therefore becomes possible – and useful for policy intervention purposes – to examine the rationale and conditions for the take-up of certain technologies in particular categories of organizations. Examples of such analyses are provided in this volume by La Rovere's research into the adoption of a set of technologies by SMEs in Rio de Janeiro (Chapter 5) and Bhatnagar's case studies of the use of telecommunication technologies in rural India and Bangladesh (Chapter 2).

Nevertheless, this conception of the diffusion of ICT innovation through the adoption of packaged products and standardized practices by a set of organizations obscures important aspects of the process through which technology artefacts are accommodated and contribute value in organizations – and economies at large. One of the insights common to the chapters in this volume is that innovation that affects ICT artefacts is constructed largely in the organizational setting of its use. The adoption of the generic technologies examined in La Rovere's research is a necessary, but not sufficient, input for the process of innovation that each company needs to pursue in order to develop new practices and products to increase their competitiveness. And the process through which artefacts and codified prescriptions of practice shape new socio-technical infrastructures is inevitably context-specific.

Several theoretical perspectives have been offered by the authors in this volume to support and elaborate on the understanding of innovation as shaped largely in context, rather than 'diffused' from the place of its conception into places where it is put into use. Almost all authors highlight the 'tacit' knowledge dimension of learning and acting. Bada (Chapter 7) analyses the institutional processes through which 'adopted' technologies are transformed to be meaningful locally and effective as information processing tools and practices. Magalhães (Chapter 10) reviews the way business economics, IS management theory and organizational maturity and learning theories elaborate on the contextualist nature of innovation. Tony Cornford (Chapter 9), Avgerou (Chapter 8) and Madon (Chapter 4) use the explanatory capacity of social constructivist theory in the sociology of technology to discuss the situated nature of the shaping of technology-based information systems and organizational practices.

C.2 THE VALUE OF INTERDISCIPLINARY DISCOURSE

The second element of the diffusion model that is simultaneously a useful abstraction and, at closer study, a challenge to rethink long-established disciplinary divisions and conceptual categories is the separation of the macro-level of the socio-economic domain from the micro-level of the organization. Within the conventional division of academic disciplines, each level is studied by different research communities: the former by macroeconomics and sociology, and the latter by industrial economics, organization theory, management, and information systems. The two levels of study have been kept distinct locally, with few weak links between them. Practically, each of them is oriented towards informing and developing the professional credentials of distinct institutions of modernity: the former serving as the knowledge platform for government policy making, the latter as the source of expertise for business management and administration.

The chapters of this book provide many indications that the historically-developed academic compartmentalization of knowledge is challenged by the study of the complex processes of ICT innovation. Studies, such as those by Bhatnagar (Chapter 2) and La Rovere (Chapter 5), indicate the inadequacy of macro-level policy analysis which considers technology as something 'black-boxed' and reduced to specific costs and effects that can be applied to organizations, themselves also seen as black-boxed units with an economic performance.

Bhatnagar shows the significance of opening the black box of the innovating organization by highlighting locally-perceived 'value'. He explains that drawing up an effective telecommunications policy requires an understanding of the peculiarities of the way economic activities are performed and how value is derived in the social conditions of the region or sector concerned. Neither technology nor organizations are controllable automata that will produce desirable economic outcomes if they are provided with the right input through policy initiatives, such as infrastructure investment, technical skills and 'awareness' programmes. As discussed by La Rovere, sector-related characteristics and competencies of organizations condition the innovative capabilities of organizations and their adoption and use of ICT. Therefore, policies devised to stimulate ICT adoption will have differentiated results. The case discussed by Prochnik and Une (Chapter 3) demonstrates that user involvement in an ICT diffusion policy is essential for its success.

The un-controllability of the organizations of production in an economy by means of conventional macro-level economic instruments is often indicated by recognizing the need for 'learning' – a cognitive process embedded in historically-developed cultural settings. The notion of 'tacit knowledge' is also one of the most commonly highlighted factors in innovation research in both economics and information systems. With concepts such as 'institutional learning' (Dalum et al., 1992), studies of national innovation policy trespass into areas that have traditionally been the territory of organizational sociology, and enrich economic instrumentality with an understanding of social, cognitive and cultural processes Although these processes are not directly amenable to policy intervention, they need to be taken into account for the design of effective government action.

On the other hand, organization-focused IS studies cannot adequately guide IS professional practice unless there is the analytical capacity to associate internal organizational processes with the broader socio-economic context. Contemporary socio-technical studies of information systems reveal that such associations are stronger and more multifaceted than those included in the mainstream micro-economic models of the business firm. These studies also point out the significance of cognitive and cultural processes, which are not isolated by organizational boundaries but are subject to broader institutional formations and transformations.

Particularly significant in this respect is the emergence of theories that span the macro-micro division. Institutional economics, evolutionary economics, resource-based theory, actor network theory, autopoiesis and structuration theory are some of the perspectives used by the authors in this volume to overcome the strict separation of the organization from the broader socio-economic context. Both economics and information systems studies therefore converge to a view of ICT innovation as a dynamic process involving multiple actors in multiple locations, codified and tacit knowledge, and instrumental and situated behaviour. While such understanding is not directly translatable to policy measures and professional skills, it does provide the basis for better judgement of policy initiatives and professional conduct.

Nevertheless, a fundamental difference between economic and IS studies[2] of ICT innovation is discernible in the preceding chapters, namely the extent to which innovation action is related to economic rationality. For evolutionary economists, innovation is essential for the survival of the firm in the new techno-economic paradigm. As innovation is considered a tool for competitiveness, economists focus on the economic rationality of innovation activities. It is important, however, to point out that although evolutionary economists look at the economic aspects of innovation, they do not consider that economic agents have full knowledge of the conditions in which they operate. In this way, evolutionary economists and transaction-cost economists reject the hypothesis of the full rationality of agents that is present in economics mainstream analysis, replacing it with Simon's (1976) hypothesis of limited rationality (Coriat and Weinstein, 1995).

According to Simon's analysis, individuals and organizations engaged in economic activities will not try to maximize economic value. Rather, they will act to obtain satisfactory results. The degree of satisfaction will be conditioned by two sets of elements. The first is related to the incapacity of individual persons to obtain full information and to calculate exactly the results of their actions. The second concerns the routines developed by organizations and the need of organizations to have a degree of consensus among their members so that their decisions can be implemented. Williamson (1985) calls the first set limited rationality and the second set procedural rationality.

However, there are also other 'rationalities' discernible in the discussion of innovation in this book. For example, Magalhães (Chapter 10), Madon (Chapter 4), Avgerou (Chapter 8) and La Rovere (Chapter 5) discuss the capacity of effective organizing, i.e., administrative rationality. Consideration of regional learning capabilities, power structures and alignments by James Cornford (Chapter 1), Avgerou (Chapter 8), Tony Cornford (Chapter 9) and Bada (Chapter 7) brings political rationality into the analysis. Not surprisingly, authors drawing from economic and business theories assume the prevalence of economic rationality in the process of innovation, although none of the perspectives taken in this book considers economic rationality in decision making and problem solving to be independent from the social context.

Overall, the distinction between economic and social theorizing made in the chapters of this volume suggests a complementarity of analytical approaches, rather than a gap that inhibits communication. Economic studies that consider the social context (whether the organization, the industry, the region, or the country) amount to a conception of innovation that encompasses both economic and institutional transformation, as conveyed by the notion of techno-economic paradigm. Moreover, there are attempts to combine technical/rational with institutional studies, such as in the combination of resource-based with structurational and institutionalist perspectives presented by Magalhães (Chapter 10) and Bada (Chapter 7) respectively.

Yet, we would argue that the value of the theoretical analyses contained in this book, and the more general contribution of the specialist fields of innovation studies in economics and information systems, lies in their differences rather than in their convergence. Theory provides a lens that magnifies and scrutinizes certain aspects of a complex phenomenon, while it belittles and abstracts others. Not only is it unrealistic to expect theoretical endeavours to reveal the whole 'truth' of socio-economic phenomena, but the contribution of such endeavours lies in exaggeration, which reveals the unravelling ramifications of complex processes. Disciplinary differences should not be ironed out. Instead, there is a need to explore the particular biases of each discipline and to create opportunities for interdisciplinary discourse and exchange of insights. And this is what we have aimed at by putting together the chapters of this volume.

REFERENCES

Coriat, B. and O. Weinstein, O. (1995), *Les Nouvelles Théories de L'entreprise,* Paris, Le Livre de Poche.

Dalum, B., B. Johnson, B.-Å. Lundvall (1992), 'Public Policy in the Learning Society', in B.-Å. Lundvall (ed.), *National Systems of Innovation: Towards a Theory of Innovation and Interactive Learning*, London: Pinter, 296–317.

Gillespie, A., R. Richardson and J. Cornford (1995), 'Information Infrastructures and Territorial Development', background paper prepared for the OECD Workshop on Information Infrastructures and Territorial Development, 7–8 November, Paris: OECD.

Simon, H. (1976), 'From Substantive to Procedural Rationality', in Latsis, S.J. (ed.), *Method and Appraisal in Economics*, Cambridge: Cambridge University Press.

Williamson, O.E. (1985), *The Economic Institutions of Capitalism*, New York: The Free Press.

NOTES

1. More information on these programmes can be found at www.cordis.lu/fp5/home.html and europa.eu.int/comm/research/fp6/index_en.html on the Web.
2. IS studies included in this book represent a particular stream of IS research. Other streams of research in the IS field adopt a business-economic perspective, or are more concerned with engineering aspects of innovation.

Index